Resisting Arrest

Resisting Arrest

Detective Fiction
and Popular Culture

ROBERT A. RUSHING

OTHER

Other Press
New York

Copyright © 2007 by Robert A. Rushing

Production Editor: Robert D. Hack

This book was set in 11pt. Berkeley Book by Alpha Graphics of Pittsfield, New Hamsphire.

10 9 8 7 6 5 4 3 2 1

Library of Congress Cataloging-in-Publication Data

Rushing, Robert A.
    Resisting arrest : detective fiction and popular culture / Robert A. Rushing.
        p. cm.
    Includes bibliographical references and index.
    ISBN-13: 978-1-59051-241-8 (acid-free paper)
    ISBN-10: 1-59051-241-3 (acid-free paper) 1. Detective and mystery stories–
History and criticism. 2. Detective and mystery films–History and criticism.
I. Title.
    PN3448.D4R87 2007
    791.43'655–dc22
                                                                    2006016275

Contents

Foreword

SAMIR DAYAL

The decline of the traditional realist novel and the concomitant rise of the modern novel constitute a major development in the annals of literary history. Indeed it is now a critical commonplace that it became impossible to write a traditional psychological/realist novel after this generic "cut" of the modern. Simultaneously, as Slavoj Žižek writes, the detective *story* gave way to the detective *novel*. And what the modern novel and the detective novel have in common is the "*impossibility of telling a story in a linear, consistent way*" (Žižek 1992, p. 49; emphasis original). In detective novels, the chain of events that constitutes the story or mystery is always reconstructed retrospectively by the detective. This act of reconstruction is often compared to the work of the analyst, the "subject supposed to know" (*le sujet supposé savoir*). Thus Žižek foregrounds the detective's essential genius and agency: he (and it is usually he) is able to identify and lend significance to the odd but apparently trivially obvious element in the set of clues, the array of evidence available to all—those enfolded within the narrative and those who number among the readership and are therefore external to it (Žižek, p. 53).

This excessive, paradoxical, or apparently "nonsensical" element shows the narrative to be lacking something critical, and therefore requiring the retrospective reconstruction of the detective/analyst, and I say more about this below. Something similar to this retrospective reconstruction also happens in the psychoanalytic clinic: detection and analysis shed light on each other, the one clarifying the procedures of the other and each showing the hidden premises of the other. The detective's reconstructive procedures, for instance, highlight the not necessarily "logical" deduction employed by the analyst. On the other hand the psychoanalyst's interpretation of the signifiers of the analysand's unconscious motivations illuminates the detective's insight into the signifiers of the criminal's motives. The excessive element is also what allows the detective/analyst to connect, as if through the process of countertransference, with the *desire* of the criminal/analysand, and thus grasp the key of interpretation. This is the insight Robert Rushing takes as structurally pivotal for his own argument. Yet his signal contribution to the study of detective fiction is that he significantly develops the original insight and shifts our gaze in a different direction, namely the dynamics of reception.

Rushing aligns his analysis explicitly with the trajectory of psychoanalytic understandings, beginning with Freud, of "misplaced and misunderstood desire." This trajectory, of course, includes Lacan and scholars who work within a Lacanian discursive framework, such as Žižek and Joan Copjec. In this tradition, some of the most compelling contemporary writing about detective fiction and film emphasizes the relationship between the detective and his criminal adversary. Copjec, for instance, identifies this relationship as "central" (1993a, p. vii). Elsewhere, she strenuously theorizes the differential relations among the class of suspects within the diegetic spaces of detective fiction. The emphasis of Copjec's analysis, then, is primarily *internalist*.

The major contribution of Rushing's book is that unlike the work of critics such as Žižek and Copjec (with whom he formally and discursively aligns himself explicitly) it refocuses our attention on the reception of the fiction, and more particularly on the relationship between detective and reader, or sleuth and *spectator*, by returning—or readdressing—readers' attention not only to the sleuth's desire but to our own, thereby straddling the fictional and the actual worlds. Whereas Žižek and Copjec emphasize the internal, diegetic relationship between detective and criminal, Rushing's analysis offers fresh insights into *extradiegetic* terrain—into certain homologies between the desire of the detective and the desire of the reader. Rushing's analysis therefore develops the mirrored circuits of desire: the desire of the detective mirroring that of the reader, on the one hand, and the desire of the critic mirrored by that of the critic's audience on the other.

What is gained by entering this hall of mirrored desires? What is important about redressing the emphasis on an internalist analysis of detective fiction to focus on the extradiegetic aspect of reception? The answer is that detective fiction and film, sometimes regarded with disdain as low forms (the counterpart of "high art") in fact reveal much about the structure of readerly or spectatorial pleasure, particularly in the "extreme" form of *jouissance*. Rushing's book delves into the reasons readers and viewers find themselves returning again and again to the pleasures of detective fiction. The implications of this discussion reach beyond the act of reading, beyond reception, to engage with questions of genre and gender, of pleasure and its sustenance through the very act of deferring satisfaction. Rushing returns us to the psychoanalytic insight that the essential nature of desire is lack, or the failure of completion. Something, as Lacan put it, "does not stop *not* writing itself." And so Rushing's exploration also highlights the crucial link between desire and repetition as the key to the vitality of detective fiction. We return again and again to "the scene of the crime," as it were, and not because we do not know "whodunit." We repeat the delicious crime of reading or watching this often-deprecated genre of detective fiction because it is a way of resisting the arrest of desire. The only alternative would be a negative, bad *jouissance*, for which another name would be the "arrest"—or stasis—of satisfaction. The first is on the side of life, the second of death. To understand the source of Rushing's title in the light of the above discussion is to grasp the productive distinction between sustaining the good enjoyment (*jouissance*) through repetition of the act of revisiting the detective fiction, as in returning to a game or a dance, or a ritual that affords pleasure, on the one side, and putting off the death of pleasure (bad *jouissance*) occasioned by the end of the game or dance, even if the end of the game or dance is a kind of *jouissance* in itself. As in sex, there is a pleasure in deferring the moment of final satisfaction, and the final satisfaction is marked not only by its specific *jouissance* but by detumescence. This is why orgasm was called "the little death." To put it in a double formulation, one might say: resisting arrest, we can put in abeyance the "end" of *jouissance*.

In his chapter on irritation, Rushing rehearses some generic definitions, following the standard division between classic detective fiction (Edgar Allan Poe, Agatha Christie, Arthur Conan Doyle) and hard-boiled fiction (Raymond Chandler, Dashiell Hammett, Mickey Spillane). He is careful to point out that the schism between classic and hard-boiled should not be understood in terms of a simple binary. Accordingly, he presents a quick synoptic tour of the proliferating smaller provinces—the subgenres—of detective fiction. Here too, he brings to light something not often discussed by critics of detective fiction: "this Great Schism, like the Protestant break, also produced a seemingly endless sequence of subsequently smaller and smaller generic denominations within the 'post-classical' world of detective fiction: the cozy, the procedural, the forensic, the historical detective novel, and so on. Within each denomination, there are still smaller generic units." Indeed, detective fiction is often like bespoke tailoring, as if customizing the detective adventure to readers' preferences. It is not above offering "a series of increasingly individually tailored settings and characters: detective novels about cats, about horse racing, about crossword puzzles, about catering, about beauticians, about chocolate . . . ." Sensitive to the nuances and ramifications of the variegations, the author nevertheless keeps before the reader the fundamental structure of classic detective fiction without falling into the trap of espousing too static or doctrinaire a definition. For serious students of detective fiction as a genre, what Rushing offers is not a mere catalogue of the genres and subgenres but a real insight into the generic dynamic that structures a libidinal economy in which detective and reader are bound together.

In developing the highly variegated subgenres of detective fiction Rushing observes that at the most general level, the received classification of detective fiction between classic and hard-boiled understands these types to be similar in some respects—presenting often legally or morally compromised detectives, a fascination with "scene[s] of *revelation*"—but it is their differences, and the efflorescence of subgenres, that have generated some of the most important commentaries on the subject. For Rushing a crucial point is that whereas classic detective fiction is "cerebral, artificial, conservative, and nostalgic," hard-boiled fiction "is set in a universe that is profoundly irrational, realistic and gritty, in such a way as to (at times) suggest a tacit social critique." Žižek would add that there is also a crucial *ethical* difference in the contractual terms under which the detective undertakes a case. In classic detective fiction, the detective is on retainer; in hard-boiled fiction, he declines mere monetary reward in preference for an incalculable ethical reward. In the former the detective is socially eccentric, a detached observer, though not necessarily detached like a scientist; rather the financial contract insulates him from the libidinal economy in which everyone else tends to be implicated. In the latter, the detective is involved in a circuit of debt or (sometimes painful) desire (Žižek 1991, pp. 60, 61, 63). Here desire—typically, the desire of the virtuous, if compromised, detective—itself seems to become hystericized, modulated as an ethical debt to the other and renamed as a self-sacrificing love or duty to that other, typically a woman with whom he cannot find self-sufficient love. In this regard hard-boiled fiction embodies the famous Lacanian precept that there is no sexual relation (*il n'y a pas de rapport sexuel*). This precept may seem counterintuitive to a casual observer of popular culture, for instance, which seems awash in representations of romantic and sexual *relationships*. The psychoanalytic principle really points to the asymmetry of the paths that desire takes for men and women. The popular cultural obsession, and generally the universal struggle, to find a completely satisfying love may result precisely from the fundamental "impossibility," which we cannot bear to acknowledge, of *the sexual relation* as such. To turn to a less trivializing gloss on the relevance of the Lacanian insight to everyday life, it might be useful to consider Renata Salecl and Žižek 's insistence that the true aim of love is the "kernel of the real," and the elusiveness of this kernel is what makes love and the sexual relation "impossible." This kernel, which takes on naturally a crucial importance in Rushing's own argument, is the Lacanian real, "what remains of the object when it is stripped of all its imaginary and symbolic features." It is a radically historicized or "historical" phenomenon, and this becomes clear when we understand that expressions of love take their concrete form in the context of a given cultural moment and milieu. And finally, Salecl and Žižek point out, love is "never really 'just love' but always the screen, the field, on which the battles for power and domination are fought" (Salecl and Žižek 1991, p. 3).

It is flexibility and variation as well as "satisfying" predictability, in fact, that make the genre of detective fiction as a whole a reliable pleasure, despite its disrepute in some critical quarters. Extending the initial definition, Rushing goes on to suggest other ways of discriminating between hardboiled fiction as emphasizing romance and adventure, and classic detective fiction, with its diet of flat or thin characters and often contrived plots, as a type of "analytic" fiction emphasizing a reliance on logic, deduction, and ratiocination. Examples of the classic form include Poe and the subgenre identified by Copjec (1993b, p. 169) as featuring the detective as "armchair rationalist"—incidentally also a model for the reader in his or her own armchair.

To this elaboration of the nature of classic detective fiction as "analytic," one might have added, for instance, D. A. Miller's formulation in

The Novel and the Police that detective fiction of the analytic variety tends to insist on a closed space with a restricted, carefully accounted (and by this accounting also relentlessly policed) set of characters. It is an additional and related condition that the perpetrator ultimately indicted is not someone produced at the last moment as a (previously) unsuspected suspect, like a rabbit out of a hat, but is invariably drawn from an already established and carefully enumerated list of suspects, ranged before the police (iconically, in a police line-up) and the rest of us from the outset of the adventure of detection. This is why it is a sine qua non that we undergo the feeling, when the truth is revealed by the detective, of wanting to kick ourselves for not having picked up on the clue right there before us: "If only the police—and we—could have seen the solution to the mystery earlier!" With both classic and hard-boiled fiction, however, it is to the reader's fascination not so much with the solution but with the process or the ritual of solving the mystery that Rushing draws our attention.

The self-evident "shortcomings" of character development and contrived plots, and the artificial-seeming restrictions imposed on the forms of detective fiction ought to point the critic's gaze elsewhere for the secret of the genre's success. After all, it is neither for complex character development, nor compelling plots, nor stunning surprises that one turns to these fictions, but rather for a different kind of enjoyment. This word, enjoyment, is the crux of Rushing's analysis, the "absented cause"—not just an absent cause—motivating the reader or spectator, and ultimately critic and reader of criticism. In the everyday sense, the enjoyment of the detective and of the reader/spectator may very well inhere in the ritualized narrative elements: the discovery of the body, the presentation of the many possible suspects or the absence, initially, of any plausible suspects, the appearance of a femme fatale, the revelations of the detective's own shortcomings or personal addictions, and so on. Yet on the other hand it is enjoyment, in the Lacanian psychoanalytic sense of *jouissance*, that must be screened or deferred by the fiction from the reader and enjoyed only as symptom. It must be guaranteed by its very secretion behind the rituals and conventionality of the progress of detection.

Theorizing the idea of *suture*, Copjec helps us to see that what is important is the crucially unsurprising, obvious element, reproduced as an *excess*, which becomes the germ of the pleasure afforded by the acts of detection, reading, and analysis. Suture describes how excess is produced as the "nonphenomenal" superaddition to a list of signifiers or clues of an element that is lacking from that list; it is this *objet a* that both marks the lack of a signifier that could complete the set of signifiers and the surplus element that illuminates the signification of the set of clues: the detective parses the clues by seeing what is that surplus element, and why it is significant though seemingly trivially obvious (Copjec 1993b, p. 176).

Rushing reformulates this surplus element, and gives the logic of the suturing excess a different gloss. He calls that surplus element the ambivalent germ of pleasure, which is at the same time a kernel of irritation, constituted by the "iconic instantiations of normal life, which irritatingly but productively interrupt the proceduralism of detection." This kernel, like the proverbial grain of sand introduced into the oyster, is the cause of the production of a pearl, the pearl in this case of what Lacanian psychoanalysis would call "enjoyment." The grain of sand enters as an irritating but perfectly ordinary and commonplace impurity; yet like the oyster it produces an estimable treasure valued for its transcendent beauty. What is remarkable about the kernel of irritation is its very banality, its participation in the untranscendent order of everyday life. The irritation manifests itself in a structure or process of *repetition*. And Rushing wants to elevate the repetition into the machinery of enjoyment or, more mundanely, pleasure. It is in this stress on repetition that he moves beyond Copjec's analysis.

In other cases, as in the subgenre of the "police procedural," it is not necessarily pleasurable in the everyday sense to encounter the kernel of irritation. The kernel can be simply irritating or upsetting; yet it is the libidinizing structure of repetition that is the guarantor of enjoyment. To shift the metaphor, it is by worrying the same, unremarkable beads again and again, by the eternal repetition of the same, that an obsessive-compulsive derives pleasure. The transcendence, if any, comes through the ordinariness of the means of extracting it. It is not the satisfaction of removing the repetition that is aimed at. Instead, it may even be from the very anticipation of repetition that the reader derives predictable "enjoyment" (not satisfaction). The idea is extended in the Lacanian logic Rushing adapts for his current purposes: satisfaction is perennially deferred, but that deferral is also a strategy of avoiding *satiation* and "arrest," the death of enjoyment. It is the play of this repetition and deferral that Rushing seeks to identify or document, sometimes in profuse detail.

Perhaps like scratching an itch, the repeated return to this kernel of irritation enables the fiction to afford a pleasurable evasion of that specific arrest of enjoyment; the question remains whether the repetition submits to an economy of marginal returns or whether it is to be thought of in terms of an insatiable drive. According to the law of marginal returns, the pleasure of the first iteration has a different degree from that of each subsequent iteration—it may be dissipated with every successive return of the same irritation. Or, if the subject is obsessive and thus exempt from the law of marginal returns, it could, on the contrary, be sustained or augmented with repetition. The question can be posed in this way: If we reread detective fiction knowing the outcome of the plot in advance, is the pleasure quotient greater or smaller than when we first discovered the secret the fiction holds? Is the revelation of the secret or the key to the mystery not the most important source of the pleasure? It would seem that these questions are to be decided on a case-by-case basis.

In some cases the pleasure of reading may derive not from the plot but from the repeated reimmersion in the language of the fiction. The preeminent example of an author whose work, though not an instance of detective fiction, provides such a textual pleasure is Shakespeare, the outcome of whose major "narratives"or plots (especially *Romeo and Juliet, King Lear, Hamlet, Macbeth*) many readers already know beforehand, perhaps even before they open the text for the first time. Arguably, the work of Umberto Eco, or for that matter Alfred Hitchcock, Michelangelo Antonioni, or Anthony Minghella might be said similarly to provide an experience of *textual* pleasure not hinging primarily on the unfolding of the mystery at the heart of the plot; the pleasure may be sustained or even increased on subsequent encounters.

It is now possible to grasp, as a gestalt, Rushing's project. Rushing wants to show that the enjoyment of the reader/viewer of detective fiction is premised not only on *returning to* the satisfying repetition, but on "*avoidance of* the real of desire" (emphasis added), and this avoidance can be facilitated by a range of means—such as an obsessive focus on rituals, a taking of pleasure in the literary or film style, the signifiers and images themselves, all mechanisms of avoiding the real and maintaining the symbolic. Such claims may seem a little strange or paradoxical because they are posed in the famously counterintuitive terms of Lacanian psychoanalysis. But there are solid precedents for the overarching psychoanalytic argument on which he draws: the *real* is revealed through, or as, the tear in the fabric of the symbolic, what we know as ordinary *reality*. Normally this tear is plugged by the *object a* of desire to afford the comforting sense or illusion of wholeness and normalcy. In this connection the key notion Rushing borrows from the Lacanian theory of desire and the drives is desire's "endless circulation around [that] always missed object"—this formulation is to be understood in the context of the understanding that the encounter with the real *must* fail. For were such an encounter to occur in fact, it would mean the dissolution of the sustaining fabric of the symbolic. The sustaining fiction of reality keeps the real at bay, fortunately.

As for what is at stake in such a project, Rushing's implied answer turns on the periodizing gesture of the New Lacanians, for whom the diacritical feature of the contemporary cultural moment is that we have graduated, or fallen away, from a social order regulated by prohibition and desire to a state of social life in which a privatized *jouissance* has been unleashed, sometimes to the detriment of civic life and public culture, to the peril of what in an earlier cultural moment was called *Gemeinschaft*. This periodizing argument is a key contribution of Lacanian psychoanalysis to Cultural Studies, and Rushing's book is an elegant illustration of the structuring and structural role of that *jouissance*, posed against desire, in detective fiction. In repeating this argument here, however, Rushing also maintains that *jouissance,* or drive and enjoyment, were constitutive elements even in classic detective fiction. They have only asserted themselves more powerfully in recent cultural texts, including more recent detective fiction and film.

In the chapter on Hitchcock (*Rear Window*) and Agatha Christie (*Murder on the Orient Express*), Rushing begins with a close analysis of Hitchcock's films and then contextualizes it within his framing conceit—"resisting arrest." He demonstrates that the romantic subplot is not "an extraneous and irrelevant waste of time." In an echo of Erik Erikson's epochal frontier hypothesis, Rushing observes that detective fiction is not just about the "free-ranging intellect of a genius detective," but also and perhaps even primarily about a "domestic arrest," the domestication of the (male) anarchic impulse, by the woman who provides "rest." Of course, this function of the woman must be counterbalanced by an acknowledgment of the "other woman" of detective fiction, namely the femme fatale, who does the opposite of domesticating the detective. She is, on the contrary, his greatest challenge, and does not hold out to him the olive branch of bourgeois domesticity.

Rushing's emphasis on *jouissance* as a crucial element in the appeal of detective fiction is an important contribution to the understanding of the way the genre captivates its fans. Yet admittedly he does not develop the difference gender makes to the appeal of the genre: he frequently does not develop the distinctions between the experience of a male and a female reader/spectator. To acknowledge such distinctions would be to understand more profoundly, for instance, the significance of the woman, including the femme fatale, in the detective fiction. Thus, it is interesting that the woman's threat in detective fiction is not, as is commonly assumed, that she will hoard *jouissance*, denying it to the hero/detective. Rather, as Žižek (1991, p. 66) points out, she is most threatening in those instances when, to turn again to the language of psychoanalysis, she "traverses the fantasy" and fully assumes her own "fate," dying a death beyond the death of her subjectivity, a subjectivity delimited as man's symptom.

Although Rushing himself does not develop this point, one could extrapolate from his concern with exploring the imbrication of the detective's desire and that of the reader/spectator to argue more generally that "the woman" is also a technology of mediation for the reader's own desire. She is a fulcrum that articulates the detective's desire with that of the reader or spectator. The figure of the woman functions as a point of condensation of the desire *simultaneously of the detective and the reader.* The male reader or spectator, for instance, is conventionally able and even encouraged to identify with the detective in the fiction, rather than with the woman, when an attractive woman or even a femme fatale is presented as the object of desire or the target of violence, voyeuristic curiosity, or projection of fantasies. By contrast it would seem harder, especially within the conventions of Hollywood filmmaking, for a female reader of detective fiction to identify with the woman against the detective to whom she is a narrative foil in some respects. It is important to stress that this asymmetry of identificatory trajectories has to do with the genre rather than, for example, with an accidentally sexist perspective on the part of the writer, although sexism on the part of a given writer or director may also be an evident problem. Detective fiction is in a specific, structural sense aimed at a male reader/viewer, and I emphasize this asymmetry to highlight a ramification of Rushing's argument.

In the next chapter, Rushing turns to Žižek to argue that detective fictions are fascinating because they reveal our otherwise unacceptable desires made "real," and thus confront us with our own "guilt"—while at the same time the generic resolution of the mystery also involves the identification of a "scapegoat" who can then take on the burden of that guilt and provide a measure of catharsis to the reader/spectator. In this tragic displacement lies the pleasure of the mystery, what Žižek terms a surplus pleasure, because we not only experience the libidinal charge of the realization of our desire but we also get off scot-free. Rushing discusses Antonioni's *L'avventura* and *Blowup*, as well as Minghella's *The Talented Mr. Ripley*. Antonioni, as Rushing presents him, is the director who "most explicitly deploys detection's generic conventions while most explicitly frustrating them." In Antonioni there is no scapegoating, and therefore no relief, and the spectator feels the need to repeat because there has been no releasing arrest. What draws the spectator in *L'avventura* is the feeling that there is something there that is always sensed in a missed encounter. Rushing asks, "Is this insistent presence of something, something illegible and incomprehensible, menacing and inhuman, not the real?" In both *L'avventura* and *The Talented Mr. Ripley*, Rushing identifies a failure of the "logic of arrest" characteristic of canonical detective fiction, the one presenting a trajectory of desire (*L'avventura*) and the other the endless repetition of *drive* (*The Talented Mr. Ripley*), so that the latter is in a way more extreme and beyond the pale of "humanity," more closely approximating the circuit of the death drive.

If this analysis brings Rushing to a diagnosis of the negative energy of drive, however, the latter half of his book also considers the positive aspect of drive: (good) *enjoyment*. In the chapter on repetition, Rushing opens with a discussion of the unnerving repetition without alteration, real repetition in a double sense, that appears at the end of the much-maligned *Teletubbies* show—a video clip is played again "exactly as before," delighting young viewers and confounding adult viewers. For Rushing this is an uncanny rather than an idiotic repetition, although the *Unheimlich* nature of the repetition may inhere in its closeness to autistic repetition, which children themselves are "so close to," and indeed the repetition may be precisely "idiotic" in the sense Lacan gives it, turning back to the Greek roots of the word. Yet, although this might seem to imply that the adult desire by contrast is for variation, detective fiction, as in the case of the classic show *Monk*, suggests that there is perhaps something atavistic, or residual, in our own adult pleasure in watching these shows.

If Rushing reads the detective as disavowing his desire—contrary to the central Lacanian imperative not to cede ground on one's desire (*ne céder pas sur son desir*)—it is also possible by the author's own logic to read the pulsion of detective fiction as always a pursuit, whether conscious or not, of one's real *desire* and perhaps not always a matter of being caught in the drive of *jouissance*. The detective, in this view, is not so much disavowing his desire but always pursuing it, even if not conscious of the implications of his choices. That is, the interesting aspect of the detective's behavior is not *méconnaissance* exactly; rather the motor, or motive, for both detective and reader is pursuit of a desire not restricted to the resolution of the mystery or the discovery of the perpetrator of the crime.

Rushing's analysis is consistently suggestive in uncovering layers of the attractions of detective fiction. He shows how the reader's desire to enjoy blood and gore, to enjoy pain, lies in the region between enjoyment of one's own pain, masochism, and *Schadenfreude*, enjoyment of someone else's pain (this latter enjoyment could be either vicarious or just the "better-him-than-me" variety). Thus, in the chapter on violence, Rushing interprets Christie's proposal to provide a less "anaemic" kind of detective story than was customary for her as a resolve to meet the desire in the reader for a kind of "displeasure." This displeasure is experienced by or vicariously *through or in the body of* another, even if the desire cannot be fully acknowledged by the reader. However, the enjoyment that is initially proffered as a pleasure permitted to roam freely, not arrested, is soon curtailed or denied, Rushing argues. So what we are talking about, once again, is enjoyment without satisfaction, or as it were, enjoyment unbound in time but strictly constrained in form. The sleight of hand is achieved precisely with the reader's complicity, and thus Rushing's reader is reminded that it is the detective fiction's reader who is the willing dupe in this strange compact of satisfaction granted through deferral.

To explain the nature of this acquiescence to being duped, Rushing posits that "the reader, far from engaging in cognitive activity, is engaged in *forgetting*, forgetting real violence in favor of a spectacle manufactured for his passive enjoyment." But we may ask: What exactly is forgotten? The real, as embodied in the "body." For though it would seem as if the addicted consumer/reader of detective fiction wants nothing more than to have the body revealed as though it were the *objet a*, that object that would satisfy desire, it is in fact thankfully screened off, denied and eternally deferred, thereby necessitating the return of the addict to the scene/"seen" of the crime, drawn by the unfulfilled desire to *see* the crime again and again, or more precisely to have it "screened," both shown and not shown.

In the final chapter the author argues that addiction is "a constitutive feature" of classic detective fiction (and here he limits his comments to the classic version, although he does say that it is important for the entire genre of detective fiction). Addiction is an imperfection that offsets the deductive capacities of the sleuth but simultaneously augments, by contrast, those presumptively extraordinary qualities. Holmes's addiction to a perception-altering drug such as cocaine or morphine (or for that matter Hercule Poirot's obsessive addiction to fastidious grooming, the television series' eponymous protagonist Adrian Monk's obsessive-compulsive behavior, or John Rebus's alcohol addiction) also sharpens the detective's ability to perceive differently from other people: the "defective detective" is thereby refigured as a super sleuth. In these fictions, the detective's dis-ease, his itch, also underscores his addiction to the activity of detection itself, something shared at some essential level with the fan of detective fiction. The spectator or reader's compulsive enjoyment, forcing a *repetitive* consumption of one fiction after another no matter how true each remains to the same formula, is a mirror of the detective's enjoyment. Rushing adroitly traces some of these doublings, perhaps displaying a third-order enjoyment in doing so: the critic's enjoyment, which is itself redoubled in the enjoyment to be had by a reader of this book. Rushing returns therefore to his main argument, that the enjoyment should remain unarrested for the genre to be successful with the reader. The detection should never be an experience of closure; the hunting must never end in the annihilation of the hunted. There is, as Rushing puts it, *"no hermeneutic component to the detective novel."* Reading, like detection, is at its core an addiction in which there is nothing to enjoy but, in Žižek's language, the symptom itself.

In a final anthypophoric movement of the argument, the author poses a question that will come up in his reader's mind: "Is there nothing after illness? Are illness and addiction all we have, all we can ever have?" Rushing's answer to this question is intriguing, but the reader will find the pleasure of this nimble book reward enough, and the answer an almost unnecessary arrest.

REFERENCES

Copjec, J., ed. (1993a). Introduction. In *Shades of Noir: A Reader*, pp. vii–xii. London and New York: Verso.

———— (1993b). The phenomenal nonphenomenal: private space in film noir. In *Shades of Noir*, pp. 167–197. London and New York: Verso.

Miller, D. A. (1988). *The Novel and the Police*. Berkeley: University of California Press.

Salecl, R., and Žižek, S., eds. (1996). Introduction. In *Gaze and Voice as Love Objects*, pp. 1–4. Sic 1. Durham, NC and London: Duke University Press.

Žižek, S. (1991). *Looking Awry: An Introduction to Jacques Lacan through Popular Culture*. Cambridge, MA: October Books/ MIT Press.

Acknowledgments

Although no list of this kind can be exhaustive, I would like to thank at least the following people. First and foremost, Lilya Kaganovsky contributed to this project enormously by reading every draft as soon as it was written, and often as it was in the midst of being written, through a constant series of discussions both theoretical and practical about the material, and, years ago, by helping to spark my interest in film studies.

I also owe a great deal to the Illinois Program for Research in the Humanities (IPRH): a semester of teaching leave, as well as a year of IPRH Fellows Seminars, in which we discussed everything from the smallest trivia to the largest disciplinary and interdisciplinary questions. This project really took shape and was largely written during my IPRH year, and I would particularly like to thank Matti Bunzl (director of the IPRH), Andrea Goulet (my IPRH fellowship partner in crime—crime fiction, that is), and Michael Rothberg and Stephen Hartnett, for their fellowship in all senses of the word.

Slavoj Žižek offered to read drafts of several chapters of this volume, engaged in a number of very helpful theoretical discussions, and was very generous with his time, energy, suggestions, and encouragement during his stays in Urbana-Champaign.

The department of Spanish, Italian & Portuguese (SIP) and the program in Comparative Literature at the University of Illinois, Urbana-Champaign, provided a semester of junior leave to help finish this project, and I would like to thank all of my colleagues in both departments for their sustained demonstration of true collegiality, but particularly Nancy Blake, for several theoretical discussions as well as feedback, Michael Palencia-Roth, for steering me in the right direction on more than one occasion, and my fellow Italianists, Antonino and Diane Musumeci, for their sustained encouragement and collegiality.

I would also like to express my gratitude to two of my colleagues at UC Berkeley, Albert Ascoli, for providing much moral and other support over the years, and Barbara Spackman, who has done the same, and who offered the seminar that was the starting point for this project.

Several chapters of this book were initially circulated among an informal writing group that included, at one time or another, Dara Goldman, Eva-Lynn Jagoe, Ann Abbott, Yasemin Yildiz, and Andrew Herscher, all of whom provided helpful feedback both inside the writing group and out.

A number of colleagues and friends both here at Illinois and elsewhere have contributed in various ways over the years, and I would like to thank them: Zachary Lesser and Naomi Reed, both for their generous enthusiasm and friendship, and significant help with this project; Nancy Castro and Gillen Wood, again for their enthusiasm and friendship, not to mention pointing me toward Other Press in the first place; Jed Esty, for his careful reading of some of the materials associated with this book; Luca Somigli, for organizing a panel at the 2004 American Association for Italian Studies (AAIS) conference in Ottawa, Canada, on Italian detective fiction that some of this material was part of; the organizers and attendees of the "Murder and Mayhem in the Mare Nostrum: Contemporary Configurations of Mediterranean Crime Fictions" conference in Prato, Italy; and Anna Westerstahl Stenport, who has since become one of my colleagues here at Illinois, for confirming the passable accuracy of my translations from Swedish.

It is hard to thank students individually because it is almost impossible to take notes during an energetic discussion on who said what, but I would not want to underestimate the collective influence of those discussions on my thinking over the years. For the purposes of this book, however, I would particularly like to thank the students in two classes: Comparative Literature 151 (a freshman seminar on detective fiction) in the spring of 2003, and Italian 290 (a history of Italian cinema) in the fall of 2001.

No such list would be complete without mentioning my family, who have contributed to this project and my intellectual life in many ways over the years.

Finally, my son Alexander/Sasha. When I finished a morning of writing and was able to go pick him up, it was a reward for the work I had done, not a distraction from further work. And no one should underestimate the powerful help that a two-year-old can give to someone trying to think through a chapter on repetition.

Early versions of several pieces of this project appeared first in journals, and I would like to gratefully acknowledge permission to reprint material. Portions of "The Real of Desire: Travel/Detection/Hitchcock/Antonioni," in *The Communication Review* 6.4 (2003): 313–326 appear in Chapters 3 (Desire) and 4 (Anxiety), and are reproduced by permission of Taylor & Francis Group, LLC., http://www.taylorandfrancis.com. A small portion of "Traveling Detectives: Verne's Logic of Arrest and the Pleasures of (Avoiding) the Real," published in *Yale French Studies* 108 (2005): 89–101, appears in Chapter 3 (Desire), and is reprinted with permission of *Yale French Studies*. Last, an early version of portions of Chapter 7 (Enjoyment) appeared in the article "From *Monk* to Monks: The End of Enjoyment in Umberto Eco's *The Name of the Rose*," in *Symposium* 59.2 (2005): 116–128, and is reprinted with permission of the Helen Dwight Reid Educational Foundation, published by Heldref Publications, 1319 18th Street NW, Washington, DC 20036-1802, www.heldref.org. Copyright © 2005.

INTRODUCTION

UNLIMITED SERIAL READING

One of the most theoretically sophisticated and nuanced studies of detective fiction is John Irwin's *The Mystery to a Solution: Poe, Borges, and the Analytic Detective Story*, and he opens it with the following "simple-minded" question: "How does one write analytic detective fiction as high art when the genre's basic structure, its central narrative mechanism, seems to discourage the unlimited rereading associated with serious writing?" (Irwin 1994, p. 1). Irwin is slightly breezy about just what "analytic detective fiction" means, but he says that it is the genre invented by Poe and it centers on analysis rather than adventure. He very deliberately contrasts it to Chandler's "romantic" version of detective fiction (i.e., the hard-boiled novel). I think we may take it that he means something like "classic detective fiction"—emphasizing logic, deduction, "ratiocination" in Poe's phrase, with thin, flat characters and contrived and *outré* situations—best known through the works of Poe, Conan Doyle, and Agatha Christie. But in a work that substantially addresses Poe, and quite famously adds yet another chapter (one revolving around the words *simple*, *even*, and *odd*) to the numerous critical interventions on Poe's "Purloined Letter," I think we are authorized to ask if Irwin's question isn't a little *too* simple-minded.

Irwin's study is dedicated to the problem of how Borges transforms classic detective fiction into "high art," but one immediately perceives a curious problem in this opposition between "analytic detective fiction" that needs to be turned into "high art": namely, that no one, *particularly* not Irwin, would want to claim that Poe, the inventor of analytic detective fiction, was not high art. How can it be that "analytic detective fiction" needs to be transformed into "high art" if the very first example of analytic detective fiction *is* high art? Here one immediately sees the opportunity for a deconstructive reading that would thoroughly explore how the opposition between "detective fiction" and "high art" breaks down, how Poe always already contains an endless *différance* that will destabilize the notion of high art, and so on, but my interests lie elsewhere. What interests me about Irwin's question is actually the second half: the claim that the genre's "basic structure, its central narrative mechanism, seems to discourage the unlimited rereading associated with serious writing." Numerous studies of detective fiction have noted, usually in passing, that detective fiction is not meant to be reread, unless it is by "people . . . with poor memories," as Irwin says (1994, p. 1), a group I have to place myself in, I'm afraid, that it is a "self-consuming artifact," although they have much more rarely explored the question of just how the genre's "basic structure" and "central narrative mechanism" discourage us from rereading. Indeed, is this even true? Where is the empirical research indicating that readers of detective fiction reread less often than readers of other genre fiction, or even literature? Might it not be the case that few readers outside of universities reread at all, that fiction whether high or low is largely treated as disposable? Is it not equally possible that ordinary readers reread their favorite texts, even if they are supposedly "self-consuming artifacts," even if they are mystery novels, or science-fiction paperbacks? What is there that would prevent readers from returning to reread mystery novels? It cannot simply be that the entire narrative is turned toward one single, shocking revelation that will eventually put everything in its place, make the truth clear, as one can think without too much difficulty of instances of "high art" that function in just the same way (*Oedipus Rex*, for instance). We often know precisely how a story will turn out, even *before* we read it the first time: Who doesn't know the fate of the "star-cross'd lovers" in advance of beginning *Romeo and Juliet*? And yet this does not impede rereading.

But what really intrigues me about Irwin's question is the phrase "the unlimited rereading associated with serious writing." Irwin presupposes here an implicit judgment about the superiority of "serious writing" over popular fiction, a preference that, in intellectual circles, appears as disdain toward popular detective fiction and its readers ("people with poor memories"), a tradition going back at least to Edmund Wilson's classic "Who Cares Who Killed Roger Ackroyd?", where Wilson says all kinds of horrible things about the mental defectives who read genre fiction, comparing them, among other things, to alcoholics and opium addicts (1950, p. 263). But where Irwin's question is really a little *too* simple-minded is that he misses the fact that there is a structure that *does* characterize the way people read detective fiction, and genre fiction more generally, a structure that is at least as interesting as the "unlimited rereading associated with serious writing." It is less esteemed than rereading, at least within the academy, but that is no reason to think it is less worthy of explanation and analysis. I am talking about the unlimited *serial* reading associated with popular fiction. This feature of detective fiction has been dismissed as precisely what marks it as contemptible and unworthy of serious attention when it is noted at all. "How," asks the outraged academic critic of detective fiction before inevitably turning his or her attention to Borges, Auster, Pynchon, Sciascia, Eco, and the like, "can readers consume one book after another after another when they are all exactly the same?" This study proposes to take that question seriously, and suggests that the genre's "basic structure" may be a withholding from the reader just what it is that he or she is looking for. This persistent return to what does not give satisfaction (a return that, in itself, may carry a certain kind of perverse pleasure) is called by psychoanalysis *enjoyment*, and I will suggest in the rest of this book that it is the "central mechanism" of detective fiction, particularly although not exclusively in its beginnings in classic detective fiction.

OVERVIEW

This is the essence of the project that I have elaborated in this book: an analysis of the role that desire and enjoyment have played, and continue to play, in crime fiction (almost entirely concerned with detective fiction, and largely centered on classic detective fiction). I am particularly interested in extending the discourse of enjoyment and drive that New Lacanian scholars such as Slavoj Žižek and Joan Copjec have brought to studies of the hard-boiled novel or *film noir* to earlier examples of detective fiction: How does enjoyment already structure classic detective fiction? But to arrive at that discussion, I also wanted to review how detective fiction has typically been understood in a psychoanalytic context, from Freud onward, as a genre of misplaced and misunderstood *desire*. To that end, the first half of this book largely addresses the question of desire, attending both to the desire of the detective, traditionally presented as pure intellect, "eccentric," outside or beyond the circle of desire, and the desire of the reader, who is instead presumed to be motivated by the basest of impulses, such as the wish to revel in sensationalistic spectacles of murder and gore. Psychoanalytic accounts of detective fiction have traditionally worked to demonstrate the genre's libidinal "bad faith," the ways in which it permits readers to avoid recognizing their own base impulses made manifest in the story. Such accounts are useful insofar as they demonstrate that detective fiction, far from being a genre of "ratiocination," as Poe calls it, is in fact a genre of misdirection, or misrecognition. Hence, the conclusion that "the butler did it" permits readers to attribute their own homicidal impulses to a fictional butler, what Žižek refers to as the avoidance of the "real of desire," where readers indulge their real, violent desires and then disavow them.

Most critical studies of detective fiction present a relatively simplified version of the genre. They organize it into a period of classic detective fiction (the genius detective variety that we know from Poe, Conan Doyle, or Christie), the hardboiled genre (Chandler and Hammett), and they may note some of the later varieties, at least in passing, such as the forensic, the procedural, and so on. In the chapter entitled "Irritation," I want to make the case, however, that the variety of detective fiction has been largely ignored or underestimated. Even fan Web sites, which tend to go in for a very exacting anatomy of the genre, don't fully recognize the types and subgenres that flourish within detective fiction. To make that case, I list and briefly discuss a number of the more obscure subgenres of contemporary detective fiction, from interior decorating murder mysteries to ancient Roman crime novels. How far can the proliferation of generic themes go in detective fiction? How marginal and strange can a detective series be and still constitute a recognizable type, a kind of microgenre? To answer this question, I will turn my attention to two genres of detective fiction that have surely gone completely unrecognized in the scholarly literature, if only because they have really only appeared in the last five to ten years: so-called "chick-lit" detective fiction, and Jane Austen-themed detective novels. To show that in this endless multiplication of genres and subgenres no possible space goes unutilized, I then discuss in somewhat more detail a series that locates itself at the intersection of these two genres: the Jane Austen-themed, chick-lit detective novels written by Laura Levine, her "Jaine Austen mysteries."

We are accustomed to talking about "detective fiction," or the slightly broader category "mystery novel," or the even broader "crime novel," as if the novels contained within this categorization actually shared some commonality. What possible connection is there between, say, Sherlock Holmes-style stories, a gritty hard-boiled novel, a science-besotted forensic television series, and a Jane Austen-meets-chick-lit tale? At first glance, it might appear that the pleasure of revelation ("Ah, that's how it was done!") is one of the only common points holding together the variety of detective fiction. The police procedural, one of the most popular and central genres, suggests that even revelation may not be common to all varieties of detective fiction, however. In the procedural it is not unusual for the reader to know immediately who the guilty party is. This is largely because the procedural strongly de-emphasizes moments of revelation, inspiration, luck, or brilliant and improbable deduction in the investigation. It does this to emphasize, in turn, that police investigation is a series of mechanical procedures, routines, forms to be filled out—in short, a great deal of work. In fact, what's really odd about the procedural is that readers enjoy it at all, since it typically depicts police work as a boring, depressing slog with little or no rewards for the investigator. What is it that captures our interest in the procedural? I look at two contemporary, popular European writers of procedurals, the Swedish author Henning Mankell and the Italian Andrea Camilleri. Although both write procedurals emphasizing routine, the social interplay of office work, obstructions from the administration above, and hostility from the people they are supposed to protect, the two writers depict radically different worlds. Mankell's protagonist, Kurt Wallander, is a depressed, diabetic, perpetually lonely soul in frigid Sweden, while Camilleri's character, Salvo Montalbano, is an energetic, social gastronome, much admired by Sicilian women. Both novelists do rely, as a structuring device, on what might seem like the most unlikely of devices: irritation. Mankell and Camilleri return again and again to minor details, an object that their protagonist has forgotten, a dinner date that has to be postponed again and again, a car that needs to be taken to the mechanic, elements that are out of place, that chafe and rub against the mind of the protagonist as well as the reader. They appear to have no other purpose. What if, I suggest, this irritation is itself the glue that holds together the detective novel? In fact, the fundamental procedure of the detective novel is inarguably irritating, since it consists in placing before the reader a crime that appears impossible and then reminding the reader of that impossibility over and over again until an explanation is offered. Although this basic procedure would appear to be profoundly unpleasurable, it obviously is not. There is something that we enjoy in it, and this is where I first suggest that the term *enjoyment* should be a key term in discussions of detective fiction, particularly in its psychoanalytic sense: returning again and again to what does not give us pleasure, always missing the same object that we thought we wanted, but obviously didn't.

In the next chapter, "Desire," I look at Alfred Hitchcock's *Rear Window* and Agatha Christie's *Murder on the Orient Express*, examining the ways in which these texts direct and misdirect the viewer's desire, facilitating the avoidance of the "real of desire." Hitchcock offers an exemplary case of this phenomenon: although *Rear Window* is very nearly explicit in a series of identifications between the protagonists and the criminal (that is, both L.B. "Jeff" Jeffries and Lisa Freemont identify to some degree with Lars Thorwald's murderous desires), and the film's spectator is neatly "sutured" into the same position, the film ultimately arrests the spreading "stain of the real" through a solution that emphasizes domesticity and immobility. The restless movement of desire—Jeff's desire for a bachelor lifestyle of unrestrained travel, unimpeded by romantic entanglements, and Thorwald's identical desire, to kill his wife and travel freely—is "arrested" as all subjects are pinned down at the end of the film: Mrs. Thorwald's body in the East River, Mr. Thorwald's arrest, Jeff's two broken legs that prevent any further travel, and so on.

If *Rear Window* is an exemplary account of the avoidance of the real of desire, then *Murder on the Orient Express* appears to pose a problem for Žižek's "exculpatory" vision of detective fiction: If classic detective fiction scapegoats our antisocial desires and thus frees us of responsibility for our darker desires, how to explain a novel in which "everyone did it"? However, I demonstrate that here, too, the "logic of arrest" is at work. Just as the characters in *Rear Window* all come to rest (or arrest) along with the solution, the Orient Express also comes to a halt when the murderer is "arrested." Although this event occurs not at the end of the novel, but at the beginning, a typical instance of Agatha Christie's astonishing ability to deceive the reader. In both cases, rest/arrest stand emblematically for the restraint or arrest of the stain of the real, specifically the "real of desire." In short, detective fiction stages a confrontation between the reader and the reader's unconscious disavowed desire—we have all experienced homicidal rage, but would prefer to think of ourselves as restrained social beings—and Žižek describes that violent desire as a "stain," a blot on the landscape of civilized society. However, in order to avoid the spread of the stain to the entirety of the social sphere, the admission that everyone has such desires, detective fiction "arrests" the stain, pinpoints all of that bad desire onto a single guilty individual.

In the following chapter, "Anxiety," I examine two cinematic examples of detection that potentially do not "avoid the real of desire": Michelangelo Antonioni's *L'avventura* (although also *Blowup*, and to a lesser degree, *The Passenger*) and Anthony Minghella's 1999 *The Talented Mr. Ripley*. Antonioni's films persistently confront, rather than avoid, this "real of desire," imagining their protagonists on the verge (or beyond the verge, in the case of *The Passenger*) of a suicidal "act," precisely the kind of desire that classic detective fiction generically turns away from. In turn, Antonioni's films demand a kind of courage from their viewers—not only the courage to confront desire, but equally how the subject that does not "give up on his desire" is led to the Lacanian *act*, a suicidal withdrawal from the social and symbolic network. In *L'avventura*, this appears principally through the character of Anna, whose disappearance initiates the question: Who would want to see her vanish? Is her disappearance suicidal or homicidal? As is his practice, Antonioni does not answer this question, and it is precisely this stubborn refusal that works against the "logic of arrest." No body is pinned down at the end of this film, and, as I argue, the final shot of the movie (Anna's friend Claudia looking out at a volcano) suggests the possibility of another suicidal act, this time on Claudia's part. Minghella's *The Talented Mr. Ripley*, on the other hand, makes use not so much of generic detective models, as is the case with Antonioni, but of the logic of *film noir*, which offers up the *femme fatale* as the embodiment of the detective's (or viewer's) desire. That desire is irresistible and yet deadly, insofar as ceding to it (it is fundamentally an antisocial and criminal desire at work) would cut the detective off from the social field and the symbolic network that define him as a subject. If in *noir's* typical formulation, the detective turns away from this desire, as Sam Spade does, for instance, in *The Maltese Falcon*, Minghella's Ripley offers an emblematic lesson to its viewers on how to find their "inner *femme fatale*," their inner abyssal dimension that is also a real of desire, both destructive and self-destructive, requiring courage. Tom Ripley is figured as a sympathetic, but still deadly, incarnation of drive, working as a kind of *homme fatal*, pushing toward a final realization of the subject not as a "fake (i.e., symbolic) somebody," but instead as a "real (understood also in a Lacanian sense) nobody." In other words, when Ripley looks within himself, he actually sees too clearly. He sees that he harbors desires that are violent toward others, and he sees his own death drive, his impulse to self-obliteration. It is that traumatic abyssal dimension inside himself, his own potential to do away with himself and literally *be no one and nothing* that Ripley refers to when he calls himself a real nobody. His tragedy is that he persistently fails, despite his talent for impersonation, to be a normal social individual who lives in ignorance of this inner abyss—a "fake somebody."

The next chapter, "Repetition," begins with a look at the television show *Monk* as a way to begin thinking about the role of repetition in detective fiction. Adrian Monk's obsessive-compulsive disorder may appear to be a mere "gimmick," but I argue that Monk's need to repeat (his tics, phobias, and compulsive behaviors) is in fact characteristic of the entire genre, especially classic detective fiction. Essentially, the role of repetition in detective fiction is summarized by an idiotic childish joke told repeatedly in one episode of *Monk*: "Pete and Repeat were in a boat. Pete fell out. Who was left?" The trick of detective fiction, I argue, is the same as that of the joke. One must con the reader or listener into saying "repeat." After *Monk*, the chapter turns to a particular fantasy elaborated in the Sherlock Holmes story "The Adventure of the Copper Beeches," in which a father imprisons his own daughter because she is about to marry and he will lose her money when she does, and hires another woman (who believes she is accepting a job as a simple governess) in order to imitate the imprisoned girl, to act as a "screen woman." Holmes eventually uses the governess to expose the father's misdeed, but the psychic structure, the elemental fantasy suggested by the story, is a different one, one that revolves around *repetition*. A father, drunk on his paternal authority, demands exclusive sexual access to his own daughter. His domination over her is repeated in his domination of the screen woman (whom he dresses and coifs like the daughter), who conceals his incestuous desire; this domination is repeated by the detective, who secretly directs the screen woman (thus, incidentally, making the father's original fear come true—the daughter is, in fact, "unfaithful" to him). The chapter then finds this entire fantasy scene repeated *again* in Hitchcock's *Vertigo*: there is again a monstrous paternal authority (Gavin Elster), his victim (Madeleine Elster), a screen woman (Judy), whom he dresses and directs, and a detective (Scottie Ferguson), who eventually dominates the screen woman to expose the father's original antisocial desire. Only, in *Vertigo*, there is already a back story set in the olden days of San Francisco involving precisely the same elements: a terrible paternal authority (a man named Ives) and his victim (Carlotta Valdes, whose history Madeleine appears to compulsively repeat). What

Vertigo makes manifest is the compulsive character of repetition in detective fiction, the way the detective brings the terrible, forbidden desire of the Father to an end, but simultaneously is compelled to repeat it.

Here the book makes its fundamental turn from desire to enjoyment, understood in the psychoanalytic sense of pleasure-in-pain, the repetitive and mechanical (at times appearing idiotic) return to what does *not* give us satisfaction. Detective fiction, in addition to being a genre of misdirected, misidentified, and misrecognized *desire*, is also quintessentially a genre of *enjoyment*. This "endless circulation around the always missed object" would presumably provide satisfaction, and indeed the various misdirections of detective fiction produce precisely such an effect, a kind of structural prohibition against the satisfaction of desire. The reader, for instance, is conned into believing that he or she might solve the crime, as if the novel were a crossword puzzle and the reader an armchair detective paralleling the detective in the text. Every mechanism of classic detective fiction, however, is geared toward "*the prevention of thought*," as Pierre Bayard has emphatically noted (2000, p. 25). The solution, then, remains the "always missed object" that the reader returns to again and again and misses again and again. Similarly, the spectacle of sensationalistic violence is another "missed object" promised by detective fiction, but rarely delivered. Again, we see a kind of deceit fundamentally at work: readers are not getting what they think they are getting out of the genre. They believe they are vicariously enjoying the genius of Sherlock Holmes, but they are actually enjoying the idiocy of Dr. Watson; they believe that the genre delivers satisfaction through the solution of the mystery when, in fact, *no one is satisfied by the solution*. Reader, sidekick, detective, criminal—all of them return again and again to precisely the same scenarios, the same rooms with dead bodies locked from the inside in classic detective fiction, the same dangerous dames in the hardboiled novel, the same grinding, unsatisfying labor in the police procedural.

The penultimate chapter, "Violence," demonstrates how classic detective fiction is predicated on a specific form of this generic deception. It promises "a good violent murder with lots of blood," as Agatha Christie writes in *Hercule Poirot's Christmas* (2000a, p. i), but this blood is immediately turned into "too much blood," an intellectual puzzle that must be solved. There is a kind of generic transubstantiation of blood in detective fiction, from a sign of furious desire and social disturbance that might satisfy the reader's secret and unspoken desires into a puzzle problem. Hence, one of the fundamental critical presuppositions about "desire" in detective fiction—that it makes manifest our forbidden, violent desires—proves problematic: violence is always both present and concealed, a "corpse to which is attached no sense of death," as Grossvogel notes (1979, p. 15). The chapter covers texts including Poe's "Murders in the Rue Morgue," Christie's *Hercule Poirot's Christmas*, and the little-known Italian modernist masterpiece, Carlo Emilio Gadda's *Quer pasticciaccio brutto de via Merulana* [*That Awful Mess on Via Merulana*]. The direct comparison of popular detective fiction (Agatha Christie) and literary detective fiction (Gadda was Italy's most difficult and rarefied high modernist) also permits a clear demonstration of how desire and enjoyment are loaded interpretive categories: by privileging a direct confrontation with desire, psychoanalysis also privileges the elite, experimental, and literary forms of detective fiction over the popular ones. Christie, on the contrary, exemplifies classic detective fiction's preference for a transgression that is not properly a transgression at all (the antisocial violence that the reader never quite gets to experience, as it arrives in a totally aestheticized and intellectualized form); this is the essence of "enjoying one's symptom," returning again and again to what did not satisfy your demand. Although I trace this structure from Poe to Christie, it equally appears in high, literary detective fiction, as Gadda's *That Awful Mess on Via Merulana* shows. Gadda's novel provides the violence the reader longs for in detective fiction, a violence that is not aestheticized, but rather functions as an irreparable trauma both for the individuals around it and to the social field itself. Moreover, because the novel ends with the mystery unsolved, there is no scapegoating onto a single suspect, no "logic of arrest" at work, and hence no avoidance of the real of desire. Although from the standpoint of traditional psychoanalytic criticism of detective fiction, Gadda's novel is exemplary because it forces the reader to confront his or her own desire, I argue that it also has a negative effect. It offers itself up as a proper and normative model of desire, one that would provide a kind of therapy for the "pathologically" repetitive behavior of the reader of traditional, popular mysteries, the reader who pursues his or her enjoyment rather than desire.

The last chapter, "Enjoyment," shows how the turn from desire to enjoyment enables us to see that detective fiction (particularly in its classic and popular forms, rather than its high "literary" adaptations), through its perverse insistence on returning again and again to what does not provide satisfaction, resists an authoritative and potentially authoritarian model of "normal" desire. Readers of detective fiction specifically and of popular genre fiction more generally have long been stigmatized for their reading habits, for consuming product after product that is basically the same; authority is on the side of literature and its eternal truths, not genre fiction and its cheap entertainment, frequently described as an addiction, a symptom of a disease. In this sense, "enjoying one's symptom," as Žižek says, becomes a perversely anti-authoritarian way of reading. It is a deliberate embrace of what is ostensibly bad for you, and, as such, brings you closer to a recognition of the operations of *drive*, your own self-destructive impulses: what Freud called the death drive. In short, drive and enjoyment are intimately connected. This last "body" chapter covers Conan Doyle's *The Sign of Four*, the television show *Monk*, and Umberto Eco's *The Name of the Rose*. It begins by looking at the question of addiction and compulsive behavior in detective fiction, using Sherlock Holmes's famous addiction to his seven percent solution of cocaine and Adrian Monk's obsessive compulsive disorder to suggest that the classic detective is *constitutively* disabled, defective, or debilitated, particularly with regard to his normal social pleasures. His sole compensation is the constant return (enjoyment in its psychoanalytic sense) to the scene of detection, the true "seven percent solution" that he cannot give up. It suggests that Sherlock Holmes with his addiction to cocaine may be a better "model" precisely in his perverse renunciation of any reward for his efforts, just as the reader is bound to receive no reward at the end of the book, than Umberto Eco's putatively liberal and anti-authoritarian stance in *The Name of the Rose*. In that novel, Eco depicts a medieval detective, William of Baskerville, who, again, reveals a constitutive feature of classic detection (true also of Dupin, Poirot, Wimsey, and the rest, up to Adrian Monk): the detective as para-authority, who stands between authority and its prohibitions following the Freudian deadlock: you must be like the father, you cannot be like the father. The fundamental prohibition of the abbey that William investigates is reading forbidden books, particularly one book (the cause of the murders he investigates), a book that would legitimize frivolous literature and enjoyment. My reading is both psychoanalytic and political, however, as William's earnest desire, equivalent to a kind of intellectual socialist liberalism, is to permit free access, within reason, to knowledge, with "the simple" proletariat receiving benevolent guidance from "the wise." William's desire to free up the paternal prohibition, however, risks turning laughter and the reading of forbidden texts into an intellectual duty, turning our subversive enjoyment into a laborious chore.

STAKES AND JUSTIFICATIONS

So, what is at stake in such a project? First, in the New Lacanian vision of history, enjoyment/*jouissance* and drive are set aside as privileged markers of contemporaneity. We have definitively moved, or at least seem to be definitively moving, from a society or culture of prohibition and desire to a society of *jouissance*. Todd McGowan's recent book, *The End of Dissatisfaction? Jacques Lacan and the Emerging Society of Enjoyment*, is probably the fullest and clearest expression of this view of history, but it is already clear in Copjec's (1994, p. 182) and Žižek's (1990, and again in 1992, pp. 48–66) accounts of classic detective fiction vs. *noir*/hard-boiled that the historical shift in the detective genre, in and out of the cinema, is precisely one from a regime of desire to one of drive, as the hard-boiled detective stages an encounter with his own death drive through the figure of the *femme fatale*. I would not want to counter this claim, although I would want to note that it is a shift viewed with implicit disfavor and a tacit nostalgia for the age of prohibition/desire and the traditional, "organic" society that went along with it by those critics who stand closer to Marx, such as McGowan. However, I do want to suggest that this privileging of drive as "where we are now" tends to obscure the operations of drive in the past, and so I argue that drive and enjoyment were already fundamental in classic detective fiction. It is true that the repetitive and self-destructive elements of detective fiction acquire a sharp visibility in *film noir* and the hardboiled novel, but part of the larger argument of this book is that this is merely a case of a structure already present in classic detective fiction being made more manifest. Assuming that enjoyment is a fundamental structure in detective fiction still leaves open the larger question, beyond the scope of this project, of whether it is not also a fundamental structure of all genre fiction. At one point in the "Encore" seminar, Lacan punningly combines the words in the phrase "the serious real" (*reel sérieux*) to form "the serial" (*le sériel*) (1975, p. 23). Might not "the serial reading" that characterizes genre fiction always be also a marker of the "serious real"?

Second, the most common psychoanalytic argument about detective fiction has traditionally been to represent it as a genre of "mistaken desire," in which the reader fails to perceive that the killer is acting out the reader's own desire. It is, in short, a genre of scapegoating. One effect of this claim, however—which is certainly true, as far as it goes—is to privilege the "high" or "literary" forms of detective fiction that do not permit the reader to easily assign his or her own hidden motives to another, just as New Lacanians have tended to esteem hard-boiled over classic detective fiction, insofar as the detective comes closer in the hard-boiled to a recognition of his own desire, even if he ultimately turns away from it. In the "high literary vein," however, one immediately thinks of a kind of "anti-detective fiction," such as Antonioni's film *Blowup*, or Pynchon's *The Crying of Lot 49*, in which there is no moment where blame can be assigned, and indeed, the guiltiest activity in the text would seem to be precisely the one that the viewer or reader is necessarily engaged in: looking for the truth of an image, interpreting a text. I first began working on this book when I had a much greater emphasis on the loftier, more literary versions of detective fiction. In fact, that was exactly the conclusion I kept coming to: Antonioni was "libidinally better" than Hitchcock, Gadda was preferable to Christie, Eco more clever than Conan Doyle, and so on. But such a "preordained" conclusion made me very suspicious, as did the automatic reinstitution of a traditional hierarchy between high and low forms of cinema, between the literary and the popular. By concentrating on the question of desire, and by largely confining discussions of enjoyment to the hard-boiled novel and *film noir*, it seemed to me that psychoanalysis was missing a potentially rewarding question: When a text forces us to confront our desire, what do we then miss out on? In other words, as the truth of our desire is revealed, is not the truth of our enjoyment concealed? My hope is that these kinds of questions, as well as the methodology I've employed in this project, might suggest that psychoanalysis and detective fiction do not necessarily stand in the relationship of analyst to patient to each other—that is, we might want to be wary of an approach that offers us psychoanalytic theory as a therapy that will "cure" popular culture. Perhaps popular culture is not as sick as all that.

This is one reason, not surprisingly, that I have found Žižek so valuable for this book. Few critics have been as "culturally promiscuous" as Žižek. From Wagner's operas to teen horror films, from Amish sexual practices to Judith Butler, everything is interesting, suggestive, rewarding, important. There are, of course, rather obvious potential problems with such an approach as well, as it could easily become a kind of mere dilettantism, or a series of sensational observations about fascinating topics that are not, at the end of the day, held together by a common thread. I hope to have avoided both pitfalls here. My own eclecticism has led me to draw on Antonioni, but also on the television series *Monk* and the Parker Brothers board game *Clue*, not only on the best known English and American authors of detective fiction, but also from a completely marginal tradition of detective fiction: Italy. The material examined also ranges widely over the field of what might be called "crime fiction." *The Talented Mr. Ripley*, by Patricia Highsmith, and its film adaptation by Anthony Minghella, for example, can't be quite properly called detective fiction because detection plays a small role, and only as a menace to the protagonist, although, as I argue, the film exploits numerous structures that come from *film noir*. I also touch briefly on the police procedural, the hard-boiled/*film noir*, and most substantially classic detective fiction and its ancestors, even, if ever so quickly, on the cozy. Again, this is partly to combat the suggestion that Lacanian theory should act as a therapeutic cure for "popular" detective fiction that somehow missed the truth of its own desire, but also in order to make fairly large claims about a genre that has had an astonishingly broad influence on culture both high and low, from Thomas Pynchon to Harry Potter.

I would also add, in justifying the presence of so much Žižek in the pages that follow, that he is often quite funny; one might even say that he is programmatically humorous, rigorously funny, so to speak. Although this might sound like a trivial or accidental quality, not to be enlisted when one turns to methodological justifications, I would claim otherwise. Humor is what happens when the truth comes at us from an unexpected direction, when it is spoken from an unlikely source. To take an example that I discuss in much greater detail in the chapter on "Enjoyment," I offer a well-known dirty joke about a bear and a hunter:

> A man goes hunting in the woods and spies a bear. He shoots at the bear, but misses, and the bear rushes over, tears the gun out of his hands, throws him down on the ground, and has sex with him. The following week, the outraged hunter waits in the woods again with a new gun, sees the bear again, and shoots. Again he misses, and again the bear throws him on the ground and has sex with him. The following week, angrier than ever, the man returns to the woods with a bigger gun with a better scope, etc. He spies the bear, shoots—and misses. The bear tears the gun away, throws him on the ground, pauses and says to the hunter: "You don't come here for the hunting, do you?"

Nothing kills humor quite like explaining a joke, but that is exactly what I will do (the only mitigating factor in this destruction of humor is that I will do it twice). Almost every reader will have realized that the comic force of the bear joke lies in our recognizing that the bear is right: this guy really isn't here for the hunting. Is this not, in a microcosm, the essence of interpretation, and not just psychoanalytic interpretation: showing how, what looked like one thing (an outraged and offended hunter trying to kill a bear) is really something quite different (an unrecognized desire that suddenly emerges with great clarity)? What I thought this was about is not really what it is about at all.

The other reason, of course, that I tell the bear joke here, is that it, too, is a neat instance of the structuring power of enjoyment in narrative, the "pleasure-in-pain" that the hunter—one might just as easily offer in his place the detective, another kind of hunter—derives from not getting what he wanted, or what he thought he wanted. For what is this incompetent hunter, this detective in the woods who keeps missing something, the kernel of his enjoyment, if not the quintessence of the subject forever "circulating around the always missed object," coming back to the same place, the same scenario, again and again? Why does he keep coming back? And why does the reader keep returning with him? Not for the detection, we may assume.

2

IRRITATION: *Levine | Mankell | Camilleri*

THE GREAT SCHISM

The goal of this book is not to give a history of detective fiction, which has been done many times before. (There are many histories available, but some of the most recent include Knight, Scaggs, Horsley, and Rzepka.) I will begin, however, by noting certain features that are common to most or all of those histories. For example, unlike other genres, modern detective fiction, that is, detective fiction that contemporary readers immediately recognize as being like the detective fiction we read today, has a conventional moment of historical origin, such as Edgar Allan Poe's "The Murders in the Rue Morgue" in 1841. With that one story, Poe appeared to invent all of the structures of classic detective fiction, from the genius detective and his average sidekick who chronicles this great intellect's adventures to the "locked room" convention—the murder victim is found inside a locked room, with no trace of the killer. Histories of detective fiction differ principally in what they consider the genre's antecedents to be, asking questions such as: Did detective fiction owe a greater debt to the gothic novel, or the *roman-feuilleton*? Does the genre emerge more from a belief in Romanticism's overwhelming and antisocial passions, or a belief in Enlightenment reason? And then one can spend hours wondering whether this or that early text (*Oedipus Rex* or the biblical story of Daniel) "counts" as detective fiction, even though it is usually clear that such predecessors did not significantly influence the birth of the modern genre.

In giving a history of detective fiction, however, it is customary to mark the presence of a Great Schism, a historical split in the genre, namely the division between classic detective fiction (Poe, Christie, Conan Doyle) and the hard-boiled novel (Chandler, Hammett, Spillane). The point here is that, although Agatha Christie is quite different from Conan Doyle or Poe, the basic "feel" of Christie or Sayers is more or less the same: the detection is intellectual and aestheticized, bent on turning a crime into a problem. Such fictions have the feel of a crossword puzzle that has been dramatized. (I will take issue with the crossword puzzle model for detective fiction at a number of points, especially in the last chapter, but it is useful to invoke it here at the beginning.) When detective fiction "returned" to America in the 1930s with the hard-boiled novel, it did so in a form that was physical, masculine, and stressed perseverance rather than genius. Although the two versions of investigation share some similarities, such as a preference for investigators who stand in an ambiguous relationship to the law (i.e., a *private* investigator) or a commitment to the scene of *revelation*, they are more diverse than alike: the one is cerebral, artificial, conservative, and nostalgic, whereas the other is set in a universe that is profoundly irrational, realistic, and gritty, in such a way as to suggest at times a tacit social critique.

What is less often noted by critics of detective fiction is that this Great Schism, like the Protestant break, also produced a seemingly endless sequence of subsequently smaller and smaller generic denominations within the "post-classical" world of detective fiction: the cozy, the procedural, the forensic, the historical detective novel, and so on. Once the universe of detective fiction split, it continued to fracture into ever-smaller units. For instance, among historical detective fiction, one finds the medieval detective novel, the ancient Roman detective novel, and so on. Among medieval detective series, the best-known is Ellis Peters (leaving aside the singular Umberto Eco entry of *The Name of the Rose*), but they have also been written by Suzanne Gregory, Margaret Frazer, Peter Tamayne, and several others. As for detective fiction set in the ancient world, David Wishart, Rosemary Rowe, and Caroline Lawrence, among others, have contributed. These historical detective novels are, generally speaking, "catholic," by the way; they tend to make use of detectives who are unusually knowledgeable and gifted, and who proceed by rational methods in the style of the classic detective.

JANE AUSTEN AND "JAINE AUSTEN"

How far can such a fracturing extend? How refined and subtle can the gradations be between one type of detective fiction—one "denomination," to maintain the conceit—and another? Quite far, as we shall see. Remaining within the historical detective novel, we find the recent invention of the "literary celebrity" detective novels. Jane Austen as an amateur sleuth! Louisa May Alcott as an ersatz Sherlock Holmes! I am referring here, of course, to Stephanie Barron's successful "Jane Austen Series," such as *Jane and the Prisoner of Wool House*, as well as Anna Maclean's "Louisa May Alcott Mystery Series," such as *Louisa and the Missing Heiress*. In each, the famous nineteenth-century novelist solves crimes when she is not penning a manuscript. I hasten to add that the "Jane Austen detective novel" is not, as one would expect, simply one author's particular fancy or branding gimmick. Carrie Bebris (*Pride and Prescience*, *North by Northanger*, and others) has also written Jane Austen-themed detective novels, although Barron is the more successful. Putting together Barron, Bebris, and Maclean, it begins to appear that the "nineteenth-century woman writer turned sleuth" detective novel is a recognizable denomination—a splinter sect, and a bit on the fringe, to be sure, but a recognizable form of the contemporary popular mystery novel. To see the real relevance of these novels, however, we have to make a quick detour into Jane Austen and "chick lit."

Barron's novels are part of a resurgence of adoration for Jane Austen, one that received a particular impetus from Helen Fielding's enormously successful and quite clever rewriting of *Pride and Prejudice* under the title *Bridget Jones's Diary*. The resurgence of adoration is for Austen generally, but for *Pride and Prejudice* in particular. The genesis of this is likely Colin Firth's charismatic 1995 appearance as Darcy in the BBC's television version of *Pride and Prejudice*, directly inspiring Helen Fielding to write her novel, which was, in turn, so successful that she was able to get Firth to play Mark Darcy in the film version of *Bridget Jones's Diary* as well. The adoration of Austen is quite radically different from that of the so-called "Janeites" in the 1920s and 1930s. Unlike that earlier adoration, it is largely by women and not men, it is popular rather than academic, and it is extremely postmodern—it takes place largely through imitation, parody, and cinematic adaptation. Since Fielding, numerous writers have attempted to continue Austen's characters and stories (invariably *Pride and Prejudice*) as if they were another example of "fanfic," such as the fiction written by *Star Trek* fans about the same characters and set in the same universe. See, for example, Elizabeth Aston (*Mr. Darcy's Daughters*, *The Exploits & Adventures of Miss Alethea Darcy*, and *The True Darcy Spirit*), Diana Birchall (*Mrs. Darcy's Dilemma*), Linda Berdoll's rather racy novels (*Mr. Darcy Takes a Wife* and *Darcy and Elizabeth: Nights and Days at Pemberly*), Pamela Aidan (*Duty and Desire*, and others), or Emma Tenant (*Pemberly: Or Pride and Prejudice Continued*). For a more parodic treatment, see Kate Fenton (*Vanity and Vexation*) or the alarmingly similar Debra White Smith (*First Impressions*). Both Fenton and Smith describe contemporary subjects doing stage or cinematic adaptations of *Pride and Prejudice* and compulsively following the roles delineated for them in their scripts, falling in love with and betraying each other, although Smith is presumably unintentionally parodic, since her novels are also intended to appeal to a Christian audience. For full-blown parody, see David Auburn and Arielle Eckstut (*Pride and Promiscuity: The Lost Sex Scenes of Jane Austen*). Almost all of these novels have appeared in just the last few years. The cinematic adaptations of Austen have been numerous and notable, but one might single out Amy Heckerling's appealing *Clueless* (also 1995) as perhaps the only example that is imitation, parody, *and* adaptation.

It is hard to underestimate the effect on the publishing industry of Fielding, other than to say it is not dissimilar to her contemporary, J.K. Rowling of the Harry Potter novels. Fielding, like Dr. Frankenstein before her, created the apparently unstoppable field of chick lit, a genre that is instantly recognizable when one enters a bookstore. With a certain degree of relentlessness, the covers appear to feature high-heeled shoes, a martini glass, and a graceful script announcing "a novel." The obligatory colors are bright pink, orange, and yellow. The formulaic character of the cover extends to the inside of the novel as well, where the stories are perhaps less inspired by Austen or Fielding than they are by the equally successful television series *Sex and the City*. Protagonists should be female, attractive and likable, in their late twenties or early thirties, professional but aspiring, single but looking for a man, and surrounded by a group of similar friends. It should come as no surprise, then, to discover that chick-lit detective fiction is a booming industry. Wendy Roberts (*Dating Can Be Deadly*), Kyra Davis (*Passion, Betrayal and Killer Highlights* and the charmingly titled *Sex, Murder and a Double Latte*), Jennifer Sturman (*The Pact*), Lynda Curnyn

(*Killer Summer*), and many others have written mystery novels in this subgenre within the last five or six years. All feature a more or less standard version of the chick-lit protagonist, and most manage to work a cosmopolitan and/or a high-heeled stiletto onto the cover art, often juxtaposed to images suggestive of murder (say, a girl with a cocktail in one hand and a pistol in the other, or a strappy sandal in the middle of a chalk outline of a body). Cementing the connection between chick lit and detective fiction is the oeuvre of Kate White, the editor in chief of *Cosmopolitan* magazine. Her most recent novel, *Over Her Dead Body*, makes sure to utilize two phrases on the back cover that are immediately recognizable to viewers of *Sex and the City* ("strappy sandals" and "a New York minute"). In addition to the mystery, White ends her book with a few pieces of advice to her readers, unrelated to the story, including "How to *Double* a Man's Pleasure in Bed."

It also comes as no surprise that these two forces in contemporary publishing, Jane Austen detective novels and chick-lit detective fiction, should have converged, as they have in the work of Laura Levine. A former sitcom writer, Levine has turned out five "Jaine Austen" mysteries in the last five years (*This Pen for Hire*, *Last Writes*, *Killer Blonde*, *Shoes to Die For*, and the most recent, *The PMS Murder*). Their brightly colored covers with a penchant for pink, orange, and yellow, cocktail glasses, and sleepy looking cats proclaim their affiliation with chick lit, as does the content. Jaine Austen (her "mother is an Anglophile, and a bad speller") is a recent divorcée (hence older and experienced, but single and looking) and a freelance writer (hence professionally ambitious). She also has the requisite best friend, a New Yorker named Kandi, who is in similar circumstances, and available as needed for heart-to-heart chats. For Levine, like Barron and Bebris, the connection between being a woman writer and detection seems self-evident. Levine's Austen is only tenuously related to the Austen of Barron or Bebris, but seems to be imagined as a contemporary version of the historical figure, a modest writer who is unlucky in love, but who enables others to fulfill their romantic dreams through her fantasies; unlike the real Austen, Levine's Austen does so, however, by penning resumes, personal ads, love letters, and the like. In the first of the series, *This Pen for Hire*, Jaine writes a love letter for a hopeless geek who wants to ask out an aerobics instructor who is decidedly out of his league. When the instructor is murdered, however, the geek takes the blame, and Jaine Austen must prove his innocence.

Naturally, the plot in "chick-lit"- or "Jane Austen"-themed detective fiction must unfold on two levels, the romantic and the detective. The romantic subplot is frequent in detective fiction, but it acquires a greater relief in Jane Austen mysteries; not surprisingly, both Barron and Bebris deploy mysteries that ultimately aim at either making possible a marriage and romance that would otherwise be blocked, or conversely, stopping an inappropriate romantic union that might otherwise go forward. How does Levine take this dual demand? Unlike Barron's Austen, who generally facilitates other characters' romances, Levine's series is fully centered on the protagonist as a kind of surrogate for the (presumably single and professionally bored) reader. Jaine is gradually drawn into detection, and the detection gradually brings her into ever closer contact with a romantic possibility, the hunky Cameron Bannick. Cameron is a fantasy come to life: he has "crinkly" blue eyes and a stylish apartment, and although he is an antiques dealer, he turns out not to be gay (much of the narrative is devoted to parsing Bannick's sexual orientation). Despite this seemingly ideal match, however, nothing happens between them. The tension grows, but Jaine is persistently left unsatisfied. She repeatedly indicates that she derives an unprecedented thrill from her activities as an illicit or unauthorized detective, however, explicitly and repeatedly describing it as a "turn-on." So where does the satisfaction come from in the novel?

There is eventually an indication that it is not from the romance. Jaine's best friend, Kandi, calls her up with a reminder. Kandi is full of ideas about how to meet eligible men, and has decided that going to auctions is a brilliant way to meet men who are both eligible and rich.

> "You haven't forgotten, have you?"
> "No, of course not. Absolutely not. Forgotten what?"
> "The auction. Our passport to eligible men. It starts at six."
> I looked at my watch. It was twenty of.
> "Damn," I said, leaping off the sofa.
> "I knew you'd forget. It's all psychological. Deep down you don't really want to meet anyone."
> "Okay, Dr. Freud. Save your insights. I'll throw on some clothes and get there as soon as I can." [p. 175]

Although the novel figures Kandi as rather scatterbrained, one can't help but wonder if she hasn't managed to say something profound here. Isn't it the case that this lack, the absence of men, is precisely the hole around which chick lit revolves and is organized, the "always missed object" discussed in the introduction? As soon as chick-lit takes on a serial format, which is virtually required by the detective genre, it is obliged to leave the romance either unsatisfied (the solution Levine opts for), or make it "provisional," that is, fated to last only until the start of the next novel (the solution employed by Fielding). Deep down, the protagonist of the chick-lit novel really doesn't want to meet anyone, since the novel ends when this happens. As it turns out, the romance is illusory, and Kandi is right—the hunky Cameron Bannick is actually the criminal. His motivations and modus operandi in carrying out the crime are too baroque to go into here, but Kandi's claims that "it's all psychological" and that Austen "doesn't really want to meet anyone" seem justified. The protagonist of the chick-lit novel doesn't happen to be without a man; she must, instead, organize her universe so that she is without a man, since that is who she is, how she is defined. An excellent solution is to choose impossible love objects. (Not only is Bannick revealed as the criminal at the end, but his disavowed homosexuality appears to return as a possibility, as well.)

Romance, however, is merely the first of two organizing principles for the chick-lit detective novel. Detection, of course, is the other. But Levine's heroine fares little better here. At a certain moment, Jaine solves the case and experiences . . . dejection. Rather than the big payoff, she feels depressed. It's worth keeping in mind that detection has been figured in the novel as Austen's sole sexual outlet, her only "turn on." But solution is not the cognitive orgasm one might have hoped for.

> I should have been happy, right? After all, I'd helped solve a major murder case. . . . I knew I had to stop fixating on this detective stuff and get back to my real job. . . . My heart just wasn't in it.
>
> You don't have to be Sigmund Freud to figure out what was happening in my tortured psyche. After all the excitement of the past few weeks, the thought of going back to my former life—churning out resumes and Toiletmaster brochures—was more than a tad depressing. Playing detective had been fun. A lot of fun.
>
> And soon, I realized, the thrill would be gone. [pp. 190–191]

This realization comes just twenty or thirty pages before the end of the novel. Essentially, Jaine believes that it is the return to a drab normalcy, or an anticipation of it, that precipitates this feeling of depression. To be precise, however, *her very first reaction* to the solution of the case is the line "I should have been happy, right?" And surely Sigmund Freud (and very likely the actual Jane Austen) would notice the reappearance of the name "Freud" here. In fact, to be precise, I have quoted the only two passages in the book in which Freud's name appears. Isn't it remarkable that the name of the founder of psychoanalysis should appear precisely at the moment when both of the major motors of the genre's plot are revealed as empty holes, gaps that produce a failure of satisfaction? Perhaps it does require Sigmund Freud to figure out what is happening here. For like the single girl seeking romance, the detective is actually constituted by the nonfulfillment of his desire: as soon as he or she solves the crime, there is no more detection and no longer a detective. "The thrill is gone," but the solution itself never produced any thrill, merely anxiety and depression. There never was a thrill—just the reflection that the protagonist "should have been happy," but was not. This structure of narrative pleasure and nonpleasure could be described in many ways, but one might easily characterize it as *irritating*. How else should we describe texts that organize themselves and our reading, our desires, around objects that are destined to be always missed?

At the true end of the novel, Jaine does derive satisfaction, but from the one place the reader cannot follow along: she makes a career change from writer of brochures and love letters to detective. Jaine plans her ad for the Yellow Pages: "Jaine Austen, Discreet Inquires. Work Done with Pride, not Prejudice" (p. 218). Remarkably, this advertising slogan essentially captures the basic psychic movement of transforming Jane Austen and her characters into detectives. First, and least surprisingly, it involves forgetting the actual Austen and her novels; even the least astute reader of *Pride and Prejudice* understands that *both* pride and prejudice are vices that the novel condemns. To the real Austen, work done with pride is just as bad as work done with prejudice. Second, it involves an unconscious rejection of the "feminine" position of Elizabeth, namely prejudice, in favor of the "masculine" position associated with Mr. Darcy, pride. That masculine position is not merely self-centered (pride) rather than other-centered (prejudice), not merely active and engaged with the world (detection) rather than contemplative (writing): it ultimately proves to be illusory, even impossible. We should recall that seriality, and the unlimited reading associated with it, demand that satisfactions be either absent, such as the failed romance with Bannick, revealed as a nonsatisfaction, such as the detection, or be provisional. That is, satisfaction can be given to the reader only to be taken away again, over and over again, until the reader understands that it is not really there at all. And so it is with Jaine's professional development. This sea change at the end of the novel, where she turns from miserable writer of personal ads and "Toiletmaster brochures" into an intrepid private investigator, disappears somewhere between the back cover of the first book in the series and the front cover of the next. When *Last Writes*, the second book in the "Jaine Austen Mysteries" begins, Jaine is a writer again, now for a dreadful sitcom entitled "Muffy 'n Me." Surely this persistent vanishing of every satisfaction presents the reader with a certain irritation.

THE DETECTIVE AS FETISH

Detective fiction seems to respond to its readership by offering a series of increasingly individually tailored settings and characters: detective novels about Jane Austen, about Jaine Austen, about cats, about horse racing, about crossword puzzles, about catering, about beauticians, about chocolate. There are, in fact, an astonishing number of food-themed mystery novels, often including recipes for some of the dishes featured within the book. Cat mysteries alone comprise an astonishing number of novels: Lilian Jackson Braun and Rita Mae Brown are the two best known names, and Lydia Adams, Marian Babson, and Shirley Rousseau Murphy, among others, have produced voluminous quantities of cat-themed mystery novels. (Laurien Berenson is one of the few to write dog-themed whodunits.) Dick Francis penned numerous detective novels about horses and horse racing. Food-themed detective fiction is surprisingly common: Susan Witing Albert, whose novels revolve specifically around herbs, Claudia Bishop, Joanna Carl (specifically chocolate—each novel is individually labeled "A Chocoholic Mystery"), Diane Mott Davidson, whose catering novels have the best/worst titles combining food and violence, from *Chopping Spree* to *Sticks & Scones*, Nancy Fairbanks, Joanne Fluke, and Joanne Pence, among others. Some of these cozy-based mysteries turn to topics that are no less conventionally feminine (Eco's "model reader" of these novels is clearly the stereotyped chocolate-eating, cat-loving under- or unemployed housewife), but seemingly harder and harder to square with a murder investigation. Laura Childs writes, for instance, "Scrapbooking Mysteries" and Nancy Cohen writes beautician-themed novels under the rubric of "A Bad Hair Day Mystery." As a culminating example of this fetishistic tendency in detective fiction, let me cite here a "trend" noted in a recent issue of *House & Garden*:

> For killer decorating tips, pick up *Death by Inferior Design*, a murder mystery by decorator Leslie Caine. Advice is woven into this whodunit

featuring rival designers as sleuths. If you like the genre, read *Tool &
Die*, the latest in Sarah Graves's "Home Repair is Homicide" mysteries,
inspired by the restoration of her Federal-style home. For more, see
houseandgarden.com. [Abramovich 2004, p. 77]

There are a number of obviously profitable avenues that one could
explore here: the evident gender, class, and social mobility issues at work
(all of which converge in the overdetermined phrase "the restoration of her
Federal-style home"), not to mention the way that this kind of detective
fiction serves at least as much to deliver "lifestyle-coordinates" to its readers as entertainment, equally true of the cooking/recipe-themed detective
novel. If these "microgenre" detective novels about cats, bad hair, beauticians, and chocolate appear to presuppose—not to put too fine a point on
it—a vulgar, superficial, uneducated housewife, with all the negative im-
agery we tend to saddle this "type" with (that is, overweight from her chocolate consumption, hysterically attached to her cats because of the lack of
sexual attention from her uninterested husband, etc.—in short, the Jean
Teasdale character invented by the humor magazine *The Onion*), we should
also note that *House & Garden* is presupposing an Internet-savvy woman
with upwardly mobile pretensions and disposable income. But what is truly
intriguing in this brief citation is the use of the word *genre*, as in "if you
like the genre. . . ." Even this brief item presupposes on the part of the reader
an automatic and easy recognition of the "home decorator detective novel"
genre and its contiguous companion, the "home repair murder mystery,"
subgenres many scholars of genre theory may have been previously unaware of. In all seriousness, this betrays a "genrification" (not to mention
gentrification) of the detective novel that has gone unremarked in scholarly literature.

It would appear that, like pornography, whatever one's taste, there is
a type of detective novel to match. This, of course, resembles nothing so
much as the *fetish* in at least three principal respects, and here I mean the
fetish less in the Freudian sense of "I know very well . . . but all the same,"
and more the fetish in its contemporary role for identity politics, the sign
of my obscene enjoyment that marks which subculture I belong to: the
apparently *arbitrary* nature of the "object of fascination" (Why a *cat* that
solves crimes? Why so few crime-solving *dogs*?); the exacting *specificity* of
the object (it is not enough that my detective should be a famous historical
figure—she must be a famous nineteenth-century woman writer); and finally, the *persistence* of the object (not one detective novel about horse

racing, but an endless series of them, or, to take an example I exploit later, Sue Grafton's "alphabet series"—*A is for Alibi*, *B is for Burglar*, and so on, currently up to *S is for Silence*).

The idea that it was the hard-boiled novel that began this ever-increasing fragmentation in detective fiction, that it began a path toward an "object of fascination" tailor-made for the reader, is true enough, but it obscures the ecumenical question of just what it is that these different denominations have in common. The problem is that the answer would appear to be exactly nothing. They all feature detectives of one sort or another (and here one runs the risk of articulating a hopelessly watered-down definition of "detective fiction" that would be applicable to almost any text—most narratives feature a character who wants to find something out), but the detectives don't seem to be delivering the same goods to the reader. What possible point of connection is there between a Dashiell Hammett novel and *The PMS Murder*? I mentioned before that classic detective fiction and the hard-boiled novel had only a few points in common: an investigator who is not state-sponsored; one who typically has a kind of partial authority, or para-authority as I call it later in the book; and a revelation at the end, albeit not necessarily the same kind of revelation. In fact, even within classic detective fiction, the revelation may have a very different character. In Sherlock Holmes stories, as in Poe's "Murders in the Rue Morgue") for instance, the revelation is typically not "who did it," but rather how something that was seemingly impossible took place, or how an apparently irrational scene or event is actually part of a rationally sensible albeit criminal world. That is, the fundamental point is a demonstration of the underlying rationality and comprehensibility of the world. Agatha Christie, on the other hand, makes use of such "impossible" scenes from time to time, but generally prefers the multiplication of suspects, so that the final revelation is, in fact, the identity of the murderer. Such a revelation is not only a proof of who the murderer is, but equally and simultaneously a proof of who the murderer is *not*. From a psychoanalytic perspective, the force of the final revelation is precisely the force of exculpation, the certainty that *we* are not the killer.

In the hard-boiled novel or its cinematic version, *film noir*, the scene of revelation has yet a different force. Although there is a sort of cognitive discharge, that is to say an explanation of who committed the crime, how, and why, this is obviously not the real point. One has only to look at a famously confusing film like *The Big Sleep* to see that a successful hard-boiled text does not even have to make sense in order to give satisfaction, to maintain its fascination. (The story goes that, after the film was released, none of the screenwriters could figure out who had killed one of the minor characters, and when pressed by the screenwriters, neither could Raymond Chandler.) Rather, in the hard-boiled, the revelation is the protagonist's near recognition of an inner libidinal weakness typically incarnated by the *femme fatale*, a woman who represents both the detective's desire for his own death as well as that of others, and a kind of amoral intransigence that allows him to say "no" to this temptation, as Sam Spade does at the end of *The Maltese Falcon*: "I won't because all of me wants to" (Hammett, 1992a, p. 215). The hard-boiled hero is not in fact motivated by values or nobility, but rather by an inexplicable, even idiotic, refusal to give in, a kind of animal stubbornness. At times, as is the case with Sam Spade, it is not even stubbornness, but a kind of perverse, almost childish, contrariness. I won't because I want to. I won't because I won't.

The tension of the hard-boiled novel is not based around what a third-person character already did (the killer and his means), as in classic detective fiction, but rather around *what the detective himself might do*: he might surrender to his desire. The novels of Dashiell Hammett typically follow this scheme, even when they do not appear to. *Red Harvest* (1992b) might initially appear to be missing the temptation of the *femme fatale*, the final confrontation, as in *The Maltese Falcon*, but here it is merely temporally disguised. In *Red Harvest*, the tension revolves not around what the protagonist might do, but what he might *already have done*: in a key scene, he (the Continental Op) awakens from a drugged and alcoholic slumber to find himself clutching an ice-pick buried in the now dead *femme fatale's* chest. The novel tacitly acknowledges, as do the other characters and the Continental Op himself, the possibility that he has given in, that he, too, has killed. Only in the final pages is he cleared of the murder. From the libidinal perspective, then, the distinction between classic detective fiction and hard-boiled is the distinction between Catholic and Protestant sin: classic detective fiction is Catholic in its insistence on the purity of *intention*— it proves that you didn't do it, and that you didn't want to do it, either— whereas the hard-boiled novel admits the sinful desire, but only counts our good (and bad) works for or against us. Also, one might note the significance of the temporal dislocation in *Red Harvest*—the Continental Op's deadly desire is what Žižek has recently called, mocking the American Secretary of Defense Donald Rumsfeld, an "unknown known" (2004, pp. 9–10). That is, it is a fact, a clear fact (either he killed the girl or he didn't) that at the same time is unknown, and unknown to the very person who most intimately "knows" it, who experienced it (or didn't). This, of course, is the unconscious.

THE "IRRITATING" PROCEDURAL

Could one then hypothesize that *revelation* is the ecumenical crux of the schismatic detective world, the point in common around which everyone agrees, even if they agree about nothing else? Here we might make a useful comparison between classic detective fiction and, not hard-boiled, but the police procedural. The procedural is one of the most popular forms of detective fiction, but this popularity might seem rather curious if one considers the deliberate banality that the genre requires: a typical procedural traces the day-to-day, mundane aspects of an investigation and of the investigators' lives. Rather than a single detective who is a para-authority, it follows a team of professional police officers, arguments around the water cooler, bad coffee, forms that must be filled out, problems with childcare, officers who are out sick. Its libidinal economy is fundamentally sadistic/masochistic in that a principal source of reader satisfaction is the suffering that the police officers must endure: hostile criminals and a hostile public "beneath" them, and a penny-pinching, uncomprehending administration "above" them, almost invariably combined with lateral or horizontal problems in their private lives covering divorce, alcoholism, memories of childhood sexual abuse, deaths in the family—a whole litany of ways in which we watch the investigators suffer only to receive meager paychecks and a heap of abuse from the people they protect in return. As for revelation in the procedural, it is often the case that there is little or none. Instead there is endless, grinding work that eventually reveals the answer that everyone knew or suspected all along.

Let me turn briefly, then, to two of the most popular police procedurals in Europe, both of which are at least moderately known in the States, although not to the degree that they are in Europe: Henning Mankell's Kurt Wallander series, and Andrea Camilleri's Montalbano novels and stories. The two series represent in many respects the two possible forms of the procedural, or at least a "higher," more literary form of it. Mankell's vision is the more typical of the two for the procedural. His novels, depicting a team of detectives in the small city of Ystad in Skåne, Sweden, led by Inspector Kurt Wallander, are dark, psychologically intense, gritty, disturbing, and very nearly uniformly unhappy. Camilleri, on the other hand, writes novels that center on Commissario Montalbano in the small Sicilian city of Vigàta, novels that are still recognizably procedurals. The investigation is a group effort, fraught with turf wars within and without, often addressing serious social issues, impeded by a Sicilian public long used to keeping quiet and mistrustful of the police, and so on, but often based on unrealistic, self-consciously ironic scenarios, frequently comic, shot through by a sunny sense of the good things in life. Besides the obvious temptation to ascribe these two tendencies to "national character" or geography (cold, dark Sweden vs. sunny, oneiric Sicily), one might also note what they have in common besides their slightly unusual preference for a provincial, rather than a metropolitan, setting (procedurals generally favor large cities).

Let us begin with Mankell: on several occasions (as in *Steget efter* [*One Step Behind*], *Villospår* [*Sidetracked*], or *Den femte kvinnan* [*The Fifth Woman*]), he begins with the crime, often presented from the killer's point of view. More to the point, in a radical contrast to both classic detective fiction and the hard-boiled novel, the reader knows who the killer is, if not immediately, then halfway through the novel, and long before the investigators do. This is, in general, not unusual for the procedural, where there is a suspect who is known positively to have committed the crime. The difficulty lies in assembling a case capable of leading to a conviction. In some forms of the procedural, such as the American television drama *NYPD Blue*, this means the viewer's sense of satisfaction can be fully elicited when the police beat, terrify, or otherwise intimidate a confession out of the obviously guilty "perp," a term that of course presupposes certain guilt (he is the perpetrator, not a suspect). The question is not "whodunit," but "how do we get him to crack?" It is rare in the police procedural that the investigator experiences a personal revelation; such an event is at odds with the fundamental character of the procedural, which emphasizes the day-to-day repetition, even the grinding routine, of the lives of policemen. The only change is that the investigators seem more and more worn down, ever more exhausted by their tireless work without reward. In every procedural, the police at some point rhetorically ask if there is any value to their work. It makes no difference if the answer is no; they continue on to the next investigation, powerless to stop the tide of crime and violence. The powerlessness of the police in the face of rising crime and social indifference fundamentally conceals a different, more radical kind of powerlessness: the ability of the investigator (and the reader of procedurals) to *stop*, to leave behind this deepest, most concealed kernel of irritation that is the investigation, the procedural itself. It is as if the procedural takes the endurance, the pure drive from the hard-boiled novel and nothing else. There is no epiphany for the protagonist, no confrontation after which nothing is the same as it was before. In fact, in the procedural, on some level, the point is that *everything is always the same as it was before.*

It is this last point that brings us to what is, perversely, the common point shared by the hard-boiled, classic, and procedural fiction: precisely the *sameness* that makes all of these formats such easily repeatable and easily imitated models. All of them establish character in the same way: by giving their investigators easily recognizable quirks or tics (Holmes's pipe or his trademark exclamations to Watson, Poirot's obsessive care of moustache and shoes, Marlowe's wisecracking and drinking, Wallander's insomnia, Monk's phobias and tics, and so on). This might appear to be an incidental feature of the genre. It is, after all, the easiest way to establish a recognizable type or character and appears in even the "highest" forms of literature, as in Homeric epithets. Moreover, it would appear to be a clear attempt at "branding," that is, at establishing your particular detective series as unique and thus memorable, based entirely around an insignificant gimmick: readers will remember you precisely because you are the writer who writes mystery novels about cats. And yet, if that were the case, why would there be so many different authors writing cat-themed detective fiction? Does one not eventually suffer from the nagging suspicion that Lilian Jackson Braun and Rita Mae Brown, the two most widely published writers of cat-themed detective novels, with their nearly homophonic last names, are in fact the same person?

Let me here turn to yet another "insignificant detail" and point out that the insistence on the quirk, the return again and again to the same thing, appears in a very different form in the police procedural, a form that one cannot claim establishes the detective as a recognizable character or the series as a recognizable brand. This is a structure that might be called "the kernel of irritation." In Henning Mankell's novels, for instance, it appears as something that the main character, Kurt Wallander, keeps forgetting: his car registration, an appointment with his eye doctor, his new diet for his diabetes, a visit with his father, a note that he needs to give a colleague—in fact, each of the Wallander novels features something of this type. It is difficult to convey how obsessively, how frequently, these details are brought up in the narrative. Such a feature seems designed to irritate the reader, as Wallander remembers *again and again*, always when he does not have time, that he needs to change his diet, disrupting the flow of the narrative, and often, the flow of the investigation as well. Eventually, these details acquire an almost uncanny charge to them, an aura of anxiety that seems larger than just realistic detail. In some instances, they suggest a mere obstinacy or insistence, as when Wallander muses that he needs a new car but regretfully concludes he will buy another Peugeot despite the problems he always has with them, or decides to buy five pairs of identical reading glasses when he recalls how prone he is to losing pens. In other cases, however, they suggest pathology, as Wallander's father paints the same painting again and again for his entire career—an autumnal landscape, the sole variation being the occasional addition of a grouse in the foreground. Indeed, these insistent, forgetful details can begin to function as a threat, such as Wallander's brief fainting spells in *One Step Behind* when he cannot remember to follow his diabetic diet. What if he should have such an episode during his final confrontation with the killer? As for the uncanny charge that is acquired by these irritating mundane details of ordinary life, in that same novel the diabetic Wallander begins to imagine the sugar in his blood slowly congealing into grains, crystals, eventually into miniature icebergs ("de vita öar av socker" [1997, p. 279], literally, the white islands of sugar, or later, "de vita sockeröarna torna upp sig som små isberg i hans vener" [p. 361], the white sugar-islands piling up like little icebergs in his veins), but there is never enough time to sleep, to rest, to pause, let alone to exercise, to eat a normal meal.

It is impossible to picture such an image in Andrea Camilleri's novels, which are set as far from a land of icebergs as European geography would seem to allow—it's just a short hop from Sicily to Africa, after all. In mentioning Camilleri, I should briefly note the revolutionary effect he has had on Italian detective fiction. As Gramsci once famously noted, national popular culture has never been Italy's strong suit, and genre literature is no exception. If you walk into a bookstore in Italy and browse the fantasy or science-fiction sections (romance and horror don't even rate their own sections, although chick lit is beginning to make some inroads), you will find only two or three Italian authors amid piles of translations from English. Detective fiction has historically been more popular than fantasy or science fiction in Italy, but tended (see the chapter on "Violence") to be parodic and literary on the one hand, or derivative and local on the other, such as a Roman detective clearly based on American hard-boiled models. In the decade or so in which Camilleri has been publishing his Montalbano novels, he has radically changed this picture. A quarter or even a third of the books in the "Giallo" (Mystery) section of an Italian bookstore will now be by Italian authors, most of them from the last several years, a phenomenon largely permitted by the runaway success of the Montalbano novels. Camilleri's immense success can be imputed to a number of factors, not the least of which is that they are extremely entertaining, with delicious characters and a deft sense of the comic, but perhaps the main one is that Camilleri finally found a purpose for detective fiction that really made sense to the Italian market. He reached back to several prior sources to do so. Numerous commentators have noted that these sources include, of course, the Spanish detective writer Montalbán, whose works were also often politically pointed, and also shared with Camilleri an interest in gastronomy. Less frequently noted, however, is a connection underlined by Camilleri himself in his latest novel (2006), *La vampa d'agosto* [*The Blaze of August*]. Readers who know Italian will note the colorful (but typically comprehensible) use of Sicilian dialect:

> [Montalbano] stetti a liggirisi fino alle unnici un bello romanzo poliziesco di dù autori svidisi che erano marito e mogliere e indove non c'era pagina senza un attacco feroci e motivato alla socialdemocrazia e al governo.
>
> Montalbano mentalmente lo dedicò a tutti quelli che si sdignavano di leggiri romanzi gialli pirchì, secondo loro, si trattava sulo di un passatempo enigmitistico. [p. 117]

> Montalbano stayed up 'till eleven reading himself a nice crime novel by two Swedish authors who were man and wife, where there wasn't a single page without a ferocious and motivated attack against social democracy and the government.
>
> Montalbano mentally dedicated it to all those who disdained reading mystery novels because, according to them, it was a mere hobby, solving puzzles.

The "dù autori svidisi" [two Swedish authors] are, of course, Maj Sjöwall and Per Wahlöö, whose entertaining novels were a relentless assault on the bourgeois welfare state. Here, of course, is the secret to Camilleri's success: he has turned the Anglo-American emphasis on pure ratiocination and logic, a faith in reason that always seemed like a source of parody at best to the Italian mind, to an emphasis on social meaning. The cognitive pleasure produced by the unfolding of a Camilleri mystery is slight; what is significant is the reader's initiation into a series of social problems, ranging from the minor (the Italian tradition of building illegal additions to the home first, and then obtaining a *condono*, or after-the-fact permission, since permission before the fact would be impossible or prohibitively expensive) to the major (intolerance of homosexuality, forced prostitution of immigrants, the mafia, and so on).

So, there is a connection between Swedish and Sicilian police procedurals. One wouldn't guess it, however, looking at the protagonists who appear in Mankell and Camilleri's novels. Unlike poor Wallander, Camilleri's Commissario Montalbano always has enough time for exercise (he swims every morning) and delicious and extravagant meals. In fact, if there is not enough time for a leisurely indulgence at lunch time, Montalbano will manufacture it with deception, as he does in a famous scene in *Il ladro di merendine* [*The Snack Thief*], and detailed descriptions of Montalbano's meals are as much a standardized part of the novels as Holmes playing violin or smoking is in Conan Doyle. Unlike the perennially lonely and single Wallander (the Wallander series begins just after his divorce), Salvo Montalbano has no trouble finding willing women. Indeed, *his* trouble is staying faithful to his fiancée. (This is an omnipresent threat in the novels, but it is not a serious one: the overall tone of the Montalbano books and stories is so light, ironic, and sunny that it would never permit a seriously self-destructive impulse on the part of its protagonist.) And yet, one finds precisely the same structure of the "kernel of irritation" here as in Mankell's works. Near the beginning of *The Snack Thief* (although the technique is already being used in *Il cane di terracotta* [*The Terra-Cotta Dog*]), for instance, Commissario Montalbano is invited to dine with his superior, the Commissioner, an invitation that Montalbano has to take a rain-check for.[1] As the action of the novel progresses, however, the missed meal returns again and again, intercutting the scenes of actual investigation. The dinner must be put off when Montalbano's Northern girlfriend, Livia, arrives unexpectedly; it is back on again when the Commissioner invites the two of them; off again when Montalbano realizes where a witness to a crime (a starving little boy, the "snack thief" of the title) is, and that he must be taken before the criminals get to him; the dinner becomes lunch the following day, postponed again on account of the little boy; the lunch becomes another dinner, canceled when Montalbano receives word that his father is dying; and finally, a last dinner invitation is kept in the novel's closing passages. All of these scenes are irrelevant to the plot of the novel and the revelation of the mystery: they seem to be there merely to remind

---

1. Montalbano's title is Commissario, and his superior is a Questore—the Stephen Sartarelli translations of the novels (Camilleri 2002 and Camilleri 2003) give "Inspector" and "Commissioner" respectively for the titles, but this is, of course, for a British audience.

us that detection serves as an irritating interruption to normal life. At the same time, one can't ignore the other kernels of irritation that structure the Montalbano novels, exemplary instances of normal life serving as an irritating interruption to detection, none more visible and cited than his endlessly deferred and postponed marriage to Livia; the necessity and urgency of that relationship manage to interrupt the investigation again and again, and yet are never resolved. The kernel of irritation, then, is not so much a delaying device (in which case it would always be "life interrupting detection" rather than its reverse) as an elementary structural necessity, the foreign object (a) that both intrudes and is missing, around which the narrative or subject organizes itself. In both Mankell and Camilleri, it appears to present only as an irritating distraction for the reader, an itch in the corner of the mind that we cannot forget, that weighs on us and distracts us as we try to follow the investigation, just as it weighs on and distracts the investigator.

It is precisely the banality of these examples that demonstrates the depth of the phenomenon. The investigations in the procedural, too, will return again and again to the same points: "Let's go over this again," the lead investigator will intone, eliciting groans from his teammates who have already been over it again and again. One eventually begins to suspect that each of these repetitions (the idiosyncratic quirk of the classic detective, the way the hard-boiled dick circles around the *femme fatale*, the series of everyday details that interrupt the investigation in the procedural, the obsessive-compulsive/fetishistic character of the "theme" in the cozy) functions in exactly the same way as a grain of sand caught in an oyster: an irritant that also produces a pearl, the kernel of our enjoyment. This is the real sense of the icebergs of sugar floating in Wallander's veins—the mineral irritant within the organism, which then secretes layer upon layer of narrative around this original "missed object."

To see this more clearly, we might return briefly to the idea that these kernels of irritation have something in common with the *fetish*. I mentioned at the beginning three particular points of commonality, namely specificity, arbitrariness, and persistence. It is the last of these, persistence, that may have the most to offer an analysis of detective fiction, as readers return again and again to the same detective with the same quirks, the same peculiar themes (chocolate-themed detective novels, beautician-themed mysteries) that gave them enjoyment before. I use the term "enjoyment" here, however, in its psychoanalytic sense, as the constant return to something that does not give satisfaction and yet gives a kind of perverse pleasure in its very failure to satisfy, and this is why the example of the kernel of irritation in the police procedural is particularly pertinent: it offers a clear instance where the repetition is both unpleasurable and has no marketing value. That is, it does not give satisfaction either to the reader or to the author. And yet it persists, nonetheless. Here it is worthwhile to note that the fetish is also basically structured by enjoyment in this technical sense. It is fundamentally organized by the avoidance of something else, by a negativity (i.e., I take a shoe as my object of erotic fascination precisely in order to *avoid* gazing on, in classic Freudian theory, the castrated female body). The fetish, to use a phrase that I have borrowed from Žižek and will use liberally throughout this book, is yet another example of the "never-ending, repeated circulation around the unattainable, always missed object" (2001, p. 48) that defines enjoyment.

3

DESIRE: *Hitchcock and Christie*

DOING SOMETHING DRASTIC—GETTING MARRIED

Rear Window (1954) is one of Hitchcock's best films. Like *Rope*, which was dedicated to the idea of making a movie with no visible cuts, *Rear Window* is based on an "ideal" formal principle: nearly every shot originates from within the protagonist's apartment, creating a claustrophobic tension ideally suited to Hitchcock's story. The film tells the story of L.B. "Jeff" Jeffries, a professional photojournalist whose work has taken him all over the world. He is injured, however, while photographing a car race; eager for a dramatic shot, he steps too close to a collision in progress between two of the cars. His leg is broken, he is confined to a wheel-chair, and has been stuck in his New York apartment for the last five weeks. This is the back story to the film, and the viewer infers it from a variety of visual clues in the opening shots of the interior of Jeff's apartment, such as smashed photographic equipment that Jeff has kept as an ironic trophy, and, in particular, the photo on the wall of the car accident that led to his own injury. We should note that the film immediately foregrounds a concern with travel, or more precisely, Jeff's inability to move freely about. The tone that dominates these early scenes is the oppressiveness of his immobility, emphasized by a close-up of the thermometer registering 94 degrees and his limp, sweaty sleep. We might also infer that this immobility poses a professional problem, as a number of the photographs show Jeff in locations that are obviously not domestic, in particular, photos that appear to be wartime documentary images. This is markedly not true of the last images the camera lingers on in this opening pan around the room: the first is a framed negative of a woman's face, followed by the image printed normally as the cover of a fashion magazine, which will be tied to the world of the home throughout the film. As the viewer will learn shortly, the image is that of Lisa Fremont (Grace Kelly), Jeff's girlfriend, and, in the ghastly, inverted image of her in the framed negative, there is already a suggestion that she and her world represent a kind of threat, that Jeff perceives her "as a negative" in his life. One can't help but note that in the first few seconds of the film, *the entire overall movement of the narrative has been revealed*, through nothing other than the camera movement. This takes place in two stages: first, as the camera pans from the active manly pursuits of the first photographs of war, travel, and car racing taken by Jeff to the feminine and domestic interests of the last images of fashion, and second, from the repellent negative Lisa to whom Jeff cannot commit to the seductive "positive" Lisa of the magazine cover.

The film's first dialogue is a conversation between Jeff and his editor. Gunnison, the editor, believes that Jeff's leg is already healed, and so calls to offer him a plum assignment photographing a violent upheaval in Kashmir, one that Jeff had correctly predicted. On learning that he is still immobile, however, Gunnison has to retract the offer. Jeff resists, telling his editor that he can shoot from a jeep or "the back of a water buffalo, if necessary," but to no avail. At the same time as we understand that his inability to travel is a professional disappointment and irritant, there is another way that Jeff's immobility provokes frustration both for him and vicariously for the male spectator: the constantly frustrated desire for sexual freedom. Hitchcock is less obvious about this, relying principally on the putatively male viewer's identification with Jeff's position: he is subjected to a parade of attractive women who remain unaware of his watchful eye. One accidentally drops her bra and bends over provocatively to pick it up, all the while dancing and dressing, while the two girls on the roof go sunbathing topless while Jeff talks to his editor. Jeff seems merely amused by the spectacle, but also follows it carefully, and the dancing and sunbathing, added to the frustration about his lost opportunities to travel, appear to have some effect. The next scene shows Jeff trying, with increasing desperation, to reach an itch underneath the cast that covers him up to the waist, finally resorting to a kind of prosthetic, a curved wooden stick. Viewers familiar with Hitchcock will recall a similar itch in *Vertigo*, under Scottie's corset. In both cases, the male subject is chafing at restrictions that exclude him from his normal position of phallic power, accentuated in the case of *Vertigo* by the fact that Scottie is chafing under the restrictions of a *corset*. "Do you suppose many men wear corsets?" he asks Midge. "More than you think," she replies archly. In part, of course, this itch also stands for Jeff's frustrated identification with Thorwald, man as held down by the "plaster cocoon" of women. This plays along with the relentless discourse of male freedom in *Vertigo*, that at some atavistic point in the past, men had "the power and the freedom" to throw women away. (For more on *Vertigo*, see Chapter 5, on repetition.) The women that Jeff watches in *Rear Window* are *unapproachable*, not in the common sense of out of his league but literally out of his reach because he cannot move.

Finally, Jeff is constantly menaced by the threat of a more dreadful, more permanent confinement. As he says to his editor, if he doesn't get back to his job soon and out of his stuffy apartment, "I'm gonna do something drastic . . . I'm gonna get married. Then I'll never be able to go *anywhere*." Although this threat sounds playful at the time, the viewer will soon learn that Jeff is in fact struggling to avoid marrying the "perfect" woman, the self-assured and capable fashion model Lisa Fremont. This is typical Hitchcock: the woman represents a trap, in this case the trap of domestic stasis, of never traveling again, and Jeff is highly aware of this danger. Numerous studies have looked at the representation of gender in the film, particularly the constellation of anxieties about masculinity that it articulates, but not through the lens of putatively masculine movement and Jeff's enforced—and putatively feminine—stasis. Indeed, the first voice we hear in the film expresses just such a concern, a radio advertisement from the musician's apartment asking: "Men, are you over forty? When you wake up in the morning, do you feel tired and run down? Do you have that listless feeling?" (This immediately follows the shot of Jeff's sweating, sleeping body and the close-up of the thermometer.) With the threat of listlessness and "never being able to go *anywhere*," it is precisely man as the mobile sex that is being called into question here, as it will be throughout the rest of the film.

There has never been any doubt that the film's two principal characters, Jeff and Lisa, are in conflict, or the essential nature of that conflict. Lisa wants marriage and Jeff wants adventure; Lisa wants the domestic and

Jeff wants to travel. One can't help but note that nearly every argument Jeff advances against continuing their relationship has to do with travel and its discomforts, with issues of money coming right behind, as he says to Stella, his insurance nurse, before we even see Lisa: "Can you imagine her tramping around the world with a camera bum who never has more than a week's salary in the bank?"

Lisa's resistance to Jeff's traveling lifestyle and her attempts to domesticate that lifestyle are numerous; she begins quite subtly, by picking up an emblematic object of Jeff's travels:

> LISA: You know, this cigarette box has seen better days.
>
> JEFF: Oh, I picked that up in Shanghai . . . (*adding with a smile of ironic regret*) which has also seen better days.
>
> LISA: It's cracked and you never use it. It's too ornate. [*Eagerly*] I'm sending up a plain, flat silver one, with just your initials engraved.

This is in the time-honored tradition of domesticating the husband, gradually replacing the inappropriately unsocialized objects of his past with more properly domestic ones: the cracked, ornate, and exotic will be replaced by the safe and bourgeois.

Lisa, as it turns out in this scene, is also a remarkably well-traveled person, highly mobile, but in a very particular way. For instance, as she describes in detail the itinerary of her day:

> LISA: I was all morning in a sales meeting. Then I had to dash to the Waldorf for a quick drink with Madame Dufresne, who's just over from Paris, with some spy reports. And then I had to go to "21" and have lunch with the *Harper's Bazaar* people—and that's when I ordered dinner. Then I had two Fall showings, twenty blocks apart. Then I had to have a cocktail with Leland and Slim Hayward—we're trying to get his new show. Then I had to dash back and change.

This is a frenetic kind of movement. Lisa *dashes* twice, and the verb is implied again for the two Fall showings "twenty blocks apart," but all within the context of what is securely established as home. Her home is the highly limited and "rarefied atmosphere of Park Avenue," as Jeff notes, the world of fashion and of fashion magazines. In fact, it's no accident that *Harper's Bazaar* holds a central position in her domesticated travel narrative, as fashion magazines represent from the film's opening shot (Lisa's photograph for the cover of a fashion magazine as the curious inverse, literally, of Jeff's other, more masculine, and more roving, photos) to the last, as we shall see.

Lisa's idea of domesticating Jeff extends beyond his clothing to his profession, and hence the most visibly mobile part of his nature. She expresses the hope that

> LISA: Some day you may want to open up a studio of your own here.
> JEFF: How would I run it from say, Pakistan?
> LISA: Jeff, isn't it time you came home?

Lisa wants Jeff to do fashions and portraits and she plants favorable items in the newspaper columns to lay the groundwork for such a career. When Jeff counters with the image of him driving to the fashion shoot in a Jeep, wearing combat boots and a three-day beard, Lisa returns the picture of him dressed in a dark blue flannel suit. This is the logic of the cigarette box again and again: the inappropriate traveling lifestyle is to be exchanged for a wholly domestic one: photographs of war and sports for fashion and portraits, combat boots for a dark blue flannel suit.

When Jeff makes it clear that he won't be trading in any of these items, and as the argument starts to heat up, Lisa counters with a different argument, namely, that all travel is already thoroughly domesticated, reducing his exotic adventures in faraway lands to the bane of all travelers: tourism. "What's so different about it here from over there, or any place you go that one person couldn't live in both places just as easily? What is it with traveling from one place to another taking pictures? It's just like being a tourist on an endless vacation." She then goes even further, seeing in Jeff's refusal to give up travel, or more precisely, his unwillingness to travel between the space of travel and the domestic space, a perverse kind of immobility: "According to you, people should be born, live and die on the same spot!" she says, which prompts an outraged "Shut up!" from Jeff.

Jeff retaliates with a list of the discomforts of travel that Lisa is ill-prepared for: eating fish heads and rice, enduring the 20° below zero of a C-54 at 15,000 feet, getting shot at and run over, little sleep, less bathing, and the telling phrase that "your home is the available transportation." This is serious uprootedness, where one's orienting point of origin is a means of transport, and it stands in profound (irreconcilable, according to Jeff) contrast to Lisa's more domestic itineraries. It also stands in marked contrast to Jeff's current immobility. As the film goes on, with virtually every shot originating inside Jeff's apartment, the viewer inevitably experiences some of his claustrophobia, and shares some of his unspoken envy for Lisa's smaller journey. In fact, all of Jeff's talk of Pakistan, fish heads, Shanghai, and C-54 transport planes begins to acquire an aura of unreality in a film whose field of view never goes farther than the courtyard and the one narrow slice of street and bar visible from Jeff's window. In other words, despite Jeff's yearning for mobility, the film's structure already indicates a cinematographic preference for restricted space and limited movement. Jeff, however, is aware that there is more than one kind of space, more than one kind of travel: there is always epistemological space, the space of detection.

PRIVATE-EYE LITERATURE

Jeff has become so bored by his long immobility that he has taken to watching his neighbors' domestic lives, inventing pet names for some. All of them represent different stages of domesticity (as Robin Wood [1965] long ago noted): the single, "Miss Torso," the unconsciously exhibitionist young dancer; a frustrated composer; "Miss Lonelyhearts," the unhappy spinster on the ground floor; the newlyweds, a recently arrived couple: the wife's sexual insatiability is used to comic effect; the married, a childless couple who lavish parental affection on their dog; and a few very brief shots of a couple with a child. Although all of these figures represent potential domestic identifications for Jeff, his attention is eventually directed in particular to Lars Thorwald, whom Jeff suspects of doing away with his invalid wife. Numerous commentators have noted the double set of identifications that the film deploys in this regard. On the one hand, Jeff (and the putatively male spectator) identifies with Mr. Thorwald, who lives out "the real of his desire"—killing the nagging wife who ties him down, freeing the male subject for further adventures including sexual ones—Thorwald's immediate destination is another woman. On the other hand, Jeff and the spectator are both constrained to play a passive role, confined to a small space, like Mrs. Thorwald. This identification might be tentative at the beginning of the film (both Jeff and Mrs. Thorwald bitterly refuse their partners' attempts to bring them a romantic dinner, for example), but will be undeniable by the end when Thorwald attempts to do away with the invalid Jeff just as he did away with his invalid wife. There is also, precisely speaking, a double set of double identifications in the film, as Lisa also must identify with Mr. Thorwald, wishing to be rid of the nagging, ungrateful invalid at her side, as well as his wife. Lisa will, after all, perversely insert herself into Mrs. Thorwald's space by taking and putting on her wedding ring.

We should note immediately that Mr. Thorwald is a *traveling* salesman who explains his wife's absence by saying that he sent her on a trip. In other words, the dysfunctional domestic space is marked precisely by its inhabitants' inability to stay in one place. It certainly suggests that travel, and by extension, the adventurous masculine impulses that traditionally prompt it, is fundamentally incompatible with the domestic space. This is a strong early indication that the film is not looking for a feel-good compromise solution (that Jeff and Lisa spend part of the year in the New York fashion world and part traveling, for instance), which we would not expect from Hitchcock in any event. Although Jeff certainly associates travel with adventure and excitement, the actual practice of travel in the film is in fact linked exclusively to injury (his leg) and death (the two Thorwalds, the murderous traveling salesman and his wife who "goes on a trip").

Because he is prevented from starring in his preferred genre, the travel narrative, Jeff turns to detection, which affords him a kind of mental exploration in lieu of the real thing. He also turns to detection, at least in part, as a ploy to distract Lisa from matrimonial considerations and the genre of the domestic romance. Numerous critics have noted that Lisa plays this game better than Jeff does: she readily assumes the part of Jeff's "moll," and eventually manages to attract his approval and sexual attention by playing along with the rules of this new genre. Lisa is quite explicit about the generic conventionality of their roles. She playfully accuses Jeff of not being sufficiently well read in private eye literature, noting that when detectives are in trouble "it's always their Girl Friday who gets them out of it." Naturally, she is also asserting the primacy of her own role in this genre, as well as the male protagonist's dependence on her. Jeff retaliates by noting that the detective "never ends up marrying" his Girl Friday, indicating that he is more up on his private eye literature than Lisa gives him credit for.

But not enough. Jeff should have read more private eye literature, or read it more carefully. He is also flattering himself by inserting himself into the place of either a classic detective like Holmes, or, more likely, a hard-boiled hero like Marlowe, Spade, or Hammer—Jeff is a far cry from such characters. Most critical studies of classic detective fiction agree that it is a fundamentally conservative genre, indeed, that this is one of its fundamental pleasures: its aims always revolve around the restoration of a prior state, the perfection of law and order, safety and security.[2] As a result, the overall ideological tone of classic detective fiction, particularly in the "Golden Age" writers like Tey, Marsh, Christie, and Sayers, is nostalgia for a diminished aristocracy and the privileges of Empire, if not the explicit dream of its restoration. Likewise, it is a critical given that classic detective fiction has a conservative epistemological function: the restoration of belief in a comprehensible universe, requiring only the presence of the detective to render the networks of cause and effect pristinely visible and manageable. Rarely noted in the list of things restored by classic detective fiction, however, is the space of the home, that despite its *outré* murders and other bizarre crimes, it is a quintessentially domestic genre. From "Murders in the Rue Morgue" onward, the classic detective narrative is largely concerned with intrusion into the home, and the detective implicitly works to restore its sanctity, its integrity. The romantic subplot of detective novels, often perceived as extraneous and irrelevant, presents only as a way of retarding the forward movement of the narrative and is in fact directly related to the ideological task of investigation—the birth of a new domesticity in a newly secure world. Van Dine formalized the rejection of the romantic subplot in his famous "twenty rules" for writing detective fiction, which I take as a neat confirmation of its necessity. (See rule # 3: "There must be no love interest." [Haycraft 1974]) Van Dine's rules are an accurate description not of detective fiction, but of how detective fiction is meant to be misconstrued by its readers. Why is it necessary in classic detective fiction that the reader should perceive the romantic subplot as an extraneous and irrelevant waste of time? That is, why do "serious" readers of detective fiction continue to dismiss, often with irritation, the romantic subplot whereas writers of detective fiction continue to include it? Does this not suggest

---

2. D. A. Miller, of course, has noted the ways that crime fiction specifically, and the novelistic form more generally, acts as a "policing agent" in *The Novel and the Police* (1989); Dennis Porter notes that "detective fiction is part of 'the discourse of the Law' that for Foucault was indispensable in the creation of the new 'disciplinary society,' which emerged in Europe . . ." (1981, p. 121); Carl Malmgren points out that classic detective fiction is willing to suppress the truth (Christie's *Murder on the Orient Express*, which I will deal with extensively later in this chapter, is a case in point) to ensure that justice prevails—a further sign of the still-centered vision of the world the genre offers. In later crime fiction, the reader must be satisfied by the truth alone; justice is often out of the question (2001, pp. 51–57).

that the romance is a necessary ingredient, but one that the reader does not wish to acknowledge as necessary? In short, it suggests that, as much as the reader might wish to believe that detective fiction is about the free-ranging intellect of a genius detective, it is also, perhaps even principally, about a domestic arrest, the capture and containment of ordinary people in the most ordinary and tame situations. The classic detective wants to go home, back to a world of aristocratic privilege, back to a world of comprehensible cause and effect, back to his undisturbed cultivation of "vegetable marrows," like Hercule Poirot at the start of *The Murder of Roger Ackroyd*.

It is a simple structural observation, however, that the classic detective is never, properly speaking, "at home." He may have a residence, even a famous one (221B Baker St.), but even a cursory glance at *The Sign of Four*, the Holmes narrative that is most clearly concerned with the establishment of domesticity, shows that Baker St. is, in its own way, as eccentric a space as Thaddeus Sholto's bizarre and extravagantly Orientalist dwelling. Both residences are counterpoised to a "proper" domestic space, one that Watson glimpses through a doorway left ajar, a beam of domestic and very English light in a world of epistemic and ideological, not to mention racial, darkness of the case that is emerging:

> As we drove away I stole a glance back, and I still seem to see that little group on the step—the two graceful, clinging figures, the half-opened door, the hall-light shining through stained glass, the barometer, and the bright stair-rods. It was soothing to catch even that passing glimpse of a tranquil English home in the midst of the wild, dark business which had absorbed us. [Conan Doyle 2001, p. 51]

Ostensibly, Watson sees Miss Morstan, already his love interest, returning to the home where she works as a governess. What Watson is really seeing here, however, is the promise of the narrative itself: "a tranquil English home." It will be his own home, of course, as the narrative will conclude with his engagement to Miss Morstan, a restoration of her very fractured home (her mother died at a young age, and her father, an officer in India, sent her to a boarding school; he disappears once he returns to England), and the tying up of another loose end, namely, Watson himself. In case after case, in fact, the Holmes stories restore domestic order: intruders into marital happiness are sent to prison ("The Dancing Men"), treasures that might stop a marriage are disposed of (*The Sign of Four*); in some cases ("The Yellow Face"), nothing at all is effected besides a reconciliation, an opening of a domestic and matrimonial truth.[3] The detective's job, in this sense, is the most mundane and domestic imaginable: to keep the house clean. The lack of attention given to this function of the detective is best expressed by Sherlock Holmes in *The Sign of Four* in an address to his chronicler that functions doubly as an address to the reader, and emphasizes the way the detective is related to the home, but does not properly belong in it: "Watson, you have never yet recognized my merits as a housekeeper" (Conan Doyle 2001, p. 79). In present-day classic detective fiction, the idea is expressed somewhat differently, but the sentiment is the same, as in the television series *Monk*, when Sharona Fleming, the sidekick, informs her boss, Adrian Monk, that "someday" he will "make someone a wonderful wife" ("Mr. Monk Goes to the Carnival").

One might observe more generally that readers and critics of detective fiction have never yet recognized the classic detective's merits as a housekeeper, an authority on domestic management who does not "properly" belong to the domestic space. And hence a litany of classic detectives who are bachelors and spinsters, but who manage, time and again, to ensure that couples are paired off, domestic ruptures repaired. In this respect, the detective bears a notable similarity to the cowboy in a classic Hollywood Western: arriving from the "outside," setting the town to rights again, and then returning to his eccentric orbit around but never within the space of the settled. More obviously, and more pertinently for this study, he resembles the figure of the analyst, that other great authority on domestic management who does not properly belong to the domestic. In any case, in both classic and hard-boiled detective fiction, the primary reason the detective must maintain his extra-domestic position is so that he may return to investigate again, a fact that, to return to *Rear Window*, Jeff has forgotten. He must also maintain a different position: that of the "subject supposed to know," free of libidinal entanglements, at least within classic detective fiction. Perhaps more significantly, Jeff has placed himself in the principal, active, and masculine role of the detective—but is his position not more akin to that of the sidekick, the one who is, after all, in the position of *relying on another to do the investigating for him?*

---

3. The point here is not that these are necessarily happy resolutions that end in the ideal middle-class English household imagined by Watson in *The Sign of Four*—this is not the case, for example, in "The Dancing Men," or "The Speckled Band"—but that all function to shut out or assimilate the foreign, to domesticate it.

The end result of Jeff and Lisa's sleuthing is double: first, Lisa rescues "proof positive" of Thorwald's crime, Mrs. Thorwald's wedding ring. As she triumphantly brandishes the ring at Jeff, who watches her through a telephoto camera lens, the viewer also understands that she is celebrating her own matrimonial triumph. Second, after a suspenseful struggle between the wheelchair-bound Jeff and Mr. Thorwald, we have the apprehension of the criminal and the consequent revelation of the full truth. Thorwald is arrested, the location of his wife's body is pinned down. So much for the traveling salesman and his wife on a trip! That overly mobile household has been brought to a standstill. This arrest functions for the viewer, as well. Although we may have identified with Thorwald as the agent who realizes our most violent desires, we are also relieved of responsibility for the crime. This is the unary logic of detective fiction that fixates on a single solution to the mystery, exculpating viewers or readers from any share of the blame. This is Žižek's logic of the avoidance of "the real of desire," a point I will return to in detail when discussing Agatha Christie. For now, having covered the arrest of the traveling salesman, of his wife "on a trip," as well as the viewer of *Rear Window*, we now have to ask: What about Jeff and his "girl Friday"? *Rear Window* aims at the "arrest" of the family that has been marked by the stain of the other. Does this economy of "travel only in order to come to a halt" also apply to the epistemic wanderings of Jeff and Lisa? That is, Jeff turns to investigation, a purely mental move-ment, because he cannot travel physically. But investigation, as we have seen in Conan Doyle, traditionally also leads to an arrest, as well as a do-mestic rest. Remember that Holmes feels that he has been underappreciated as a housekeeper.

In an ironic reversal of the film's opening sequence, the final shot is a slow pan around the courtyard, now largely depicting contentment and quiescence: the thermometer registers 72° (Is it not also a sign of Hitchcock's total domination of the narrative that the thermometer registers precisely "official" room temperature, neither a degree more nor less?), and the camera moves inside Jeff's apartment, where we see his comically smiling, con-tented face. The camera tracks down to his legs and the viewer discovers that they are now *both* broken. This shot never fails to elicit amused laugh-ter from the audience: Jeff has really been had (*two* broken legs!); he has fallen into the domestic trap and discovered that he loves it. Lisa has her man, and however much he may have been immobilized before, he is even more thoroughly removed from the realm of travel now. There is no longer any of the sweating, frustration, or itching that characterized the film's beginning. Unlike Scottie in *Vertigo*, Jeff has learned not to chafe under his corset, a difference that has everything to do with the very different ways the two films end: *Vertigo* is the tragic triumph of man's desire; *Rear Window* the comic triumph of woman's.

The camera moves from his plaster-encased legs to Grace Kelly's rather less encumbered ones. Perhaps the viewer has lingering doubts; perhaps she will, after all, participate in his traveling lifestyle once he is out of the wheelchair (she is wearing pants, after all). Indeed, Lisa is reading a travel book, whose title—*Beyond the High Himalayas*—is clearly visible in these final shots. Lisa's clothes have become progressively more practical throughout the film, and never more so than now, down to her sensible shoes. We should note that here, at the end of the movie, physical movement is again equated with interpretive play. That is, travel as a possible discourse at the end of the film represents the possibility of an incomplete closure: further adventures could await Jeff and Lisa, and, in a gross violation of the rules of detective fiction, the detective, despite having acceded to the domestic, might return to investigate again. Desire might become mobile again.

But there will be no lingering doubt for the viewer: our knowledge, including our knowledge of their relationship, will be apprehended in a totalizing stillness. Lisa peers at Jeff to confirm that he is asleep, and discards the book to replace it with a more domestic piece of reading: *Harper's Bazaar*, of course. Securely encased in his plaster cocoon and a life of fashions, portraits, and dark blue flannel suits, Jeff is not going anywhere. Lisa smiles slyly, and the viewer is treated to a literal closure, the blinds rolling down to cover the window. Fade to black.

EXCULPATION AND IDENTIFICATION

The domestic bliss afforded by the ending's double arrest of Jeff and Thorwald also has a psychic counterpart, however, a specifically libidinal counterpart—it is mirrored by the solace of Žižekian exculpation. Žižek claims in *Looking Awry* that classic detection is based on "avoiding the real of desire." We watch mysteries precisely so we can see our unacceptable desires made real, like the murder of the nagging wife in *Rear Window*. The recognition of this is to be found in a structural element of classic detective stories: the scene of revelation, where the detective sits everyone down at the table and says to the assembled suspects: "Any one of you could have committed this crime!" This is the most suspenseful part of the narrative for the viewer precisely because, according to Žižek, *the spectator recognizes him- or herself in that call.* The pleasure comes from our release from culpability, as the detective then goes on to demonstrate with infallible logic that the blame lies elsewhere, with one specific character.

> Herein lies the fundamental untruth, the essential falsity of the detective's "solution": the detective plays upon the difference between the factual truth (the accuracy of facts) and the "inner" truth concerning our desire. On behalf of the accuracy of the facts, he compromises the "inner," libidinal truth and discharges us of all guilt for the realization of our desire, insofar as this realization is imputed to the culprit alone. . . . The immense pleasure brought about by the detective's solution results from this libidinal gain, from a kind of surplus profit obtained from it: our desire is realized and we do not even have to pay the price for it. [1992, p. 59]

Žižek's formulation nicely explains certain features of detective fiction, such as the imperative of complete closure; to prevent a nagging remainder of guilt, an incomplete consolidation of all blame onto the scapegoat, it is vital that all the narrative possibilities heretofore multiplied be reduced to one. Detection makes the "real of desire" spread like a stain across the entire narrative landscape (a kind of universal culpability) by progressively multiplying narrative possibilities. Alibis fall through, motives emerge, and everyone seems to have been carrying a suitable weapon the night of the murder. The suspense of detection is largely created by maintaining the equality of guilt, the uniform thickness of the stain of the real, which accurately reflects the libidinal economy of the genre. On some level, everyone has desires that are secret, repressed, unacknowledged, misrecognized. Where Žižek sees a kind of bad faith is in the collapse of narrative possibilities, the reduction of the stain to a minute dot, an eccentric singularity in the narrative landscape. What this amounts to, of course, is an "arrest" of the spreading of the stain, an arrest that parallels and coincides with the real arrest in the film. Such an arrest is always at the same time a "rest," a literal and libidinal quiescence or stasis, typically figured as the restoration or establishment of domesticity. Not surprisingly, it is also figured as the end of travel, an end to the mobile and potentially disruptive movement of desire, the potential of the stain to turn "free range," move beyond the edge of the frame, and "denature" the spectator as well.

What about Jeff's identification in *Rear Window*? Is he principally identifying sadistically with Mr. Thorwald, displacing his own aggressive resentments against Lisa onto the murderous man in the couple across the courtyard, or is he masochistically identifying with the invalid Mrs. Thorwald? The answer is that he is doing both, and what is particularly clever about this double identification is that both forms provide Jeff with satisfaction, and in both instances he can shift any guilt over his sadism or his masochism onto Mr. Thorwald. Jeff gets to witness the real of his own desire: through his identification with Mr. Thorwald, he gets to kill the nagging wife he dreads at the beginning of the film, and through his identification with Mrs. Thorwald, he can also eliminate his own weak, immobile self. (This double identification and double desire is expected to play itself out at the level of the putatively masculine—and sedentary—spectator.) Jeff gets to have his desire (a double desire, even) and eat it, too: the unary logic of investigation and arrest absolves him of responsibility, reduces the stain of the real of desire to the singular point of Thorwald's glowing cigarette in the apartment across the courtyard. (In a particularly famous shot in the film, Jeff can see nothing but Thorwald's cigarette in the dark window frame, a slow pulse of murderous satisfaction, one which, not coincidentally, links murder of the woman and a satisfaction of sexual frustration, not to mention addiction and compulsive, repetitive activity.) This is just as true of Lisa's desire. She does, after all, promise Jeff "a week [he'll] never forget" early in the film, and her resentment and frustration with him are amply paid back through Thorwald, who tellingly asks, "Your friend, she could have had me arrested. Why didn't she?"—a question Jeff cannot answer. That is, Lisa also identifies sadistically with Mr. Thorwald, whose attack on Jeff amply repays her for Jeff's shabby treatment of her earlier in the film, and masochistically with all of the suffering female characters in the film (Miss Torso, Miss Lonelyhearts, Mrs. Thorwald). Moreover, the film substantially recounts Lisa's triumph, the victory of feminine domesticity through the substitution of the fashion magazine for travel literature. One might note the femininity of classic detective fiction and its domestic solutions, written so markedly by conservative women—Agatha Christie, Dorothy Sayers, Ngaio Marsh, Josephine Tey—as compared to the masculine genre of the hard-boiled that does not know a domestic solution. *Rear Window* is obviously "post-classical"; however, it is emphatically not hard-boiled (as much as Jeff wishes he were in a novel by Chandler or Hammett); the "amateur sleuth" genre that it belongs to has always been much more closely aligned with the tropes of classic detective fiction.

In other words, detective fiction generally, and *Rear Window* specifically, conjured up the threat of the spread of the stain of the real of desire only, in Grossvogel's terms, in order to "effortlessly dissipate" it (1979, p. 15). Here one thinks quite naturally of the obvious instance of the spread of the stain in *Rear Window*, when Jeff attempts to defend himself against Thorwald's intrusion into his apartment by triggering a series of flash bulbs that temporarily blind the killer. As each bulb goes off, the viewer is treated to a POV shot from Thorwald's perspective, as a red stain appears and expands across the frame, obscuring "our" view of Jeff. An exemplary instance of what Žižek has called "the Hitchcockian blot," it is no accident that it appears as a spreading stain precisely at the moment of greatest mobility in the film, when the killer quite literally "comes over to our side," or perhaps more correctly and more literally still, *we find ourselves on the same side as the killer.* That is, the spreading stain appears at precisely the same moment that the real of desire spreads over the border of the putative frame in the film, and appears in such a way that the spectator is "sutured" into Thorwald's position, forced, albeit temporarily, to recognize that desire as his or her own, to "recognize him- or herself in that call." (We might also note that this "blot" that denatures the frame appears much earlier in the film—indeed, in the first scene—in the photograph that Jeff has taken of the car race: it is the wheel flying directly at the viewer that has already marked Jeff's desire as too mobile, too dangerous, even if, evidently, one broken leg is not enough to get the message across, not enough to contain or arrest it.) As Miran Božovič has noted, the wheel flying out of the frame at Jeff undermines "the photographer's position as 'neutral,' 'objective,'" effectively photographing Jeff, making him too the object of a gaze (1992, p. 171). The recognition of the viewer's implicated position is what mobilizes the logic of "arrest" that demands the constriction of the stain, its fundamental displacement; it equally demands an end to the free roaming of desire. It must be clearly located in one place, arrested, imprisoned by the viewer's misrecognition and misattribution.

Žižek's description of exculpation in *Looking Awry* is concerned specifically with classic detective fiction and hard-boiled/*noir* ("the Sherlock Holmes way" and "the Philip Marlowe way" of avoiding the real of desire). *Rear Window* is, of course, neither classic detection nor hard-boiled, but it still evinces the comforting solace of arrest and exculpation, and its domesticity is already an indication that its libidinal structures, if not all of its generic structures, are principally indebted to classic detective fiction. (Again, Jeff was reading the wrong kind of detective fiction when he accused Lisa of not being up on her private eye literature.) Here I would like to turn to an exemplary instance of classic detective fiction, perhaps the most obvious example of the theme of travel in classic detection: Agatha Christie's *Murder on the Orient Express.*

Christie is certainly a paradigmatic example of classic detective fiction. Her novels feature detectives who defend the domestic without properly belonging to it (the "eccentric" position of the detective), reasoning, frequently sedentarily, by logical deduction, and they certainly evince complete narrative closure. In other words, Christie fully subscribes to the "domestication of investigation" or "truth without remainder": this is virtually the defining characteristic of classic detective fiction. We might profitably compare Christie's distant, exiled, eccentric detectives to the haunted and obsessive ones of a modern writer who still writes in the classic vein such as Ruth Rendell, or contrast their approaches to the recuperation of the domestic space. In a novel like Rendell's *No More Dying Then*, Inspector Burden is faced with a choice between two women, one an appropriate object choice, the other inappropriate. Not only does he obsessively pursue the inappropriate woman, but at the end he is left with neither (also true of Detective Constable Drayton's love interest in *Wolf to the Slaughter*). In Christie, there is almost invariably an explicit or implied resolution of the love story (Mary Debenham and Colonel Arbuthnot in *Murder on the Orient Express* or Flora Ackroyd and Major Blunt, not to mention Ralph Patton and Ursula Bourne, in *The Murder of Roger Ackroyd*).

Moreover, the scene of exculpation that Žižek describes clearly comes from Christie. Although he refers to the procedure as the "Sherlock Holmes way of avoiding the real of desire," the gathering of suspects and the dramatic claim that "any one of you could have done this!" is not a scene that appears anywhere in the Holmes stories. Poirot, however, regularly gathers all the suspects around the dinner table, accuses them each in turn, and then reveals the true killer. In so many respects, Christie is the paradigm of classic detective fiction, but her work tends to be obscured by and to reside behind the more memorable icons of the deerstalker cap, the pipe, and the magnifying glass. The Holmes stories, by contrast, hardly ever work on the standard Christie method of the multiplication of suspects, in which it is possible, all too possible, that each character should have committed the crime, but instead on the seeming impossibility that any character could have committed the crime and hence, the occasional "cheating" ending in Holmes, as in "The Dancing Men," in which the criminal appears for the very first time only at the end. What Žižek describes, then, is the Hercule Poirot way of avoiding the real of desire. At times, Christie's language, as with Borges's "Kafka and His Precursors," even seems to be echoing Žižek's, as when the characters in *And Then There Were None* discuss who among them might be disqualified from suspicion. One character concludes that the murderer "is one of us. No exceptions allowed. We all qualify." Another states, as if performing an impromptu Žižekian reading down to his particular use of italics, of the genre at hand: "My point is that there can be no exceptions allowed on the score of *character, position,* or *probability*" (Christie 2004, p. 136).

It is perhaps curious that Žižek should have formulated this notion of exculpation based on a scenario from Christie, however, as Christie's most memorable novels are still today the ones where she spreads the stain of "the real of desire" into spaces that had previously been thought eccentric to the space of investigation. Consider the case of *Curtain*, the last Poirot novel. In this novel, we find that the *detective*, the eccentric subject par excellence, is guilty of the murder. He retains some semblance of the "subject supposed to know," however, as not only is he omniscient, but he acts in the interests of the Law, killing in order to stop a killer so fiendishly clever that he will never be caught. I will return to the problem of *Curtain* in quite a different way in the chapter on "Enjoyment."

But this is not the most troubling part of *Curtain.* What leaves a more permanent mark on the reader's hopes for exculpation is the fact that Hastings, Poirot's longtime friend, none-too-bright sidekick, and narrator, has also killed. Unlike Dr. Sheppard of *Roger Ackroyd*, however, Hastings was not even aware that he was causing someone's death. When all of the others are distracted by a display of shooting stars, Hastings idly spins a kind of rotating table, actually a rotating bookcase, with two cups of tea on top; what he does not know is that one cup is poisoned, and now the poisoner will inadvertently swallow her own medicine, as it were. Even if Hastings were not the quintessentially average "everyman" that he is, designed to elicit the reader's identification, surely the endless spread of guilt in this novel, where even the most trivial of actions is charged with murderous results, will not release the reader in the end. Note how brilliantly Christie handles the scene where Hastings recalls a tender scene with his dead wife, Cinders, and is interrupted by his daughter, Judith:

> I bent closer over the paper. For I was remembering . . . A clear tropical night—frogs croaking . . . and a shooting star. I was standing there by the window, and I had turned and picked up Cinders and carried her out in my arms to see the stars and wish . . .
> The lines of the crossword ran and blurred before my eyes.

A figure detached itself from the balcony and came into the room—
Judith.

Judith must never catch me with tears in my eyes. It would never
do. Hastily I swung round the bookcase and pretended to be looking
for a book. I remembered having seen an old edition of Shakespeare
there. Yes, here it was. I looked through *Othello*. [1993, pp. 151–152,
ellipses original[4]]

What is remarkable is that the nostalgic recollection of his wife, the
shooting stars, the eyes blurring over with tears, Judith's sudden arrival,
and the need to look for a prop as a distraction—all these touching elements and the only elements of any importance to the reader are just so
much distracting fluff to Christie. They only exist to draw our attention
away from an action that is already astoundingly forgettable, banal, and
trivial: the turning of the bookshelf.

The Murder of Roger Ackroyd presents an equally interesting case, as
Christie spreads the stain of guilt onto the narrator, who is also Poirot's
sidekick. Such a procedure has been called cheating because Christie has
concealed the third-person answer to "whodunit" underneath the voice of
the first-person narrator, who faithfully narrates events—with certain key
omissions. Wouldn't such a procedure leave a residue of narrative possibility and potential "surplus guilt" that might not be adequately pinned
down? More intriguing still, Pierre Bayard has argued quite persuasively
that *The Murder of Roger Ackroyd* demands a careful rereading (a clear violation of narrative closure) in order to demonstrate, as he does, that *the
narrator is not the killer after all* (Bayard, 2000). I will return to this point
shortly, but let us first consider the trope of travel and its relation to closure in *The Murder of Roger Ackroyd*.

The first thing that Dr. Sheppard (our narrator, Poirot's sidekick, and—
according to Poirot at the end of the novel—the killer) says to Poirot is an
expression of his desire and inability to travel. Poirot suggests to the doctor that, after years of work, a man in retirement might wish for nothing
more than to return to his old job, and Sheppard replies:

---

4. Naturally it must be *Othello*—the killer is uncatchable because he works like Iago,
poisoning the minds of others so they will kill for him. Naturally, the lines Hastings finds
for the "clue" (poor Hastings believes it is only a clue to his crossword) are spoken by Iago,
and the lines that Judith responds with—"all the drowsy syrups of the world"—are about
poisons.

"Yes," I said slowly. "I fancy that is a common enough occurrence. I myself am perhaps an instance. A year ago I came into a legacy—enough to enable me to realize a dream. I have always wanted to travel, to see the world. Well, that was a year ago, as I said, and—I am still here." [2000b, p. 17]

As we saw in *Rear Window*, the desire for travel is already enough to mark a desire that potentially sets one outside the normal, outside the domestic—in other words, potentially in the eccentric arena of the criminal and the detective. It is always also "desire as such," that is, desire as a manifestation of the symbolic slippage of the signifier, desire as the quintessentially mobile part of the psyche, always going "somewhere else" as its *goal* is always different from its *aim*. Unlike Jeff in *Rear Window*, however, Dr. Sheppard has no Lisa to exert a centripetal force and draw him back in, because he lives at home with his sister. Caroline Sheppard occupies a curious place in the text, as Bayard has very astutely noted.[5] To begin with, Christie acknowledged Caroline not only as her favorite character from *The Murder of Roger Ackroyd*, but also the basis for Miss Marple, so she would seem to occupy a kind of privileged position. That position appears to be the "subject presumed to know." Like the detective, she possesses a knowledge that is uncanny, as when she knows about Mrs. Ferrars' death before he does. (He is the village doctor, and hence should have privileged information about such subjects.) Her information resources are, like the detective's, extensive, and she is also an astute judge of human nature. She understands at once that Mrs. Ferrars' death is suicide, not an accident, correctly deduces her motivations for killing herself, and even knows that Mrs. Ferrars will have left a letter explaining the situation. Dr. Sheppard likens her curiosity to that of the mongoose, whose motto is "go and find out," and, just like the detective, Caroline seems to be capable of occupying an eccentric space, circulating and picking up information unseen by others. In other words, she seems unusually *mobile*, a stark contrast to her rather slow and unimaginative brother.

---

5. In fact, there is an indication in the text that Dr. Sheppard's relationship with his sister may be "eccentric." Bayard makes much, and rightly so, of Dr. Sheppard's reference to Kipling in Chapter 1, but, perhaps because he prefers to take a detour through Oedipus and see Caroline as a mother figure, he ignores Dr. Sheppard's reference (2000b, p. 28) to George Eliot's *The Mill on the Floss* and that novel's intense sibling love.

The male characters in the text seem to have an interest in restricting that mobility, however, in domesticating it. Dr. Sheppard suggests that the motto of the mongoose according to Kipling ("go and find out") would be quite appropriate to her, only "one might omit the first part of the motto" (2000b, p. 2). On the following page, he reminds the reader again that "there is no need for Caroline to go out to get information. She sits at home and it comes to her" (2000b, p. 3). This is, of course, literally untrue, as Caroline is frequently out of the house, on one occasion going through the woods to eavesdrop on Ralph Paton and an unknown woman. It is equally untrue, however, at a more metaphorical level, where Caroline stands in the eccentric space of the detective.

This is obviously unacceptable to Poirot, who will successfully "arrest" and domesticate Caroline at the end of the novel by constraining her to remain at home. We should also note the aggressive misogynistic violence done to Caroline in the process:

> Caroline was in the hall. I think she hoped that she might be invited to accompany us. Poirot dealt with the situation tactfully.
> "I should very much like to have had you present, mademoiselle," he said regretfully, "but at this juncture it would not be wise. See you, all these people tonight are suspects . . ."
> We went out, leaving Caroline, rather like a dog who has been refused a walk, standing on the front door step gazing after us. [2000b, p. 215]

The foolish Dr. Sheppard does not realize that Poirot leaves Caroline behind because the detective already knows that Dr. Sheppard himself is the killer, and wishes to spare her feelings. Bayard notes quite correctly that this is a moment of profound error on Poirot's part, as a number of literary and psychoanalytic cues indicate that *the real conflict in the book—detective and psychic—pits Poirot against Caroline*" (2000, p. 217, emphasis original). Bayard suggests that Poirot misidentifies the criminal, and presents an entirely plausible scenario (at least as plausible as Christie's) in which Caroline Sheppard, and not her brother, is the killer. There is no need to cover that argument in detail here. Suffice it to say that Bayard is quite devious in exploiting all of the tropes of detective fiction in making his case, not to mention literary criticism and psychoanalysis; what interests me here is that *both* Bayard's and Christie's solutions obey the classical rule of full closure and arrest. Discussing the kernel of subjectivity that inhabits every literary text, Bayard writes dramatically:

For if it is true that an intermediary world exists between the text and the reader, it is likely that the murderer of Roger Ackroyd has found refuge there. He has been living there secretly, perhaps, since the creation of the work, in a deceptive tranquility that is about to end. [2000, p. 110]

If, on the one hand, the passage suggests that Bayard's revelation that Caroline is the killer will disturb a certain tranquility, on the other hand it also suggests that a hidden person's location will be pinned down, that a fugitive from the law will be seized—in other words, Bayard, too, wishes to arrest Caroline Sheppard. No one at the end of the novel, neither the would-be traveler Dr. Sheppard, nor his sister, pinned down, left on the threshold of the home like a dog refused a walk, can escape this arrest.

EVERYBODY DID IT

But more than either *Roger Ackroyd* or *Curtain*, *Murder on the Orient Express* seems tailor-made to test Žižek's reading of the avoidance of the "real of desire" and hence the question of closure and arrest. In this novel, Christie examines yet another structural possibility of the detective novel: What if *everybody* did it?[6] Briefly, the novel tells the story of a murder committed on a train trapped by a snowdrift. It is conclusively demonstrated that the killer is also trapped aboard the train by the snow. Poirot, who happens to be on the train, undertakes the investigation. The victim, Mr. Ratchett, turns out to be a well-known criminal, the kidnapper in the Armstrong kidnapping case. (Christie based this on the infamous Lindbergh kidnapping.)

---

6. We should note that even the very first detective story relies on a similar structural trick to effect the reader's surprise: What if *no one* (i.e., an orangutan) did it? Christie's *And Then There Were None* also mirrors the gimmick of *Murder on the Orient Express*: all but one of the characters bear the guilt of a prior death. All these former killers are brought together on an island and picked off one by one. The only character who is *not* stained by the guilt of a prior crime is, perversely, the character committing the current crimes. However, as we shall see in *Murder on the Orient Express*, the consecutive murders of the victims are all revealed as non-crimes, delayed justice carried out by the aptly named Justice Wargrave. Paradoxically, and here quite unlike *Murder on the Orient Express*, although "everyone is a killer" in this novel, too, Wargrave still functions as the scapegoat. The whole book turns on the question of "which of the ten is the killer" (although they are all killers), and his identity is revealed only through his final suicide note.

Even though he received the ransom, the kidnapper had killed his victim, the three-year-old Daisy Armstrong (Daisy's mother then died of heartbreak and the father committed suicide), and then was acquitted on a technicality when captured. After much investigation, Poirot discovers that *all* of the passengers on the train are former members of the Armstrong household bent on delivering justice to the certainly guilty Ratchett. Having drugged him, each passenger entered his cabin and blindly stabbed at him, as a result of which none of them would ever "know which blow actually killed him" (2000c, p. 241). The suspects admit this is true. Curiously, however, Poirot offers another explanation, one that does not involve any of the passengers, but instead a stranger who entered the train, killed Ratchett, and left. This other solution, though somewhat satisfactory, does not fit many of the facts, but Poirot leaves the decision as to which of the solutions is the correct one to his friend M. Bouc, a director of the train company. Bouc, having heard the heart-rending stories of the Armstrong household, elects to proffer this other explanation to the police.

Poirot does not miss his chance to gather all of the suspects around a table here, but there is no exculpating moment of a hallucinatory projection of guilt onto a scapegoat. "Any of you could have committed the crime! And, indeed, all of you did." Our desires to kill are made real, and we are found guilty of them. This certainly sounds like a real challenge to Žižek's scene of exculpation, which is in turn a challenge to the "arrest" of narrative closure. We might note other problems, as well: the novel privileges indeterminacy, as Poirot, against his usual habit, offers two solutions to the mystery; it privileges deception over truth, as the solution that will eventually be proffered to the police is the false solution; it seems to suggest that murder is the solution to, as much as the cause of, domestic trauma (the act of revenge clears the way for Mary Debenham and Colonel Arbuthnot); and finally, if we are looking for the investigation's end to coincide with an arrest of travel, we will be disappointed: the train stops when the investigation begins. *Murder on the Orient Express* begins to look like a good "limit case" for an analysis of narrative closure and arrest, travel and domesticity.

Let's begin with this last point. The Orient Express comes to a stop, at least insofar as the narrative is focalized through Poirot, precisely at the point at which the crime is committed:

> He awoke some hours later, awoke with a start. He knew what it was that had wakened him—a loud groan, almost a cry, somewhere close at hand. At the same moment the ting of a bell sounded sharply.

Poirot sat up and switched on the light. He noticed that the train
was at a standstill—presumably at a station. [2000c, p. 32]

Still, there should be nothing terribly surprising in this—*Rear Window* is also the story of a frustrated travel narrative becoming a detective narrative. For that matter, *Rear Window* starts its domestication of travel at the beginning of the narrative. What is more surprising here is that the novel does not *end* with an arrest—of either kind. There are two responses to this "problem," the first trivial and the second more telling.

The first is that, unlike the ending of *Rear Window*, we don't doubt for a moment that the Yugoslavian police will soon arrive, the snowdrift will be cleared, and everyone will return home. If not, we would be left with quite a remainder: a train full of killers, albeit motivated by the desire for justice, on a voyage without end. Not surprisingly, the 1974 film version[7] concludes with the clearing of the tracks and the train's resumption of its interrupted journey, as does the BBC radio version.[8] The return home is not explicitly narrated in the text, either, but is certainly implied, and with it, a return to normalcy and the domestic, exemplified in the text's desire to unite Miss Debenham and Colonel Arbuthnot.

Mary Debenham and Colonel Arbuthnot occupy a privileged place in *Murder on the Orient Express*. They are presented in the first chapter entirely on their own. Poirot encounters most of the other characters in the novel *en masse* a few chapters later. They are the first objects of curiosity for us and for Poirot, who overhears a number of curious private conversations between them that suggest they have a prior, even intimate, acquaintance, despite the fact that they behave in public as if they have just met. They are substantially less caricatured than the other characters in the novel (I say less caricatured because it is rare in Christie that characters have anything like real depth), and they represent a recognizable "type" in Christie's work: the practical English girl and her suitor, the stolid and extremely reserved military man. In *Roger Ackroyd*, they are Flora Ackroyd, "a simple straightforward English girl" (2000b, p. 27), and the aptly named Major Blunt. Here, in *Murder on the Orient Express*, Mary Debenham is possessed of "a kind of cool efficiency" (2000c, p. 7), whereas Colonel

---

7. Directed by Sidney Lumet, and featuring quite an assembly of stars: Lauren Bacall, Ingrid Bergman, Albert Finney, Sean Connery, John Gielgud, Anthony Perkins, and Vanessa Redgrave.

8. Broadcast originally from December 28, 1993 to January 1, 1994.

Arbuthnot is blustering, but always well intentioned. Both are notably well traveled, the Colonel returning from India, Mary from Baghdad with an air about her that "bespoke a knowledge of the world and of travelling" (2000c, p. 7).

Perhaps more importantly, they represent the romantic, and hence domestic, possibility in a novel where the domestic space has been entirely destroyed: the baby killed by kidnappers, the mother dead of a broken heart, the father a suicide. In fact, what is left is literally a series of remainders, the remainders of the Armstrong household. If we are to bring our text to a full conclusion, we can't have this residue of domesticity, but if the domestic can be reestablished and recuperated, those remainders could be subsumed, returned to place (who knows, perhaps around a hopefully happier Arbuthnot household). After a few meals of proper British reticence together, the Colonel makes an endearingly clumsy overture to Mary:

> The Colonel inquired whether she was going straight through to England or whether she was stopping in Stamboul.
> "No, I'm going straight on."
> "Isn't that rather a pity?"
> "I came out this way two years ago and spent three days in Stamboul then."
> "Oh! I see. Well, I must say I'm very glad you are going right through, because I am."
> He made a kind of clumsy little bow, flushing a little as he did so.
> He is susceptible, our Colonel, thought Hercule Poirot to himself with some amusement. "The train, it is as dangerous as a sea voyage!" [2000c, p. 9]

Poirot refers to one of the classic potential gains of travel, romantic or erotic, which is also one of the ways that travel has been used to strengthen the domestic. A few pages later, Poirot learns that their relationship is more profound than he had previously suspected, but there is something blocking the promise of a happy return to home and a newfound domestic bliss.

> It was the voices which gave him the clue to the two indistinct figures standing in the shadow of a traffic van. Arbuthnot was speaking.
> "Mary—"
> The girl interrupted him.
> "Not now. Not now. When it's all over. When it's behind us— then—"
> Discreetly M. Poirot turned away . . . [2000c, p. 10]

As we can see, the novel does not need to narrate the train pulling into London because it is explicitly promised in its opening pages: when it's all over, *then* an end not only to the investigation and the eccentric and marginal life they have lived, but an end to travel and its disruption of domesticity.

FULL STOP

I had said that there were two reasons the novel does not end with an "arrest," either metaphorical or literal, of the criminals, and the second reason is also why *Murder on the Orient Express* is not a counterexample to the Žižekian principle of the avoidance of the real of desire after all. Poirot does not arrest the criminals because they are not criminals. There is only one true criminal in *Murder on the Orient Express* and that is the abominable Mr. Ratchett. The "Cast of Characters" tells us the literal truth of the novel before it even begins, in describing Poirot: "the Belgian sleuth illustrates the efficacy of his methods when he comes face-to-face with a murderer on an international express" (2000c, p. vii). This has a triple function within the narrative, typical of Christie's slippery structural irony. First, it misleads the reader to expect a typical detective narrative with a single guilty party indicated by the indefinite article "a murderer"; second, it appears ironically untrue at the novel's ending when we understand everyone was in on it; third, it appears literally true again once we accept Ratchett as the singular murderer. Poirot verbally confirms this literal truth when he refuses Ratchett's request for protection in what is the book's most "face-to-face" encounter: "If you will forgive me for being personal—I do not like your face, M. Ratchett" (2000c, p. 28). A further confirmation can be found in the rather extensive exposition given over to Ratchett's past and his current psychology. Poirot has several somewhat unnerving encounters with him before Ratchett is killed. Classic detective fiction is normally uninterested in the victims (consider the way the victims in "Murders in the Rue Morgue" are forgotten by the end of the story), but considerably more interested in the criminal's past and motivations.

Taken under this light, we can understand Poirot's final gathering of the passengers in an entirely different way: this is a scene of exculpation in which *no one* is guilty. The mathematical operation of the novel is the reduction of all the suspects to none, the number that you cannot divide by, that can leave no remainders. Poirot, like all classic detectives, represents a *higher* agency of the Law than the police, who are so frequently incompetent bumblers. Similarly, Poirot's two solutions are actually united in that *both* of them exculpate the passengers: one does so in the eyes of the readers, the other in the eyes of the police. The pleasure of *Murder on the Orient Express*, then, is the pleasure of the exoneration of the vigilante. We get to see the realization of our vigilante desires and be freed of guilt for having them, not because we are not guilty of having them, but because there is no guilt in having them. Murder doesn't repair the ruptured domestic space—execution does (there are twelve passengers to match twelve jurors), along with the inevitable stillness and quiescence that results from it.

If we return to the scene we cited a little earlier, we can now understand Christie's real structural playfulness:

> He awoke some hours later, awoke with a start. He knew what it was that had wakened him—a loud groan, almost a cry, somewhere close at hand. At the same moment the ting of a bell sounded sharply.
>
> Poirot sat up and switched on the light. He noticed that the train was at a standstill—presumably at a station. [2000c, p. 32]

This is the moment when the final arrest of the novel appears, and it does indeed take the metaphoric form of a cessation of travel along with the literal stillness of Mr. Ratchett: a death cry, the chime of a bell, the stopped train. Although it is structured like a traditional investigation, everything that follows Ratchett's "arrest" only serves to bring out the background story, to slowly exculpate not a few, but ultimately all of the passengers. This is the figure of *hysteron proteron*, the inversion of the normal order of events. In fact, the standard detective novel is already an example of *hysteron proteron* because we begin with the final effect in a chain of events—a murder—and then gradually trace our way back to find its cause. The reduction of *all* the suspects to *none* in *Murder on the Orient Express*, however, does not impinge on the unary logic of the detective's single, correct solution. The image on the cover of the novel, in its somewhat fancier incarnation as a trade paperback, is a silhouette of the snowbound train, enclosed on either side by braces. Just as in *The Murder of Roger Ackroyd*, where Christie hid the normally third-person culpability behind a first-person narrator, here she conceals it between the parentheses on the cover. From the execution of Ratchett on, the moment in which the detective novel's insistence on a unary logic of guilt affirms itself, the action in the novel is a long parenthesis, ending in, as the British say, a full stop.

4

ANXIETY: *Antonioni and Minghella*

COURAGE

In the Fall of 2001, I was teaching a course on the history of Italian cinema. About halfway through the semester I received an e-mail from an Italianist colleague who was teaching much the same sort of class at a different university. She had primarily written to discuss and compare the current choices in textbooks for such a class, but along the way, she complimented me on my *coraggio* (bravery or courage) for showing the students Bertolucci's *Il conformista* (*The Conformist*). No doubt she was referring to the movie's complex series of flashbacks, and the chorus of student complaints that would come from the disorientation they would produce. After screening the Bertolucci, I met with the students for discussion, and thought it might be a good way to begin by telling them about the e-mail. Had I been brave, I asked them, in showing them *Il conformista?* No, said one student wryly (referring, no doubt, to the film's slowness, its inconclusiveness, its "boredom"); what took courage was watching Antonioni's *L'avventura*.

Here one does indeed learn something about *Il conformista:* the difficulties that the film presented to audiences when it was first released in

1970 were entirely assimilable. Its multiple flashbacks and disordered temporality are frankly old hat to undergraduates whose formative cinematic experiences include films like Christopher Nolan's *Memento*. Nolan's film begins at the chronological endpoint of the story and then moves gradually backwards in short narrative pieces, very literally one step forward, two steps back, to arrive at a beginning that radically transforms our understanding of what we saw initially (i.e., the character we thought was a sympathetic vigilante trying to avenge his wife's murder is actually a serial killer bent on a revenge that can never be satisfied, a beautiful instance of the denaturing transformation of desire into drive). I mention this only to note that Bertolucci's "radical" narrative technique was already remarkably domesticated by the time *Memento* was released, having previously been used in such mainstream venues as *Seinfeld* in the 1990s and *thirtysomething* in the 1980s. One can fairly confidently predict that this technique will eventually have lost any aura of difficulty or surprise that it may have once had, if it hasn't lost it already. Bertolucci's film is beautiful, but not dangerous—it requires no courage.

On the other hand, one learns that showing or viewing *L'avventura* is still a risk, that whatever structures govern Antonioni's film have not lost their aura of difficulty. Something about Antonioni requires courage on the part of the viewer, if only in the form of heroic perseverance. I am of course interested in the way Antonioni's films are informed by detection and the question of how a detective story might induce anxiety and require courage—certainly classic detective fiction and its cinematic analogues do not. They seem entirely designed, on the contrary, to provide various kinds of relief and reassurance. Sam Rohdie writes that "detection . . . informs all of Antonioni's films" (1990, p. 45), also noting that "there is hardly a single film of Antonioni's which does not involve an investigation . . ." immediately adding that it is "an investigation which inevitably loses its way, becomes diverted, displaced; interest in it dissolves . . ." (p. 113). Before discussing *L'avventura* in depth, however, it is worth looking at the Antonioni film that most explicitly deploys detection's generic conventions while most explicitly frustrating them: *Blowup*.

In that film, the viewer is treated to a long series of seemingly senseless episodes in the life of Thomas, a young, arrogant photographer, played by David Hemmings. But just as boredom seems definitively to set in for the viewer, Thomas notices something strange about a photograph he has taken, another ideal example of the "Hitchcockian blot" that denatures the frame (ostensibly a couple frolicking in the park). He begins to enlarge the photograph, again and again, until he can see a figure holding a gun in the bushes, apparently the woman's lover, about to do away with her husband.[9] This is without question the film's most engaging sequence, one that promises a kind of salvation from the glacial slowness and apparent non-narrativity that preceded it, as if to say: I thought I was watching Antonioni, but thank goodness, it turns out I was watching Hitchcock! The sequence ends with a final enlargement revealing the "real blot" (also literally the blot of the real), an amorphous tangle of white blobs and strings stretched out on the grass, now so enlarged as to appear virtually like static, an image that is essentially illegible, that could be anything at all: the corpse of the victim, or at least so Thomas believes. Like the viewer, Thomas charges out, revitalized by his discovery, to photograph the corpse and pin down the "real of desire" he has glimpsed. But it is Antonioni and not Hitchcock after all: the corpse vanishes, the photographs and enlargements are stolen from his studio, and the film ends, quite famously, with Thomas watching mimes play an imaginary tennis game, and learning to "see" the imaginary ball. If, as I hope to have shown in the previous chapter, *Rear Window* demonstrates the generic insistence on "arrest"—the need to locate and then fix the position of all its protagonists, from Mrs. Thorwald's body to Jeff's two broken legs—*Blowup* provides an exemplary instance of mobility: a corpse that continues to move, desires that cannot be finalized, even a tennis ball that must be returned to the game, put back into play, into motion.

If we return, then, to the framework from the previous chapter, we can immediately perceive that such a formulation of investigation radically

---

9. As in other scenes of cinematic enlargement in a detective context—specifically, *Blade Runner*—the film seems to depend on an *impossible* blowup. In *Blade Runner*, Deckard uses a computer to "see around" a corner into a space that is not actually within the photograph, one of the two moments in the film when still photography "comes alive," a kind of animation, also in its etymological sense, that gives these robotic characters a soul for a moment, precipitates them into the symbolic, and its concomitant desires. In *Blowup*, Thomas hangs the final enlargement, the one that reveals the gun, next to the original image that produced it in which one can apparently see the face of the killer. Try as one might, one cannot, however, find the hand and the gun in the original, nothing that even *might* be the hand and gun—another impossible enlargement. The naïve question to ask here is, "Is it all in Thomas's head, a phantasmatic projection onto the film of his internal desire?" which misses Antonioni's fundamental procedure: to disregard the detection, its causes, its results, the issue of desire and its consequences, altogether. What matters exclusively is the short-circuiting of the viewer's narrative expectations, the film itself as the object (a) disrupting our enjoyment.

upsets the reassurance normally offered by detective fiction. Antonioni's films never offer a solution to the investigation, never conclude, and, as a result, offer no scapegoat for the various forms of desire that go awry at the beginning, setting off the need for the investigation in the first place. This would indicate that the stain of the "real of desire" spreads out to include not only the characters, but the spectators of the film—and is this not part of the most common reaction to Antonioni's films, namely boredom? Are they not intended to arouse bafflement, frustration, even hostility in the viewer? Is this not already an indication of what might require courage in a viewing of these films?

To answer these questions, and move toward an analysis of *L'avventura*, let us return to the notion of "avoiding the real of desire" from the first chapter. Recall that, in *Looking Awry*, Žižek claims that we watch mysteries precisely so we can see our unacceptable desires made real. In Hitchcock's *Rear Window*, for instance, this took the form of Lars Thorwald killing his nagging wife. If the murder represents the reader or the viewer's unacceptable desire made real, the avoidance that Žižek refers to becomes evident in a staple of Agatha Christie mysteries, namely, the scene of revelation. Here, the reader is threatened with possible guilt, as all the characters seated around the dining room table are shown to be potential suspects, but then is released from any real culpability as one of the characters is shown to bear the burden of all the guilt. It is as if the reader can say: "I didn't do it—the butler did!" Permit me to cite again the relevant passage from Žižek.

> Herein lies the fundamental untruth, the essential falsity of the detective's "solution": the detective plays upon the difference between the factual truth (the accuracy of facts) and the "inner" truth concerning our desire. On behalf of the accuracy of the facts, he compromises the "inner," libidinal truth and discharges us of all guilt for the realization of our desire, insofar as this realization is imputed to the culprit alone. . . . The immense pleasure brought about by the detective's solution results from this libidinal gain, from a kind of surplus profit obtained from it: our desire is realized and we do not even have to pay the price for it. [1992, p. 59]

The courage required of *L'avventura* may not be in watching a film in which nothing happens, but rather in watching a film in which something quite specific does not happen: the avoidance of the real of desire. This non-event marking the end of the film leaves a stain of guilt across the visual field, a stain which, Žižek argues, certainly includes the spectator. This stain makes it impossible to mark any position as eccentric, outside the film's libidinal economy. In other words, to return to the language of the previous chapter, there is no "arrest" here, neither the literal arrest of the guilty party nor the more metaphorical arrest of the spread of the "stain" of desire. This is Lacanian "anxiety," which is produced not when our desire is about to be disrupted or destroyed, but precisely when we approach its satisfaction too closely. To see how this plays out in possibly the most restless of Antonioni's cinematic texts, let us turn now to *L'avventura*.

DESIRE AND THE REAL

L'avventura tells the story of a dissatisfied and restless upper-class Roman girl, Anna (Lea Massari), who goes on a cruise with her indolent lover Sandro (Gabriele Ferzetti) and her working-class friend Claudia (Monica Vitti). They are also accompanied by a few of Sandro's friends and business associates. On a small island called Lisca Bianca between the mainland peninsula and the island of Sicily, Anna vanishes. They search the island, bring in the police as well as Anna's father, and Claudia and Sandro continue their search in Sicily. As they investigate the disappearance, Claudia and Sandro become progressively more involved (Sandro has already tried to kiss her when they were on Lisca Bianca), and it becomes increasingly clear that the movie is not in fact about Anna at all, but rather more concerned with Claudia. She and Sandro become lovers, and eventually arrive at the San Domenico Palace in Taormina. There, Sandro makes love with an American prostitute while Claudia sleeps. She discovers them in the morning, after she awakens, worried that Anna has returned. The final sequence of the film shows Sandro crying on a bench and Claudia approaching him from behind. After some hesitation, she reaches out to touch his shoulder and hair, and the film's final shot has the two of them— she standing, he seated—facing, respectively, Mount Etna in the distance and a stone wall.

As is typical for an Antonioni film, everything is structured in such a way as to short-circuit our normal narrative expectations. Characters, such as Anna's father, hint at back stories that are never elaborated, hurl themselves into relationships that appear unmotivated (Sandro shows no interest in Claudia before Anna disappears; thereafter, he appears to be in love with her), and no motivations are ever offered. Most notably, however, Antonioni's films activate generic expectations, particularly those of detection and investigation, that drift off, become lost or abandoned. *L'avventura*, on paper, is a mystery: the unexplained disappearance of a young woman. And yet, within the film as it is actually played out, this disappearance does not even function as a pretext for some other story. One begins to appreciate the degree to which the absence of a McGuffin (which, being a placeholder for an absence, is not precisely an absence itself) is equally the absence of a narrative.

The origin of the term "McGuffin" is a joke: two men were traveling on a train from London to Scotland; one is carrying an oddly shaped bundle. "What's that?" the second man asks. "It's a McGuffin," says the first. "What's a McGuffin?" queries the second. "A device used for capturing lions in Scotland," says the first. "But there are no lions in Scotland!" objects the second. "Well, this isn't a McGuffin either," concludes the first man. (The variant on this punchline is: "See, it works!") And so the McGuffin fulfills its function, generating exchanges and stories, only to vanish under erasure at the end. It was never there at all.

As Geoffrey Nowell-Smith observes, Anna's disappearance is "not so much an event as a non-event (Anna has not done anything, she is just not there) . . ." (1997, p. 130). What does emerge, however, with absolute clarity, is that *something* is no longer with us (Anna, narrative, naturalistic characters, motivations . . .).

At the same time, it also emerges that, as a kind of dreadful, uncanny compensation, something *is* there. The massive presence of architecture, outcroppings of rock, the volcano at the end all suggest something pervasive and menacing, as if the motive for doing away with Anna that would normally be at the heart of a classic detective narrative has been loosed on the world, or better still, is now in the world. In one of the strangest and most compelling sequences in Antonioni's works, Claudia and Sandro stop in a deserted fascist-era town, reminiscent in its architecture and absolute desolation of one of De Chirico's paintings. Antonioni's signature tracking shots are already at work in this film, and one can't help but notice that the camera prefers to track the characters until they are gone from the frame, and then linger on the empty space, to "see" their absence. (This is, of course, a prelude to the two most famous tracking shots in Antonioni, namely, the nonexistent tennis ball at the end of *Blowup*, and the extended, circular tracking shot at the end of *The Passenger*.) In this, there is already a kind of murderous drive within the camera movement itself, a diffuse desire in Antonioni's films to establish a point of view outside of the symbolic, an inhuman gaze on a thoroughly depopulated world. More obviously threatening, however, is the last shot of Claudia and Sandro's visit to the town: here the camera is positioned within an alleyway, and as they turn to head back to the car, we realize that the apparently neutral camera view is in fact a POV shot as it begins to move menacingly toward them, a remarkable instance in which the Hitchcockian blot lies within the camera itself, lodged within the eye, inside the point of view—more precisely, within the camera's *movement*. To return to the discourse from the previous chapter, the camera emerges as a threat, as a threatening other, precisely when it abandons its static position and demonstrates that it is mobile.

But whose point of view? Or better still, the point of view of what? For the viewer immediately realizes that this is not a *human* perspective at all, as whatever is looking begins to move menacingly forward toward the two searchers before slowing and stopping as it gives up. Even this shot, however, cannot be inserted into a coherent story, or even a style: it is never repeated. Is this insistent presence of something illegible and incomprehensible, menacing and inhuman, not the real? Moreover, is it not the "unhinged" real of desire, no longer attributed to the level of character (as character effectively dissolves in Antonioni, where a whole sequence of protagonists play at being others, indeed often die at being others), but now diffused throughout the film—in short, the stain of the real of desire now imbuing every frame?

It may very well be the case that Antonioni's nonanthropocentric camera would like to see all of the characters vanish, and that the frustrated viewer of his films might like to see not only the characters, but the entire film, disappear. But to return to the more specific desire in the film, we must ask, whose desire is it to see *Anna* vanish? Certainly no one accuses anyone of having killed Anna. However, it is precisely the accusation that makes exculpation from the real of desire possible; without it, we would expect the stain of the real to remain, along with the guilt of having the desire in the first place.

All three of our primary characters have reasons to want Anna's disappearance: Sandro, the playboy, though too lazy to have ever done away with Anna, is certainly not in the least put out by losing her. He makes a pass at Claudia before they have even left Lisca Bianca, during their search for Anna's body. He accompanies Claudia on her search for Anna in Sicily in order to continue his seduction. Similarly, his betrayal at the end of the film demonstrates that another substitution—Claudia's disappearance —wouldn't be unwelcome. The real of his desire is indicated explicitly in the film, when a character says: "Io non lo conosco, questo Sandro. L'avrà fatta fuori lui, per caso?" [I don't know him, this Sandro. Might he have done away with her?]. The question is greeted only with laughter, and a scene that was part of the screenplay but not included in the film alludes to Sandro's indolence and incapacity as sure indications that, although he may have desired her disappearance on the libidinal level, he wasn't responsible for it on the literal level (Amberg 1969, pp. 171–172).

Claudia is a more interesting case, as she is the only character to show any real regret about Anna's disappearance and any motivation to find her, and is the only possible target of conscious audience identification. Not surprisingly, she is also the character who should most devoutly wish for Anna to vanish, the only one who, in a scene late in the film at the hotel, acknowledges that she is afraid that Anna may come back. She is brought along on the yacht trip as a kind of "poor relation." There are a number of references to her lesser economic status in the film and she clearly enjoys Anna's lifestyle. That Claudia might fill Anna's place in the symbolic network is made clearer by a scene several minutes later: after Anna returns from her swim, the two change clothes in a cabin. Claudia tries on one of Anna's shirts (identity exchange is a favorite topos of Antonioni—there is also an exchange of shirts in *The Passenger*). Anna tries to give her the shirt, and Claudia reluctantly refuses the gift, but when Claudia leaves the cabin, Anna stuffs the shirt in the other woman's knapsack. Of course, Claudia's desire is made real; Anna disappears, and the next morning she finds herself with both her friend's shirt and boyfriend. This symbolic promotion is verified later in the film when Claudia tries on a brown wig (her blonde hair is her clearest remaining demarcation from the brunette Anna). By the end of the film, Claudia will admit that she doesn't want Anna to come back.

However, it may fundamentally be the real of *Anna's* desire, to vanish, perhaps to die, to take herself out of the narrative, such as it is, and out of her place in the symbolic. (Rohdie is careful to note that suicide and acts that resemble it are another constant in Antonioni's films [1990, pp. 106–107].) One should note, of course, the involuntary character of Claudia's "promotion" through the exchange of shirts; Anna puts her shirt in Claudia's bag once Claudia is out of sight. In other words, it is not what Claudia wants, not even what she asked for, to take Anna's place in the symbolic network. Although it may seem strange at first, this last point, that the film is stained with the real of *Anna's* desire, brings me to Antonioni's use of landscape and architecture. His landscapes, and not just in this film, are repeatedly marked by the alarming, often menacing, presence of the real, from the immense bleakness of the desert or the sea to the monumental Baroque architecture of Noto. Homay King writes in her discussion of *The Passenger* that "Antonioni is helping us to conceptualize a non-egoic look, a way of seeing that avoids anthropomorphism both in its movements and in what it attributes to its objects" (1999, p. 120). One of these non-anthropomorphic objects is the looming outcropping of rock near the island where Anna vanishes, a smaller island called Basiluzzo. From onboard the yacht, the passengers observe the crisscrossing vertical and horizontal striations marking the massive rock, giving it an otherworldly and inhuman look, the "non-anthropomorphic" look that earlier was lodged in the camera's movement. Claudia rejects the idea of swimming here, calling the outcropping *pauroso* (frightful). This appears to be one of those moments in the film that calls for the bravery I discussed earlier. As the passengers watch, Anna becomes increasingly restive, until she exclaims: "Uffa! Quante storie per un bagno!" [Ugh! So much talk over a little swim!], before leaping off the boat into the water.

The rock is marked as a frightful intrusion of the Real: this is already an impulse toward self-obliteration. To throw yourself at the Real is to do just what Anna does: take yourself out of the network of symbolic circulation. It is what Žižek calls the *act* in his discussion of Rossellini's *Stromboli* (1949) in *Enjoy Your Symptom!* "The act," Žižek writes, "is that of *symbolic suicide*: an act of 'losing all,' of withdrawing from symbolic reality, that enables us to begin anew from the 'zero point,' from that point of absolute freedom . . ." (2001, p. 43). (In fact, the gesture we see here was very nearly a literal suicide for the actress Lea Massari. Because of weather and finance-induced delays, these scenes were shot in November. After repeated takes in the frigid water, Massari suffered both renal failure and a heart attack, and had to be hospitalized. As a result, the figure we see from behind leaping into the water is not Massari at all, but the assistant director, Franco Indovina, a man.) In other words, the real of Anna's desire is not necessarily to die per se (although it may be), but to escape her place in the symbolic, to *manquer à sa place*, to risk everything for the possibility of something else. This is precisely the interpretation given in the scene I mentioned before that was not included in the film, where a minor character, Ettore, imagines Sandro asking Anna: "Why don't you do me a favor and get rid of yourself on your own?" This scene, either never filmed or removed in editing, is already "missing from its place," and the comment engenders "complete, dead silence" (Amberg 1969, pp. 171–172). Anna's "suicide" has truly taken her outside of the symbolic, a radically undomesticated journey.

In Rossellini's *Stromboli*, the heroine *acts*, in the Žižekian sense, at the end of the movie by ascending the slopes of the volcano Stromboli, a "terrifying 'encounter with the Real'" (Žižek 2001, p. 42), where she is enveloped in smoke and fumes. The film ends inconclusively (although the American release featured an inevitable happy ending and pedantic voice-over about redemption). *L'avventura* also ends (or refuses to end) with a volcano, and the possibility of some future *act*.

> What is namely an act? Why is suicide the act *par excellence*? The act differs from an active intervention (action) in that it radically transforms its bearer (agent) . . . after an act, I'm literally "not the same as before." . . . the act involves a kind of temporary eclipse, *aphanisis*, of the subject. Which is why every act worthy of this name is "mad" in the sense of radical *unaccountability*: by means of it, I put at stake everything, including myself, my symbolic identity; the act is therefore always a "crime," a "transgression," namely the limit of the symbolic community to which I belong. The act is defined by this irreducible *risk*. . . . [Žižek 2001, p. 44]

In the film's final shot, the screen is neatly divided in two. On the right side, there is a stone wall, extending well above the top of the frame. On the left, there is a vista, largely open sky, but also including the distant volcano Etna. Claudia and Sandro stare out at this vista, but in markedly different ways. The weak Sandro is seated on a bench, hunched over, placed on the right, and hence linked to this blind wall, a dead end. Claudia, on the other hand, is still standing, and to Sandro's left, the side of this open vista with the distant volcano. Might Claudia, too, be drawn toward a volcanic act? Rather than merely changing places within the symbolic, she could risk everything by effacing her self; perhaps more radical than, or at least equivalent to, a journey without end would be the experience of no place at all. We will never know, of course, because the temporality of the act is always, necessarily, *before*, before the annihilated subject assumes a new place within the symbolic network. Antonioni leaves us with this enigmatic glimpse of the Real, a volcano and a blank, sheer wall, as well as the anxiety-inducing "real of our desire," and the rare nondiegetic music that swells without resolution, just like his film.

THE NON-HITCHCOCKIAN BIRDS

If Antonioni's films require then a certain "courage" in order to confront the free-floating anxiety of unarrested desire at work, the same could hardly be said for a director who is undeniably popular: Anthony Minghella. I have shown his 1999 *The Talented Mr. Ripley* to students in courses on detective fiction on several occasions, and they find the film at times unnerving but largely appealing, and it is the sort of film that almost invariably makes for a good discussion. They have just one complaint: the film is too long. The last twenty minutes seem to be an unnecessary repetition of previous scenes (more killing, more fleeing, more of Tom Ripley's anguish). In other words, the viewer's resistance seems to be located not at the level of content (what is, after all, one more heart-wrenching murder of a loved one on board a boat?), but at the level of structure (why yet *another* heart-wrenching murder of a loved one on board a boat?) We already got the point. Or did we? This chapter focuses precisely on the issue of spectatorial resistance, those cinematic moments that appear to induce a kind of anxiety requiring courage (and so I maintain my ironically self-congratulatory conceit, although one might just as easily talk about boredom and perseverance, or even bloody-mindedness, in both senses of the term), so we would do well to examine more closely what precisely it is in this film and its ends that challenges the viewer's desire, paying particular attention to the level of structure rather than content.

The Talented Mr. Ripley is a remarkable, if not particularly faithful, adaptation of Patricia Highsmith's novel of the same name. The film tells the story of the poor Tom Ripley (Matt Damon), dressed in a borrowed Princeton jacket, who meets the wealthy shipping magnate Herbert Greenleaf. Mr. Greenleaf mistakenly assumes Tom went to school with his son, Dickie (Jude Law), and sends him off to Italy to bring his errant son back to America—an all-expenses paid vacation, and a chance for this "real nobody" to become a "somebody." Tom's natural talent is impersonation (forgeries, voices, mannerisms), part of his yearning to be someone, anyone other than himself. He clearly loves Dickie (Tom's latent homosexuality is strongly suggested in Highsmith's novel, and explicit—and manifest—in the film) and his money, his lifestyle. Tom obsessively identifies with Dickie, copies his every move, an alarming appropriation of Dickie's identity that culminates in Tom killing Dickie when Dickie explicitly rejects him. The second half of the film details Tom's ultimately successful quest to become Dickie Greenleaf, to assume his place in life, necessitating at least two other murders, the last of which is Tom's lover, Peter Smith-Kingsley.

Tom Ripley picks up Italian with remarkable ease, obviously another one of his talents, all of which revolve around an ability to assume and exchange a variety of masks or alternate personas. But he is not immune to making occasional errors. Immediately after arriving in Mongibello, he watches Dickie and Marge (Gwyneth Paltrow), Dickie's girlfriend, with binoculars from his hotel room as they play in the water. At the same time, he practices his Italian, describing what he sees and what the viewer sees. These are point-of-view shots through the binoculars alternating with counter-shots that look back at Tom, *à la Rear Window*, the gold standard for cinematic depictions of voyeurism. Ripley's Italian is notable here for a novice. He very carefully pronounces the double consonants, his correct use of possessives is unusual for a beginner (Italian, unlike Spanish or French, requires the definite article to make a possessive), and the succession of phrases is highly methodical, so it is quite striking when he makes a mistake, and his facial expressions telegraph that mistake to the English-only viewer:

> [Looking through binoculars] *La fidanzata ha una faccia.*
> The fiancée has a face.
> *La fidanzata è Marge* [looking at Marge and Dickie diving off the boat].
> *Questo è la faccia di Dickie* [looking at Dickie].
> *Questo è la mia faccia* [swings the binoculars over to look at Dickie's sailboat, named "Bird"]. Bird.
> This is *my* face [close-up of Dickie].
> [Looks down at the book, then ruefully and emphatically corrects himself] *Questa è la mia faccia.*

There is nothing wrong in the content of what Tom says in Italian, even if it is a little strange: "The fiancée has a face / The fiancée is Marge / This is the face of Dickie / This is my face." He merely makes a grammatical error of the kind that is so common for native speakers of English learning a romance language. He should be saying "*Questa è la mia faccia*," but twice says instead "*Questo è la mia faccia.*" It is the difference of just one letter, an *-o* instead of an *-a* at the end of *quest-*, but it is a letter that generates grammatical significance.

The scene is clearly intended to unnerve, as it sutures the viewer into Tom's position. We see through his eyes, engage inevitably in the same voyeuristic act that he engages in, and we are aware that something is not right from the very first line of dialogue: "*La fidanzata ha una faccia*, the fiancée has a face." This curious phrase—surely not a sample phrase in any language textbook or dictionary—can only acquire meaning in contrast to Tom's "facelessness." More unnerving still is Tom's ready assumption of the face of the other, his appropriation of Dickie's face that is a prelude to his much more literal assumption of Dickie's identity. Again, what renders these activities so unnerving is that the "face of the other" that Tom assumes here, and that the viewer is constrained to see as the face of the other, is precisely the face of normalcy, a face that is both heterosexual and social, in direct contrast to Tom's solitary and masturbatory voyeurism. The final line, then, functions as a kind of throwaway comic relief that "re-marks" Tom as normal and human: like everyone, he, too, makes mistakes while learning a foreign language. As strange as his behavior may seem, he is fallible, prone to error, and his embarrassment at his mistake, his recognition of the limitations of linguistic mimicry, endear him to the viewer. It is not too early to point out that this is central to Minghella's overall project in the film, eliciting the audience's sympathy for a figure that is ultimately inhuman and monstrous, the faceless yet wrenchingly pathetic figure of Tom Ripley.

One should, however, beware of such throwaway lines, and always remain attentive to the way jokes work to simultaneously conceal and reveal the truth. In essence, I am recalling the Lacanian imperative to pay attention to the most literal aspects of the text. In attempting to appropriate Dickie's face, to insert himself into a space that is both heterosexual and social, Tom bungles the *gender* of the word: what he believed was masculine ("my face" or "la mia faccia") is in fact feminine, and hence he must correct the pronoun to match ("que*sta* è la mia faccia"). As a kind of first glance at the error, this proves quite satisfying; after all, Tom is unable to sustain a heteronormative masculine identity, thus leading to the series of criticisms of the film as yet another instance of Hollywood perpetuating the stereotyped figure of the frustrated homosexual as serial killer. Yet this reading ultimately proves to be insufficiently literal, *insufficiently superficial*, for it ignores something much more curious about Tom's appropriation.

When Tom asserts that "questo è la mia faccia" (this is my face), he is *not* looking, as we might expect, at Dickie at all—he is looking at Dickie's sailboat, specifically the name of the boat. In fact, when Ripley asserts that he has Dickie's face while looking at him, he does so in English, and hence

without an error of gender. It will take some time to elaborate the significance of this visual error, this apparent misalignment of dialogue and shot/
counter-shot, but we have to begin by looking at a scene that occurs just a
little later. Tom's initial attempt to befriend Dickie has fizzled out, but he
goes to say goodbye to him and Marge armed with a bag of jazz records
that he drops at an opportune moment. Dickie can't help his enthusiasm
for jazz, and as Tom had hoped, this turns into an occasion for male bond-
ing, explicitly marked as such, as Dickie makes fun of Marge's conception
of jazz as insipid, bourgeois, conventional, white:

> DICKIE: Marge says she likes jazz, but she says Glenn Miller's jazz.
> MARGE: I never said that!
> TOM: Bird. *That's* jazz.
> DICKIE: Bird? [Growing excited] Ask me the name of my sailboat.
> TOM: I don't know—what's the name of your sailboat?
> DICKIE: Look. Look. *Bird!*
> MARGE: Which is ridiculous. Boats are female. Everyone knows you
> can't call a boat after a man!

"Bird" is the nickname for the male jazz musician Charlie Parker, and
boats are traditionally named after women, or at least gendered as female.
It turns out, then, that Dickie has also made an error of gender, and it is no
surprise that whereas Tom's slip reveals a concealed feminine (he thought
his *faccia* was masculine, but really it's feminine), Dickie's slip is public
evidence of a willingness to disregard the feminine.[10] That is, the difference between these two lapses is not in the slip itself (both attempt to mark
something as male that is "properly" feminine), but in their response to
"grammatical authority." Tom responds with embarrassment and self-
correction, looking in the dictionary, marking himself as subject to linguistic discipline. Dickie ignores Marge's admonishment, indeed seems

---

10. One could just as easily, and correctly, I believe, describe Dickie's disregard for
the custom of naming boats after women as evidence of a kind of blind spot, an inability
to perceive his own femininity, that is, his own castration. However, normative masculinity is characterized precisely by the unwillingness to perceive one's own symbolic castration. In this respect as well, Tom's position is essentially feminine. He is brought up short
by the authority of the book that informs him that his *faccia* is feminine; in other words,
he recognizes his own linguistic and hence symbolic castration. The properly "male" response would be to ignore the dictionary and go on saying the incorrect "questo."

unaware that she has spoken, reentering the conversation only when Tom asserts that the rule wouldn't apply because Charlie Parker "isn't a man, he's a god."

Here my analysis becomes somewhat convoluted, but necessarily so, as these two "errors" revolving around birds turn out to be a nexus of cultural and linguistic references that will require multiple translations. "Bird" has another meaning besides Charlie Parker, as in "giving someone the bird." In this context, "bird" functions as a potential concealed reference to the phallus.[11] Now that we understand this scene of gender confusion as related to Tom's earlier mistake, we might also consider the inter-linguistic dimension operative in that earlier scene: "bird" in Italian is *uccello*, which turns out to be the most common metaphorical term for the penis in that language. Or, to translate it back into English more properly, *dick*—Dickie. In other words, Tom's mistake in looking at the boat while saying "questo è la mia faccia," isn't precisely a mistake: he is indeed looking at "Dick" when he sees the boat. His mistake here is not looking up the English word he says out loud—"bird"—in the dictionary, a translation that would allow him to begin to understand how Dickie is already multiply determined as his impossible object of desire. In both senses Tom wants Dick, or more precisely, he "misses" Dick, fails to get Dickie, and, by missing the translation game at work around him (Bird = *uccello* = dick) locates himself in the position of nonmastery.

DICKS, DUPES, AND "DESUBJECTIFICATION"

The question of the "real of desire" as formulated by Žižek with respect to classic detective fiction (the "Sherlock Holmes way of avoiding the real of desire") doesn't directly involve the question of gender. Classic detective fiction rigorously excludes the detective from the circuit of desire, transforming the hero into a largely asocial and asexual eccentric for whom the question of gender or sexual orientation is largely irrelevant. The detective's sidekick, however, functions as a kind of supplement to this icon of pure

---

11. "Bird" also functions, of course, as a metaphor for "girl" in British English, and Minghella is, after all, British. I would point here to the previous note: Dickie's ignorance of the sexual ambiguities inherent in his nomenclature is evidence not of his own ambiguous sexuality, but precisely of his normative masculinity.

thought; the sidekick is all libido (Watson and Hastings never met a shapely ankle they didn't admire). In any event, gender comes up centrally in any analysis of *noir*, where the detective is placed squarely within the circuit of desire (and hence the consistent lack of the sidekick in the hard-boiled novel). More to the point, not only is *film noir* inevitably gendered through its opposition of the male protagonist, who is often, but not always, the detective, to the *femme fatale*, but this opposition directly implicates both "the real of desire" and the question of courage, as the *femme fatale* embodies a kind of radical danger to her male counterpart. Žižek writes:

> Why is this ambiguity, this deceitfulness and corruption of the universe embodied in a woman whose promise of surplus enjoyment conceals mortal danger? What is the precise dimension of this danger? Our answer is that, contrary to appearance, the femme fatale embodies a radical *ethical* attitude, that of "not ceding one's desire," of persisting in it to the very end when its true nature as the death drive is revealed. [1992, p. 63]

Where classic detective fiction avoids the truth of desire by introjecting an imaginary scapegoat, whose gender is irrelevant, who takes the blame off the reader or viewer, the hard-boiled text or *noir* film revolves around the male detective's avoidance of the tempting but ultimately destructive *femme fatale*. However, the protagonist's relationship to the *femme fatale* can follow two different models: the dick and the dupe. The dick, is of course, the private dick, a "positive" and masculine model such as Sam Spade in *The Maltese Falcon*. Tempted by the abyssal dimension of the *femme fatale*, he is capable of simultaneously acknowledging his desire for her and turning away from it at the same time—in Spade's words, "I won't because all of me wants to" (Hammett 1992a, p. 215). He recognizes that the *femme fatale* represents a literal death, but also a kind of willing acceptance of abjection, principally through symbolic and potentially literal castration. Again, Spade notes to Brigid O'Shaughnessy that "I couldn't be sure you wouldn't put a hole in me some day." Spade "gives up on his desire," then, but explicitly marks that renunciation as such: "I won't because all of me wants to." It is perhaps impossible not to see this as an "advance" with respect to classic detective fiction, whose principal aim, in Žižek's view, is to conceal the reader or viewer's desire from him- or herself. The dick acknowledges the "real of his desire," explicitly avows it, and turns away from it all the same.

The dupe (Joe Gillis in *Sunset Boulevard* or Al Roberts in *Detour*) is the negative dimension of the protagonist, who, perversely, occupies a much more normatively masculine niche. (One cannot help but notice the way Sam Spade in *The Maltese Falcon* rids himself, at every opportunity and as rapidly as possible, of all of the most potent phallic symbols: money, guns, the Falcon itself.) The dupe is presented as having been trapped by the *femme fatale*, and hence is able to disavow or ignore his desire. Joe Gillis is perhaps the ideal example of this type, as he finds himself unable to extract himself from Norma Desmond's mansion, despite the fact that all the locks in the house have been removed for years, as if saying "I know very well that I could leave at any time, but all the same I am fated to remain here." Because the dick acknowledges his desire and recognizes his own self-destructive impulses, he survives his encounter with the *femme fatale*. The dupe, however, is doomed. One can perceive that, from a Lacanian perspective, there is a fundamental failure in both the dick and the dupe to "not give up on desire": the first acknowledges his desire but turns away from it; the second does not acknowledge his desire and so persists in it.

Here we begin to realize the essential perversity of *The Talented Mr. Ripley*: Tom Ripley functions as a kind of *homme fatal* within the economy of the film. He represents the abyssal dimension of identity, the fear that when all the masks come off, what will be revealed is nothing at all, a sort of tear or open wound in the tissue of the symbolic, a rip that turns out to be Ripley, as it were. Ripley is himself terrified of this possibility and strains against it for almost the entire film, neatly made into a kind of aphorism in one of the film's tag lines: "I'd rather be a fake somebody than a real nobody." Ironically, Dickie plays the role not of the dick, but of the dupe: he remains steadfastly unaware of the degree to which Tom represents a kind of suicidal attraction for him, that his attempt to break free of Tom's pull on him, which masquerades throughout the first part of the film as Dickie's pull on Tom, will end exactly the same way that Joe Gillis's attempt to leave Norma Desmond does. Dickie's blindness is so thoroughgoing that one cannot understand him as "avoiding the real of desire" so much as "missing entirely the real of desire." Minghella's film takes the next step, then, in the evolution of *noir*: the possibility that the threat of "suicidal desire" (abjection, castration, weakness—in short, non-normative masculinity) might be incarnated in anyone, not only in the extravagantly eccentric and obviously loony cinematic *femmes fatales* (Carmen Sternwood in *The Big Sleep*, Vera in *Detour*, Norma Desmond in *Sunset Boulevard*, and so on). But of course, it is not Dickie's desire that concerns this film.

Indeed, the psychic threat posed by Tom Ripley is much more significant. His true significance lies in the fact that the viewer is placed in an entirely new relationship to this *homme fatal*: he is "our character," the character who solicits our pity and empathy, our identification. This is true not only because the movie tells, after all, Tom's story, and hence elicits our apprehension, our suspense and fear when the police close in on him, but also because it constantly makes use of subjective camera to make sure that the viewer sees through Tom's eyes. Hence spectators are invited (compelled) to speculate on their own abyssal dimension.

This invitation (or demand, or compulsion) appears most clearly in the final sequences of the film in which Tom realizes that he is in the same place again, in the position of having to kill his beloved Peter just as he killed Dickie Greenleaf. The point here is that the film has constantly presented Tom with just two possibilities: being a "fake somebody" and being a "real nobody." Peter, of course, is the third possibility, the dream of a perfect union, the ideal partner with whom the subject could be a "real somebody." "You're not a nobody," he reassures Tom, "that's the last thing you are"—but we may read these words literally, as a "nobody" is precisely the last thing that Tom will be in the film. Peter is not judgmental, not tortured, the person with whom Tom can "be himself." As always, this ideal sexual harmony, the sexual relationship that Lacan said was impossible, is disrupted here seemingly by chance—Meredith Logue, who has only known Tom in his disguise as Dickie, is on board the same ship. Tom cannot "be himself," but must continue to play the role of Dickie, the "fake somebody." But here is the crucial revelation of the film: to play the role of someone, to assume the alienating armor of identity, is the same as to be a real nobody, to be no one in the real. And so Tom has Peter tell him "good things about Tom Ripley," be precisely that ego support that will let him be himself, and as Peter recites the list of Tom's good qualities (the qualities that scroll by, too rapidly to read, in the film's opening credits, "beautiful," "talented," and so on), Tom strangles him.

One cannot help but notice that these murders, the killing of Dickie and Peter, are quite different in character from Tom's vengeful murder of the odious Freddie Miles (Philip Seymour Hoffman). The killing of Freddie is quintessentially a murder of desire, rather than drive, a true burst of rage that gives everyone, the viewer as much as Tom, real satisfaction. The murders that frame the film, on the other hand, seem compulsory, demonic, in part because they are inevitably acts of self-castration for Tom as well. Tom literally cuts himself off from his beloved Dickie, his beloved Peter. The gradual process that takes place during the course of the movie is something like an extended version of what Žižek describes as occurring at the end of *The Maltese Falcon*, where Brigid O'Shaughnessy tries on and abandons a whole series of "inconsistent hysterical masks" (1992, p. 65) only to eventually reveal the nothing, the "real nobody" that stands behind the masks. This moment is the moment in *noir* that permits the detective to turn away from the *femme fatale*: her revelation as nothing, "an entity without substance," a tear in the tissue of the symbolic; it turns the detective to disgust, permitting him to gain "a kind of distance toward her" so that he can finally reject her. The true threat in the *femme fatale* lies in the possibility of the detective's identification with her stance (Žižek 1992, p. 66), an entirely willing acceptance of one's subjectivity as a passive object. This is arguably already what happens at the end of *Sunset Boulevard*, where Joe Gillis reveals his own "fan of hysterical inconsistent masks" before engaging in a kind of suicidal gesture.

One could note that the two types of *noir*, which respectively feature the strong male who rejects the *femme fatale*, and the weak male who is horrified but does nothing to escape from this threat, embody the two distinct reactions to the sight of the castrated female that Freud describes in "Some Psychological Consequences of the Anatomical Distinction Between the Sexes" (1925b). The first reaction, the "heterosexual" reaction, is disgust and contempt, which is precisely the affect that Sam Spade arrives at; the second reaction, the "homosexual" response, is horror and disavowal, as in Joe Gillis's relationship to Norma Desmond in *Sunset Boulevard*—I know very well that I can flee this horrifying older woman at any time (again, the "servant" Max, has, with pointed irony, had all the locks removed), but all the same I am doomed, trapped. In this respect, however, *The Talented Mr. Ripley* seems to be genuinely "queer"—that is, its position is more perverse and destabilizing than "mere" homosexuality, as it does not situate the spectator in either of those two positions. Far more perversely, it seems to invite the spectator, in the language of New Age psychology, to discover his "inner *femme fatale*," the abyssal dimension in which he, too, is a "real nobody." This is, by the way, why the reviews that condemned the movie for repeating the stereotype of the frustrated homosexual who turns to murder were off the mark—Ripley attains the far more "queer" position at the end of the film of *having no orientation at all*, a creature of drive with no direction, and hence no orientation—"I'm lost," he says at the end.

One might just as easily say, continuing to parody the discourse of pop psychology, that the film also offers a different, equally heartwarming lesson at the end: Tom discovers his inhumanity. The pathos of this film is watching precisely the "desubjectification" of the protagonist, his earnest yearning to belong to a social and symbolic network which, although admittedly founded on a metonymic slippage (a fake somebody), still seems preferable to its alternative, a real nobody. However, in order to fully grasp how this happens, how Tom becomes an "abject" rather than a subject, we will need to reflect for a moment on desire and drive.

Žižek writes that desire "implies a dialectical mediation: we demand something, but what we are really aiming at . . . is something else" (1992, p. 21). In other words, desire (and here it is distinguished from need) is always about something beyond the object of its desire, the object of its satisfaction. This is why desire can never be fully sated, because its *goal* is something other than its *aim* (see Žižek 1992, p. 5). It aims at one thing, but as a kind of trope for something else. Money is, of course, the quintessence of the slippage between goal and aim, as well as the perfect embodiment of the social and economic character of desire. Let us say that I desire to be wealthy—my *aim* is to be rich. But surely that is not my *goal* in wanting money, as made obvious by the fact that no one would wish to be incredibly wealthy but trapped with no means of communication on a barren, desolate, deserted isle barely capable of sustaining life. No, I want money in order to buy things, which in turn I do not desire for themselves, but rather for the recognition they will bring me from others, and so on. One can already see in this the Lacanian formula of metonymic slippage of the signifier, and the fundamentally *symbolic* character of desire/demand: the goal is always "somewhere else," beyond the aim. In this respect, we could say that desire is both linguistic and social (that is, it belongs to, reciprocally constitutes, the symbolic register), ostensibly "normal." Drive, on the other hand, manifests itself in the abandonment of the goal, or perhaps it is better to say that the goal loops around and becomes the aim itself, hence the "idiotic," circular, and mechanical quality of drive: I want to be rich in order to be rich in order to be rich. Drive is thus autistic, pathological, ostensibly abnormal. The persistence of drive lasts "to the end," wherever that may be. If desire models the metonymic slipping of the symbolic, drive, on the other hand, is part of or associated with the real, because, like the real, *it is always in the same place.*

Žižek's quintessential cinematic example of drive is the Terminator, at least insofar as it was represented in the first movie: relentless, implacable, literally mechanical. The Terminator does not want to kill Sarah Connor in order to accomplish something (although the machines that sent it into the past may have had a larger *goal* in mind): it wants to kill her in order to kill her. This is precisely what makes it such a monstrous adversary and what removes it entirely from the realm of the human: hence the obligatory scene of unmasking that occurs near the end of the film, where the Terminator's human face is stripped away to reveal a hollow metallic cranium, a death's head. (Other great science fiction nemeses obviously share this implacable and relentless character of embodied drive, from the aliens of *Alien* to the Borg of *Star Trek*.) Of course, the Terminator returns in the second film, *Terminator 2: Judgment Day*. The nemesis of incarnated drive is even more alarming, now made of liquid metal, able to assume any form, offering up a terrifying mimicry of life. Once again, the film comes perilously close to suggesting that every subject contains an inner, abyssal dimension of the real, but it is fundamentally amorphous, faceless, precisely in its capacity to assume any face, any mask. The original Terminator (played by Arnold Schwarzenegger, of course) also returns in this film, in quite a different guise. The second film details the story of the Terminator's "resubjectification," as Žižek says à propos of a different science-fiction film (*Robocop*), the gradual process of reinserting this inhuman machine into the symbolic, and hence into desire. (Without going into detail, it is enough to note that this resubjectification is a staple of science fiction's robotic and alien heroes. The most successful characters of *all* of the *Star Trek* franchises, for instance, have all been such "resubjectified" aliens and androids, and what makes *Blade Runner* so effective is the fact that its human characters are so robotic, asocial, and without empathy, whereas the "replicants" are tragically full subjects).[12]

If these latter films recount the triumphant story of the reinsertion of subjects into desire—which is, fundamentally, a fable or allegory of therapy in which the sociopath cut off from the normal social field is renormalized, rendered nonpathological—*The Talented Mr. Ripley* offers up yet another kind of perversity. Its story is fundamentally a tale of *desubjectification*, the extraction of the subject from the field of the symbolic, its transformation into the unspeakable real. For Tom Ripley is indeed, like the real, like drive, "always in the same place" in this film, quite literally, as the opening and closing shots of the film demonstrate. Both are the same scene, a scene we do not recognize at the beginning of the movie, namely Tom Ripley in his

---

12. The extended DVD version of *Terminator 2: Judgment Day* includes an additional scene in which Sarah and John Connor reset the "friendly" terminator's chip from the "not learning" to "learning" position, a moment that marks its acquisition of memory, or more precisely, the use of memory as an anticipation of the future, an acquisition that also marks it as a split subject, and hence part of the symbolic, subject to desire.

cabin, alone, just having killed Peter Smith-Kingsley. If we set these two shots alongside the climactic midpoint of the film, the murder of Dickie Greenleaf, it becomes clear that Tom has always just killed someone on a boat, is always excluded from the social network of the symbolic.

It is this insistence on the importance of boats that might bring us back to where we began: Tom's curious identification of his face with Dickie's boat, "Bird." Here we find that the complex series of references that the shot allows the viewer to elaborate (Charlie Parker, the phallus, *uccello* as dick, Dickie, and so on) is a reading that is *still insufficiently literal*, insufficiently superficial. For what renders the shot strange is that Tom's pronouncement "Questo è la mia faccia" [This is my face] is matched not with a shot of a human face, or even, properly speaking, with an animal reference ("Bird"), but with a *thing*. Ultimately, his identification in this scene speaks to the question of drive rather than desire, Tom's eventual inhuman loss of all faces. Dickie is Tom's impossible object of desire not because Dickie is straight, but precisely because desire is itself structurally outside of Tom's purview. The image of Tom that opens the film is that of a face broken into pieces, crossed by black fracture lines, like a piece of broken glass, a clear reference to a whole series of shots that reflect, as it were, Tom's impossible relationship to the specular symbolic.

In one instance, Tom drives through the streets of Rome on a *motorino*, only to see the dead Dickie Greenleaf's reflection in a mirror instead of his own. He crashes in his shock at this specular misalignment, and his fall naturally breaks another mirror, in what is the clear basis for the fracturing black lines in the opening credit sequence. In another shot, Tom is forced to give up the expensive apartment he has held in Dickie's name, forced to kill off Dickie Greenleaf, to forge Dickie's suicide in order to conceal Dickie's murder. As he closes the lid to the grand piano he has bought for himself, his amorphous reflection in the lid splits in two, a marked demonstration of the way the psychotic real cannot be assimilated into the specular symbolic, its quintessential illegibility—in short, Tom's impossible relationship to his own desires. Finally, there is the shot that ends the film, a reflection of the opening shot: Tom realizes that he is always in the same place, quite literally a real nobody, the subject annihilated by its contact with the real, its own inner abyssal dimension. This fully desubjectified Tom stares blankly forward, oblivious to his own reflection in the mirrored doors of a cabinet that swing with the rocking of the boat, gradually closing, and, more importantly, gradually closing the viewer within this very queer closet, this abyss that the film's spectators must gradually learn to inhabit, if they have the courage. (The uncanny effect of this "always being in the same place" is intensified for viewers of *The Bourne Identity*, where Matt Damon reappears, still on an Italian boat, with clear traces of having been recently involved in a deadly altercation; he suffers from amnesia, and sits in front of the mirror in the boat, speaking to himself in a variety of languages with the same chameleonic and desubjectified linguistic mastery Tom Ripley showed in a different film: "je ne sais pas qui je suis" [I do not know who I am].)

POINTLESS EXCESS

Let me now return to the question that we started with: Why is this film twenty minutes too long? The film comes to a climax and resolution, after all, when Tom successfully convinces Dickie's father and the private investigator he has hired of his innocence, thus confounding Marge, who now suspects and even openly accuses Tom of killing Dickie, and reducing her to a kind of Cassandra who speaks the truth but is ignored by everybody. This is, after all, the point in the film in which the investigation concluded: everyone, including the Italian police who have hounded Tom, particularly with their suspicions of his homosexuality, accepts that Dickie committed suicide and that Tom is innocent. (It is at this point in the novel that Tom attempts his last, most audacious forgery—Dickie's will, leaving everything to him, Tom; naturally, the forgery is accepted.) In the film, Tom takes another sea voyage with his new lover, Peter Smith-Kingsley, but on board the ship he is seen by the most "superfluous" character of the film, one who hardly exists in the novel: Meredith Logue.

The point of Meredith is that she alone, of all the movie's principals, knows and accepts—indeed, loves—Tom as Dickie, as what she believes is a "real somebody." For a brief moment after Meredith greets Tom enthusiastically, the solution seems clear. There she stands, next to the railing, the aft deck of the ship deserted. What could be easier than to push her over? And Tom/Dickie asks her if she is traveling alone. But she is not: her relatives suddenly appear on an upper deck overlooking them, disapproving, severe, an instant manifestation of the prohibition of the social field that creates Tom's "enjoyment," the thing that really persecutes and pursues him in this film. And so there is only one way Tom can reconcile the two opposing world views, only one person on the ship who knows him as Tom Ripley, namely his own lover.

It is precisely the pointlessness of the last twenty minutes that is the point, a demonstration of the excessive experience of drive. It is as if the film is saying to the viewer "I know that you got the point (Ripley is trapped in his 'closet,' a 'real nobody'), but you have not understood the nature of drive, to repeat and repeat and reappear again, to be always in the same place, *precisely to be a pointless excess*." And after all, won't Tom have to kill Meredith anyway—this most pointless, superfluous, or *excessive* of characters—and all her relatives after her? I mean "have to" not in the conventional sense of some inner compulsion to kill, but as an external, precisely *structural* necessity, a compulsion that acts from the outside, pushing the film toward more of the same. The twenty minutes too much at the end of the film is precisely the excess of drive. Could not one say that, if the motto of desire is "never enough," the corresponding motto of drive is "always too much"?

This "pointless excess" of the too-long ending may have another effect, however, one that pertains to the question that opened this chapter. It also works to drive an identificatory wedge between the viewer and Tom. At the point of the "first ending," the logical endpoint where Tom convinces Dickie's father of his innocence, the libidinal structure of the film is quite different, and in fact resembles the "avoidance of the real of desire" of classic detective fiction. Tom has, after all, gotten away with murder, a source of perverse anti-authoritarian enjoyment for the viewer. The viewer, however, *must* identify with Tom up to this point in the film. The narrative is focalized through him; in the best Hollywood tradition, he is a working-class common man, sharply contrasted to the indolent aristocrats who surround him, and the basic plot structure—pursuit—always encourages identification with the one pursued. The true sign of this identification is that Tom, for this brief moment, stands on the side of sanity; it is Marge who appears mad with her paranoid accusations against Tom. Her madness is, of course, conditioned by an "other scene," the killings of Dickie and Freddie, that Tom effectively owns, that no one else has any conscious access to. Marge here appears as insane precisely for this reason; her speech is conditioned by an other scene that she has no access to. In any event, this identification means that the viewer would suffer from anxiety in watching Tom get away with it, and this is, in fact, the source of the film's suspense: we approach ever more perilously close to an ending in which our desire would be satisfied. The reason that films are unsatisfying when the killer gets away with it is not that our desire for justice has been thwarted, but that our actual desire has been satisfied. So, the final twenty minutes of *The Talented Mr. Ripley* work to alleviate that anxiety. As Tom becomes more and more inhuman, running on auto-pilot, our identification diminishes until it turns out that *our* desire was not satisfied, and in fact, as the film insists on repetition and drive, it turns out that the desire was the desire of *no one at all*, Tom Ripley as the "real nobody." This is why viewers of the film do not experience it as radical, threatening, anxiety-inducing.

What, then, have we learned from *L'avventura* and *The Talented Mr. Ripley?* Both films seem to require a certain kind of courage on the part of the spectator, a certain perseverance in the face of a desire that is not pinned down to the East River of *Rear Window* or the snowbound train of *Murder on the Orient Express*. Both Anna and Tom function as libidinal agents still at large, no longer subject to the "logic of arrest" that typifies more canonical instances of detective fiction, especially in its most rigorous, if not actually rigid, form in classic detective fiction. But it is not too early to notice that this other kind of detective fiction, as seen in the examples in this chapter, presents at least two faces: if we can still reasonably speak of desire and its operations in *L'avventura*, we inevitably turn to a consideration of drive in *The Talented Mr. Ripley*. Drive in that last example works like a kind of desire gone awry, entirely negative, inhuman, desubjectifying, relentless, menacing, and dismissible as alien and other, perversely the reason that film does not provoke the same anxious, restless boredom that characterizes Antonioni's films.

Moreover, the overall structure that I've outlined in these last two chapters—the real of desire and the logic of arrest—duplicates the "standard" psychoanalytic reading of detective fiction, in which it is seen as a way for us to mask our desires from ourselves, to see and yet not see at the same time. And this is no doubt the case. However, it also has a different, perhaps less desirable effect: popular forms of detective fiction (Hitchcock or Christie) become "libidinally inferior" whereas high art forms that make use of the genre (Antonioni, for instance, or, to a lesser extent, Minghella) begin to function as a kind of therapy for more popular forms, demanding a confrontation with the desire that was avoided in the popular forms. In the next chapter, I will examine this issue in more detail, asking how drive in its more positive, benevolent form—that is, *enjoyment*—is also at work in detective fiction, and how it may complicate the traditional psychoanalytic scenario of detective fiction.

5

REPETITION:
Monk | *Conan Doyle* | *Hitchcock*

PETE AND REPEAT

When my son was two years old, he generally preferred to watch Russian cartoons, but he did enjoy two English-language television programs. The first was *Teletubbies*, a British show that had the distinction of being the first television program to target prelinguistic children. Its characters are brightly colored, puffy, plush, toy-like creatures that—as if this world were designed by a sunnier, happier David Cronenberg—sprout antennae from their heads and have television screens implanted in their abdomens. What invariably astonishes adults who see the show, however, is not this blatant and shameless exposure of the terrible truth of children's television (i.e., that the television screen is effectively being "implanted" into our children, that the postmodern subject is transformed into a kind of blank, passive receptor for the transmission of the voice of the Big Other, and so on), a truth that they long ago learned to live with, but a structural element of the show. At some point, one of the Teletubbies is selected to receive that day's transmission. (Each one preens and postures in the hopes of being the recipient, and they all congratulate whoever is chosen.) A video begins to play in the chosen Teletubby's belly screen, and the camera zooms in until the image fills the viewer's screen. What follows is the generic multicultural stuff of children's television—kids in Argentina feeding chickens, in Korea looking at snails, in Russia filling a bottle with colored sand—for four or five minutes. Then the video ends, and the Teletubbies express disappointment, before excitedly chanting "again! again! again!" Sure enough, the video comes on again, but here is the part that shocks the adult viewer: when it repeats, *it repeats exactly as before*. Not a single shot is truncated, abbreviated, given from a different angle; there is no change in the voice-over, *no variation whatsoever*. For adults, something about this repetition seems unfair, as if the producers of the show had obtained—which, to be sure, they have—twice the air time for the cost of just one video. "And then, when it repeats, it's exactly the same!" they yelp in outrage. The point here is that there is something uncanny in the repetition, uncanny precisely because the repetition is identical. We normally think of the *Unheimlich* as the return of something familiar in disguise; this is the return of something familiar in no disguise whatsoever, but it carries its own uncanny charge. (One might hypothesize that what gives rise to the uncanny in perfectly identical repetition is its nearness to autistic repetition, which children are so close to, at times, perilously so; "normal" adult repetition is defined by its reliance on variation.)

It won't surprise any parent to learn that young children enjoy the repetition of the *Teletubbies* video; the penchant that children have for exact repetition has long been noted. And so I was surprised when my son began to repeatedly ask to watch a more adult show that he had seen part of, the USA Network's detective fiction/comedy show *Monk*. "Papa, watch *Monk*," he would say, pulling at my sleeve. One day his first words upon waking were shouted from his bedroom: "Papa, more *Monk!*" The show is about a detective, Adrian Monk (Tony Shalhoub), who suffers from obsessive/compulsive disorder (in the politically correct world of medical acronyms, OCD), which gives him a suite of phobias (he can't drink milk because he perceives it as "dirty," for instance) and compulsive behaviors (in one episode, he accidentally steps on a very, very long sheet of bubble wrap and pops one of the bubbles, and then sighs in anticipated exhaustion because he now has to pop *all* the bubbles). The humor of the show lies in the way these phobias and compulsions interfere with the detection, so that Monk has to rescue a clue from a garbage truck, or stop pursuing a suspect in order to fulfill some compulsion. The Lacanian anxiety in the show, however, is how close it steers to the truth—namely, that these tics, phobias, and compulsions, rather than interfering with our putative desire for narrative and epistemological closure, *are* the point of the show, that our engagement with classic detective fiction is fundamentally an obsessive-compulsive urge to repeat.

My son only wanted to watch one episode, the one that featured one of his chief interests at the time: airplanes ("Mr. Monk and the Airplane"). In this episode, Monk is compelled, despite his overwhelming fears, to fly on an airplane, but in the midst of his terror, he can't help but deduce that a murder must have taken place back at the airport and that the killer is on the plane. The episode alternates between his attempt to prove the crime and the obligatory litany of irritations that confront the modern air traveler: angry, spiteful flight attendants; overly chatty seat-mates: recirculated air; turbulence; and bratty children—all of them rendered more excruciating by Monk's OCD.[13] One of these unbearable moments occurs when the annoying child seated in front of him turns around and asks him if he likes riddles. The nature of the riddle she tells, however, is indicative not only of the kind of repetition that appeals to children, and is perhaps the reason, along with the presence of airplanes, my son was so attracted to the episode, but also the kind of repetition that I will argue typifies detective fiction, especially classic detective fiction.

GIRL: Do you like riddles?

MONK: Why, yes.

GIRL: Good, 'cause I have one.

MONK: Did I say yes? I meant no.

GIRL: Pete and Repeat were in a boat. Pete fell out. Who was left?

MONK: [*Cautiously, as if the answer is too obvious*] Repeat.

GIRL: Pete and Repeat were in a boat. Pete fell out. Who was left?

MONK: [*Getting the joke and giving a weak smile*] Repeat.

GIRL: Pete and Repeat were in a boat. Pete fell out. Who was left?

MONK: [*Realizing the situation he is in, but unable to stop*] Repeat.

GIRL: Pete and Repeat were in a boat. Pete fell out. Who was left?

---

13. The episode was made just about a year after the September 11 hijackings, and although there are some specific references to security measures that were implemented after the event, by and large the episode leaves unspoken a central anxiety for the normative viewer of the show: a nervous Arab American (Tony Shalhoub) on an airplane.

At this point, the camera cuts away for a while to Monk's assistant, Sharona Fleming (Bitty Schram), but later cuts back to Monk and the girl, obviously after a significant amount of time has elapsed that has been filled with more and more repetitions:

> GIRL: Pete and Repeat were in a boat. Pete fell out. Who was left?
> MONK: [*Now in agony, whispering*] Repeat.
> GIRL: Pete and Repeat were in a boat. Pete fell out. Who was left?
> MONK: [*His neighbor, Nathan, is now watching with interest*] Repeat.
> GIRL: Pete and Repeat were in a boat. Pete fell out. Who was left?
> MONK: [*Nearly in tears*] Repeat.
> GIRL: Pete and Repeat were in a boat. Pete fell out. Who was left?
> MONK: [*Turns to Nathan for help*]
> NATHAN: Repeat.
> MONK: Thank you.
> GIRL: Pete and Repeat were in a boat. Pete fell out. Who was left?

There are several things to notice in this scene, or pair of scenes. The first is that it begins with the detective's disavowal—"Did I say yes? I meant no"—and that this disavowal is in response to a question that should produce an unambiguous "yes" when directed to a detective. Are we not invariably given to understand that the detective, especially the classic detective like Holmes, Poirot, or Wimsey, likes riddles? This disavowal is not merely a reflection of Adrian Monk's personality (I do like riddles, but I find social contact, especially with strangers, unbearable.), but also a kind of anticipation of what follows. The detective likes riddles, but does not want the truth of his enjoyment—its repetition—to be made too clear. The second element here, more obviously, is the idiotic nature of the riddle that the child proposes. What makes this scene so brilliant is that—and this is typical of the show *Monk* as a whole, as I argue here and in the chapter on "Enjoyment"—the childish riddle proposed by the girl only *appears* to be the "other" to Monk's mature detection. That is, her riddle is radically pointless, without consequence, obvious, whereas the conundrum that Monk is investigating is important and difficult. The editing of the episode, which alternates mere airline irritations with investigatory moments, reinforces this opposition. This, again, is the reason for Monk's disavowal about riddles. He likes them and does not like them at the same time, which is to say that he compulsively pursues riddles; he cannot stop saying "repeat," but does not obtain satisfaction from them: in short, he *enjoys* them in the Zizekian sense. The brilliance of *Monk* is that it explicitly stages the truth of the classic detective as a character *at the mercy of* the riddle, persecuted by his *jouissance*. Finally, one also can't help but note that this seemingly idiotic and insignificant riddle simultaneously stages all the basic scenarios of detective fiction: a mysterious death or disappearance ("Pete and Repeat were in a boat. Pete fell out."); the locked room or enclosed scene (the boat in this story); the survivor on whom suspicion is naturally cast (in the riddle, it is Repeat—why is he not helping Pete? Did he push Pete overboard?); and finally, the ingenious twist at the end that puts everything in a different perspective, makes us realize that what we thought we had witnessed was in fact something completely different, that Repeat is not a character at all, but the imperative of drive, a kind of autistic, mechanical repetition. Is this not the elemental formula of classic detective fiction? Someone vanished, someone suspicious was left behind—repeat.

In this chapter, I will argue that this last point—the imperative of drive, the trick of getting your interlocutor to say "repeat" at the end—is not an incidental feature of the girl's riddle, but an essential element in detective fiction. Detectives and readers of detective fiction alike "enjoy" their riddles, enjoy precisely their seemingly meaningless content. We follow these riddles to the end, and, like Monk, we don't know how to stop saying "repeat." This point is made clearly in another episode of *Monk*, "Mr. Monk Meets Manhattan," in a scene where Monk, nearly overcome by the bustle and noise of Manhattan (as if San Francisco were a small village!), attempts to talk to his former boss, Captain Stottlemeyer, about a possible deal with the district attorney. Their conversation is repeatedly interrupted at exactly the same point by a man using a jackhammer at a nearby construction site. No matter how long Monk pauses, the man with the jackhammer cuts him off at just the same point. As I argue in the first chapter about the police procedural, the scene appears to be designed only to irritate. It is only briefly funny, then irritating, and finally agonizing. It does not develop the plot or the characters, nor does it foster audience identification: it seems only to embody the obsessive-compulsive nature of the genre. But it also indicates something more. If Monk's obsessive-compulsive disorder is normally portrayed as his personal and internal persecution, here it is clear that *the world itself is obsessive-compulsive, persecutory*, unwilling to let us be in peace. This is true, of course, even of the girl on the plane. I reproduce the scene below, but offer as a final observation that the sentence that Monk is attempting in vain to articulate over the noise of the jackhammer is indicative of the entire character of the show, and of the genre of classic detective fiction:

STOTTLEMEYER: Whaddaya think?

MONK: Well, I guess I don't have—[*he starts as the jackhammer goes off. Monk leads Stottlemeyer a few feet away*] I guess I don't really—[*jackhammer*] I guess I don't really—[*jackhammer; Monk tries to get the sentence out quickly*] I guess I don't—[*more jackhammering; close-up of Monk*] I guess I don't really—[*cut to man jackhammering; long pause*] I mean, I guess I don't—[*jackhammer in close-up; camera cuts back to Monk and pulls in a little tighter*] I guess I don't really—[*here Monk interrupts himself and turns defiantly to the now silent jackhammer; the operator keeps trying to get the position right, so Monk turns back to Stottlemeyer*] I guess I don't really have—[*jackhammer cuts in again*] I guess I don't—[*jackhammer*] I guess I don't really have—[*jackhammer; they move farther away*] I guess I don't really—[*jackhammer; Monk begins to shout over the now continuous noise of the machinery*] I guess I don't really have a choice.

DETECTION AND PSYCHOANALYSIS

There is a long-standing and, to some degree, mutually beneficial relationship between psychoanalysis and detective fiction. Detective fiction and its literary antecedents have long informed psychoanalytic theory; here one need only think of the signal importance of the story of Oedipus for Freud, Poe's "Purloined Letter" for Lacan, or Hitchcock's investigatory thrillers for Zizek. Indeed, Freud turns out to have been a regular reader of the Sherlock Holmes stories, not so much for entertainment, evidently, as for pure methodology (Zizek 1990, p. 29). The parallels between the work of the analyst and that of the detective are too well-known and too numerous to fully enumerate, but I will mention a few of them here. Detection and analysis both aim to uncover a hidden truth, both assuming that they must pierce a veil of deliberate or unconscious deception that has been erected to forestall the endeavor. In other words, they are both fundamentally *cognitive* activities, concerned with knowledge, but they are also both *intersubjective* undertakings in their shared emphasis on deception. Detective fiction, especially in its classic form, is elaborated through a series of scenes, often highly artificial or even fantastic, each of which conceals but still hints at some traumatic, prior "primal" scene that can only be fully revealed through the "subject presumed to know"—the detective or the analyst. The sequence of seemingly pathological, crazy, and impossible scenes that confront the detective bear a significant resemblance to both the patient's apparently meaningless dreamwork, concealing an unconscious repression as well as a latent content, or his or her logically inexplicable behavior, which will make sense only once the patient has worked back to this original trauma. We might further note that detection and psychoanalysis privilege form over content. Both recognize that the hidden primal truth is concealed by a seemingly insane deception, but that it is revealed precisely through the particular *form* that this deception takes, precisely because it is the content that must be guiltily repressed. This is particularly true of excess and lack. Consider, for instance, the methodological similarity between Holmes noticing the "dog that didn't bark in the night" or Dupin realizing that the purloined letter is "a little *too* self-evident," and Freud noting that his patient is answering a different question than the one that was asked. In each instance, what the detective/analyst notes is not what was said, but the way in which the utterance, or lack thereof, does not fit certain formal criteria.

At times, the detective's client frames the urgency of the case precisely in the language of madness, as with the "unhappy" John McFarlane in Conan Doyle's "The Adventure of the Norwood Builder"—"you mustn't blame me. I am nearly mad" (1986, p. 683), he exclaims on entering Holmes's studio. Indeed, one of the Holmes stories, "The Adventure of the Beryl Coronet," suggests that his clients all appear insane, that it is their constitutive feature. Watson spies a man in the street behaving strangely and says: "Here is a madman coming along." Holmes replies dryly, "I rather think he is coming to consult me professionally. I think that I recognize the symptoms" (1986, p. 408). That is, madness is a symptom of the need for detection. More often, to stay with Conan Doyle, the client seeks Holmes's help in order to resolve the apparently pathological behavior of the other, as in "The Adventure of the Solitary Cyclist" (a young woman is followed by a strange figure on a bicycle, every day, for precisely the same stretch of road), "The Adventure of the Six Napoleons" ("a queer madness" afflicting an individual, such that he smashes a series of plaster busts of Napoleon), or "The Adventure of the Copper Beeches" (a woman who seeks employment as a governess is asked by her employer to wear a certain dress, sit in a particular chair, and cut her hair quite short). All of these investigations are responses to the *che vuoi?*, the question of the other's desire: What does this person want of me? Again, both psychoanalysis and detection (particularly in its classic form) emphasize a truth that emerges out of form rather than content, from the superficial features of an apparently meaningless text. To return to some of the examples from Conan Doyle, Holmes perceives in "Six Napoleons" that the motivation is not a pathological hatred of Napoleon, but a completely literal instance of *agalma* (a treasure hidden inside statuary [the image appears again in "The Adventure of the Blue Carbuncle."]). In "Copper Beeches," he understands that the seemingly insane requirements of the employer are in fact the attempt to stage a scene in order to fool some observer (once again, the shared emphasis on the theatrical, and on bringing to light the "other scene" that conditions the visible, mundane scene). It is even true that both detection and psychoanalysis reconstruct the hidden "primal scene" as a form of therapy for the individual in the case of psychoanalysis, and for the disrupted social field in the case of detection.

Rarely has the relationship between psychoanalysis and detection been as clearly articulated as in another episode of *Monk*, "Mr. Monk Goes to the Asylum." The series generally participates, occasionally parodically, but usually seriously, in the tropes of classic detective fiction; Adrian Monk is clearly modeled on Sherlock Holmes. Indeed, in one episode, "Mr. Monk and the Other Detective," a rival detective (Jason Alexander) invites Mr. Monk to pose for a photograph with him, saying: "Philip Marlowe meets Sherlock Holmes." Unlike Holmes, however, Monk's full deductive capacity is only released by a psychological trauma, the murder of his beloved wife, Trudy. Monk feels intense guilt over his wife's death because he believes the car bomb that killed her was meant for him, and this guilt also precipitates a latent obsessive-compulsive disorder in the detective, the gimmick that the show revolves around. In "Asylum," Monk must spend 48 hours being observed in a psychiatric clinic because he mistakenly walked into his wife's old house and began to cook dinner, alarming the current inhabitants. In the asylum, he meets with the humane and warm Dr. Morris Lancaster for an initial evaluation, and Monk immediately asks him if he caught anything on his fishing trip in South America the week before. The psychiatrist is amazed by the precision and speed of this deduction, and Monk goes on to demonstrate the pieces of evidence that led to his conclusion (the customs mark on the cigar box dated the previous week, the blister on the doctor's index finger above the knuckle, and so on), adding a touch of Sherlockian pride when he says: "unless I'm wrong, which . . . I'm not." Dr. Lancaster's response initially places detection and psychoanalysis on an equal footing, but it develops in a way that is emblematic of psychoanalysis's response to detective fiction, including returning the detective's language, "unless I'm wrong, which . . . I'm not," back to him:

LANCASTER: Well, that's very impressive. We both have similar jobs, we both analyze clues, both solve problems. Only you look outward and I look inward. So now it's my turn! Sit. [*They sit*] What were you doing in Trudy's old house yesterday? [*Monk says nothing*] Your late wife lived there for—

MONK: Yeah, I know. I don't, I don't know why I go there.

LANCASTER: Well, I'm going to hazard a guess. I think you went there yesterday to cook Trudy dinner.

MONK: To cook—. Ah, well, that's absurd.

LANCASTER: Your file says that you're allergic to tomatoes, so the chicken cacciatore was for her, wasn't it? [*Monk looks uncomfortable*] And I'll bet you it was her favorite meal . . .

MONK: [*Pauses, then gives in, as if only now remembering*] That's right. [*Really beginning to remember*] That's right.

LANCASTER: So, what was so significant about yesterday?

MONK: N–Nothing. [*Shrugs*]

LANCASTER: August twelfth. Unless I'm wrong, which, you know, I'm not, the date has some significance.

MONK: [*With difficulty*] Our anniversary.

. . .

LANCASTER: I think your analytical powers, they're—they're dazzling. But I think you use them as a prop.

MONK: A prop?

LANCASTER: As a way to avoid dealing with your real problems. So, while you're here, do me a favor: don't be the detective. Let me be the detective.

As made clear here, psychoanalysis has always had a somewhat patronizing attitude to its own literary inspiration. I don't mean here the sort of critique elaborated by Derrida in "Le facteur de la verité" (that psychoanalysis looks at literature and sees, rather than literature, only and always the truth of psychoanalysis), but something much simpler. Psychoanalysis looks at detective fiction with a kind of bemused frustration: the figure of the detective comes so close, but still misses the mark attained by the analyst. Psychoanalysis gives detective fiction a perennial grade of "A–," almost, but not quite there. Hence, Dr. Lancaster offers his own Sherlockian deductions that equal Monk's (allergic to tomatoes, so the chicken cacciatore could not have been his own dinner) and then surpasses them, precisely in the turn from looking outward to looking inward to a higher, inner truth. It regards detective fiction as a patient in need of therapy, and says: "Do me a favor: don't be the detective. Let me be the detective." And the problem with detective fiction for psychoanalysis, as I indicated at the close of the previous chapter, is always the same. Detective fiction operates according to a unary logic of absolutely individual guilt. "Whodunit?" Which *one* of these characters is responsible? Which *one* will bear the burden of antisocial, violent, pathological desires? It deploys the specter of universal guilt, universal pathological desire, only in order to reduce that stain of guilt onto a single subject, missing the universal guilt, the universally antisocial desire, elaborated by psychoanalysis. And it is precisely this structure that is the prop Dr. Lancaster refers to, the real problems that Monk desires to avoid, which are precisely the problems of the real of desire.

Detective fiction is not willing to simply give up in its confrontation with psychoanalysis: Monk discovers a murder was committed four years ago in the asylum and begins to investigate. And the logic of their investigatory competition also dictates that the murderer should finally be revealed as Dr. Lancaster. Once the police have the psychiatrist (now dressed in a Santa Claus suit, reduced to a ridiculous figure of derision rather than the trusted subject we are supposed to know) trapped on the roof of the asylum, Monk concludes their therapy sessions with a genuinely heartfelt sentiment that is an equally perfect summation of the stance of detective fiction to psychoanalysis. He says, without any trace of irony or guile, "By the way, in case we don't get a chance to talk later, I just wanted to let you know—except for the murders, and your trying to kill me—you really were the best doctor I ever had." Its message (that is, the message of detective fiction in competition with psychoanalysis) appears in luminous form in the episode when Monk's assistant sends him a seemingly innocuous photograph of Trudy. (Dr. Lancaster already realizes that Monk is on to him and stages a series of deceptions designed to make the detective believe that he really is going mad.) The photograph has a message in glow-in-the-dark ink, however: "YOU'RE NOT CRAZY!" In other words, both detection and psychoanalysis have their own apparently insane surface (What could appear less superficially rational than psychoanalytic treatment?) that may be explained through recourse to the other discourse. In every drama, there is always an *andere Schauplatz*, an "other scene." For detective fiction, it is the psychoanalytic scene (Monk's obsessive guilt over his wife's death, which he tries to remedy through the touching, and entirely unconscious, gesture of cooking her a favorite meal), whereas for psychoanalysis, it is the investigatory scene (Dr. Lancaster's criminal guilt, or, in strictly Lacanian terms, the way Lancaster uses the discourse of the Analyst to conceal the discourse of the Master). If indeed both discourses are examples of a "higher truth," it would not be a truth that would stand on one side or the other, as *Monk* so ably demonstrates: the truth is always elsewhere. As the *X-Files* would have it, but only if we read the slogan in its most literal way, "the truth is out there," but not in here where we are.

If it is in fact true that Monk uses detection to avoid his real problem, it is a clear breach of the Lacanian maxim of desire, the Lacanian imperative: *ne ceder pas sur son desir*—never give up on your desire. This means pursuing one's desire to its end, and necessarily comports a full recognition of that desire, in all its social negativity. Detective fiction permits an isolation and a foregrounding of the desire in its full social negativity, but without a recognition of that desire as one's own. In standard psychoanalytic treatments of detective fiction, this is precisely what accounts for the appeal of the genre, this near miss of libidinal recognition. In this respect, then, the detective comes to stand for a perverted, albeit inspirational, version of the analyst. The detective always directs the reader's desire in the wrong direction. In maintaining the stability of the social field, he necessarily introduces an element of bad faith, a *méconnaissance*, into the field of desire. This is the psychoanalytic version, if you like, of a more common sociological argument about detective fiction: that it is inherently conservative in its longing for social order, for the rule of law, for an older, more aristocratic, way of life. My own perverse suggestion here would be to reverse the usual direction of the argument and ask if the analyst, especially in contemporary American-style ego-reinforcing therapy, is not a perverse figure of the detective, who does, after all, precede him chronologically. The analyst's obsessive interest in provoking a confrontation with the patient's desire introduces a kind of *méconnaissance* into the social field; the patient comes to perceive his antisocial desires as somehow normal. It is true that society disapproves of them, but they are in fact not an aberration at all; *everyone*, as it turns out, is at least neurotic or perverted, if not actually psychotic. As a result, the patient no longer "enjoys his symptom," can no longer experience the symptom as the transgressive threat to social authority that it was. In turn, the patient takes up a new obsessive activity to which he returns again and again without satisfaction: therapy itself. In short, the site of his *jouissance* has been relocated from symptom to therapy.

FANTASY AND REPETITION

Let's return to one of the Conan Doyle stories mentioned above, "The Adventure of the Copper Beeches." As is often the case, the story begins with Holmes's boredom, the simplistic nature of the cases that have been offered to him, the suggestion that detection has become commonplace and trivial. As always, however, *this* case proves to be different, to offer some "points of interest" or "particular features." Initially the case of the Copper Beeches, however, appears principally to offer confirmation that Holmes has "hit bottom," that he has been reduced to "recovering lost pencil leads" (1986, p. 431), as the young lady who arrives to engage his services merely wishes to know whether she should accept a particular situation as a governess. But her story proves to be unusual.

Miss Violet Hunter, whose economic needs are becoming pressing, has been seeking employment as a governess for some time through an agency where a prospective employer calls, and is shown the women seeking work one by one. This employer, a Mr. Rucastle, takes one look at Miss Hunter, and, without interviewing her (indeed, he shows no interest in her qualifications), declares that he "could not ask for anything better!" He offers her a magnificent wage, provided she accept some curious conditions: she must agree to wear certain clothes that will be provided for her, sit where her employer desires, and cut her hair short. Losing her hair is a sticking point for a time, but when Mr. Rucastle increases the wage still further, she accepts the post. Holmes, oddly, does not dissuade her, although he implies that there might be some danger, and agrees to come if she should call. Having taken the job, Miss Hunter takes care of the young child, a disturbingly large-headed and sullen creature who loves to kill insects, and on several occasions she is arranged by Mr. Rucastle in a kind of tableau; her back to the window, she sits in a chair, and is told amusing stories, or asked to read aloud. Eventually she conceals a mirror in her hand, and sees that she is being observed by a man outside the house during these scenes. Her employer asks her to gesture to the man to go away, and she complies. She also learns that there is, as there always is in these stories, a wing of the house that is kept locked and shuttered at all times. At this point, she wisely decides it is time to call in Holmes.

Holmes deduces that Mr. Rucastle has a daughter whom he has imprisoned in the unused wing of the house. Miss Hunter was hired to impersonate the imprisoned girl, whom she closely resembles, especially the distinctive color, although not the original length, of her hair, and the tableau is arranged to convince the daughter's fiancé that she is at liberty and chooses to see him no more. (The ostensible reason for this imprisonment and subsequent charade has to do with income that was willed to the young woman, and the father's fear of losing it if she were to marry.) Holmes has Miss Hunter trap the servants in the basement while Mr. Rucastle is out of the house, and he, Miss Hunter, and Watson all break into the locked wing to free the girl, only to discover that, rather anticlimactically, her fiancé has just freed her.

This rather long summary is necessary in order to perceive the more abstract structure that stands behind the story, and reveals it as a *mise-en-scène* of a particular fantasy. The father, drunk on his paternal authority, takes possession of his own daughter, demanding exclusive "economic" rights over her—that is, exclusive sexual access to her. (The sexual nature of this dominance is even more clear in another Holmes story from the same volume, "The Adventure of the Speckled Band," where the paternal figure, about to be deprived of his stepdaughter's income, sends a snake to bite and kill her; his desire for exclusive sexual possession of her is also revealed when he bolts her bed to the floor.) The father-of-absolute-authority then exercises his domination over another girl, dressing her up, commanding her to hold herself just so, cutting her hair, and so on, transforming her into a shield or "screen woman" who conceals his obscenity. Naturally, the fantasy must suffer a breakdown in order to restore the social field, a breakdown that is brought about by the figure of the detective. What is crucial about this scenario, however, is that every figure within it is doubled, repeated: the father and the daughter are mirrored in the detective and the screen woman. The obscene father of enjoyment masters first the one girl by imprisoning her and then the other by treating her like a living doll, dressing her, arranging her pose, and so on. The detective, in turn, unconsciously mirrors the actions of the father, as it is ultimately Holmes who turns out to be manipulating the scene and the actions of Miss Hunter, not Mr. Rucastle. One could also say that the control of the "other scene," the invisible and unknown scenario that conditions the visible world, passes from Mr. Rucastle to Holmes; at the end, the "other scene" is precisely Holmes's suborning of Miss Hunter, a betrayal that Rucastle is unaware of.

In this way, Holmes makes manifest, makes real, the fear that first set Mr. Rucastle on his perverse path: the fear that his girl might belong to another. Note that here the detective can hardly be seen as the paragon of rational behavior and thought who sets everyone's mind at ease because he reveals that underneath the insane appearance of the world is a logical order. On the contrary, his function is to show that *the father's paranoid sexual suspicions about his daughter were all true.* To see how this fantasy and its dissolution appear in the most literal manner possible, we must turn to a scene near the end of the story. Holmes, Watson, and Miss Hunter force their way into the wing of the house where they believe Rucastle's daughter is imprisoned but they find it deserted. Holmes believes that Rucastle has entered through a skylight and, knowing he was about to be discovered, moved his daughter to some other location, or possibly killed her. Holmes hears Rucastle on the stairs and reminds Watson to have his pistol ready, as Rucastle is a dangerous man:

> The words were hardly out of his mouth before a man appeared at the door of the room, a very fat and burly man, with a heavy stick in his hand. Miss Hunter screamed and shrunk against the wall at the sight of him, but Sherlock Holmes sprang forward and confronted him.
> "You villain!" said he, "where's your daughter?"
> The fat man cast his eyes round, and then up at the open skylight.
> "It is for me to ask you that," he shrieked, "you thieves! Spies and thieves! I have caught you, have I? You are in my power. I'll serve you!" He turned and clattered down the stairs as hard as he could go. [1986, pp. 449–450]

There is a barely noticeable non sequitur concealed here, typical of the logic of Freudian negation (Freud 1925a): Rucastle does not answer Holmes's question, but rather returns it to him. Let us treat Rucastle's words when Holmes asks him the location of his daughter literally: "It is for me to ask you that . . . you thieves!" It is for *me*, Rucastle, to ask *you*, Holmes: "Where is your daughter?" Where is Holmes's "daughter" here? We should recall that it is only at this moment that Rucastle's suspicions that Miss Hunter is "serving another" rather than him are confirmed. Is *she* not the daughter that Holmes has stolen from him? Moreover, does his returning of the question to the sender not suggest that Miss Hunter now stands in precisely the same fantasy relation to Holmes as she (and the daughter) previously did to Rucastle? That is, as the fantasy daughter who may be commanded, dressed up, *arranged in a tableau in order to deceive the rival?* Holmes is revealed here as the uncanny double of the obscene father figure, as the rival who provoked the father's jealousy in the first place, even if the detective only appeared afterward.[14] All of this plays out precisely as the mythic past Freud describes in *Totem and Taboo* (1913): the primal father claims for himself *all* the women of the horde, effectively arrogating to himself every scrap of *jouissance*, until he is murdered by his own sons. Whereas it is true that the sons of the primal father institute a social order and a series of prohibitions to prevent this sort of excessive, antisocial enjoyment, it is also true that they are responsible for instituting a different kind of enjoyment as well: the ever-accessible guilty pleasure of the fantasy of the murder of the father, a fantasy scenario to be played out again and again and again.

The entirety of Rucastle's reply is filled with the kind of strangeness that indicates it is being conditioned by an "other scene" not immediately visible to the reader. After returning Holmes's question back to him, in its most literal form ("Where is your daughter?"), he makes three further statements that contradict each other and themselves. We begin with the exceptionally bizarre "I have caught you, have I?" whose tag question at the end threatens to reduce the discourse to the level of total incoherence. This kind of uncertainty ("I have caught you, have I?") is seemingly belied by the positive, if obviously false, affirmation "You are in my power," which is then directly contradicted by the delicious ambiguity of the phrase "I'll serve you," as well as Mr. Rucastle's running away. This hysterical vacillation obviously revolves around precisely the fantasy the story articulates in the first place—the daughter, servitude, power—and marks the total breakdown of the fantasy scenario. As always, when the father's secret enjoyment is made manifest, made public, it transforms him from a stern figure of authority into a pathetic figure of ridicule, or as Watson says of Rucastle later in life, "always a broken man, kept alive solely through the care of his devoted wife" (1986, p. 451). This is the basic difference between Rucastle and other fathers of excessive enjoyment (what Zizek calls

---

14. Miss Hunter also has a strangely familial relationship to Holmes, as the detective twice refers to her as his sister. When she asks if she should take this strange assignment, Holmes replies: "It is not the situation which I should like to see a sister of mine apply for" (1986, p. 436).

the "anal father") and the mythic primal father: the primal father's enjoyment was not secret, but absolutely open, a fantasy, and an impossible one,
at that, of enjoyment without prohibitions.

If we return to the basic structure of this fantasy (the father oversteps
the Law and possesses a woman in a way not permitted to him; he then
dominates another woman and transforms her into a screen for his obscene
behavior; the detective discovers and reveals the crime, but only through
his own domination and transformation of the screen woman) we may be
surprised to discover that it is exactly the plot of Hitchcock's *Vertigo*. The
two texts describe precisely the same fantasy, the absolute paternal control over female sexuality. We have two paternal figures, in love with the
idea of an absolute masculine freedom, who exercise a control over their
women, a control that oversteps the Law. In *Vertigo*, the obscene father-
of-enjoyment is Gavin Elster, who murders his wife, Madeleine, precisely
in order to obtain more enjoyment; in "Copper Beeches" it is Mr. Rucastle
who imprisons his own daughter, Alice. These are two "screen women"
who uncannily double the female victims (both Judy, in *Vertigo*, and Miss
Hunter, in "Copper Beeches" are made up to resemble the victims), and,
of course, this obscene and excessive paternal figure is doubly doubled
in the figures of the detectives, where both Holmes, unconsciously, perhaps, and Scottie Ferguson, more obsessively and pointedly, in *Vertigo* re-
duplicate the fantasy of absolute paternal control. Both Holmes and Scottie
direct their damsels in distress, command them, demand from them an
unquestioned obedience as these "secondary fathers" direct a scenario that
will reveal the truth of the father's obscene enjoyment (all the more so in
Vertigo, where it is the *detective* who becomes the pathetic figure, weakly
pleading with Judy to change her hair, to dress differently). In both cases,
there is the same logic of the impossible Freudian imperative, "you must
be like the father; you cannot be like the father," where even the original
paternal figure (Rucastle, Elster) is subject to certain limitations, all the more
so for the incomplete authority of the detective, who is never fully authorized to perform his investigations. (Holmes is, of course, completely un-
official; Scottie has retired from the force because of his vertigo.) At the
end of "Copper Beeches," aware that they are guilty of breaking and entering,
Holmes remarks to Watson that "it seems to me that our *locus standi* now
is a rather questionable one" (1986, p. 451). The classic detective's *locus
standi* is always a rather questionable one insofar as he is para-authority,
only partially authorized to "be like the father." And is not this questionable *locus standi* precisely the sensation that one does not stand on firm

ground, that—literally now—"the place in which you stand" is precarious, ready to give way? In other words, what is this questionable *locus standi*, the ground under our feet about to collapse, if not *vertigo*?

Again, the standard psychoanalytic reading of detective fiction—the avoidance of the "real of desire"—will initially stand us in good stead with *Vertigo* and "Copper Beeches." Each element of the fantasy (the father, the daughter, and the repetition) is doubled precisely so that the reader will not see that *this desire is doubled in him as well*. In other words, the fantasy was always already doubled; the original scenario is doubled again precisely so that the reader may recognize himself in the detective, in this outside figure who discovers the forbidden desire in another. The reader can take comfort in having located the desire on the outside, in the *arrest* (to return to the language of the first two chapters) of desire's movement. Again, making use of Dr. Lancaster's terminology, the problem with detective fiction is that it locates the truth by "looking outward."

Not surprisingly, the last sentence of "The Adventure of the Copper Beeches" is an emphatic disavowal of the detective's repetition of the original scenario, a disavowal of the real of his desire: "As to Miss Violet Hunter, my friend Holmes, rather to my disappointment, manifested no further interest in her when once she had ceased to be the centre of one of his problems, and she is now the head of a private school at Walsall, where I believe that she has met with considerable success" (1986, p. 452). The unusual character of Holmes's admiring comments toward Miss Hunter (he repeatedly praises her bravery and intelligence in a manner most unusual for the detective, almost unique in the Holmes stories, in fact—"a very brave and sensible girl . . . a quite exceptional woman" [1986, p. 447]) has not gone unnoticed by Watson, but Watson also has the power to retroactively annihilate Holmes's desire. As the narrator, always speaking from a point later in time, even years after the adventure has played itself out, Watson may perform a kind of libidinal absolution on Holmes that extends to the reader, as well, to say: "we were never interested in this spirited and intelligent young woman, with her face that was bright, quick and freckled." We certainly never wished to dress her up, cut her hair, arrange her in this or that pose, make her do whatever we wished. A desire that broadly stained all the protagonists in the story is reduced to a minute dot, the pathetic figure of the now invalid Mr. Rucastle.

Vertigo makes this disavowal of desire rather more difficult, as the detective does not give up on his desire at all, nor does he explicitly disavow it; he pursues it to the very end. He *wants* to be this obscene father of enjoyment, to push his wife from the tower, to fully act out the fantasy of total dominion over women, which in Vertigo always takes the form of a literalized "throwing away" of woman. But perhaps "wants" is the wrong term to apply to Scottie Ferguson. It is not so much a question of his *desire*, but a hollow acting out of Elster's scenario; Scottie goes through the motions in a mechanical, automatic way, behaving as if he is driven or possessed. (This is one of the most remarkable aspects of the film; it exposes one uncanny possession as a fraud, namely "Madeleine" possessed by the spirit of Carlotta Valdes, only to have the uncanny possession return in another guise, undeniably "real," in both senses of the term this time.) He does not seem in control of his own actions, which is precisely what gives this film its powerful sense of the uncanny. After all, Gavin Elster and his wife quickly vanish from the film, leaving the impression that Scottie and Judy are possessed, animated by this "other scene" that we do not have direct access to until Scottie reenacts it at the end. Strictly speaking, we never see Elster's wife alive, only glimpse him hurling her already dead body off the Mission bell tower. This uncanny reanimation of the principal characters is also, however, what permits the kind of minimal disavowal necessary in the film: because Scottie is "possessed," somehow externally compelled to restage Elster's scenario, he can still be surprised at how the scenario ends (i.e., this time with the death of Judy dressed as Madeleine). But his surprise necessarily has the character of a kind of horrified recognition, as if to say: "If I had only stopped to think, I would have realized this is where my desire was taking me." It is only this minimal flinch from a full recognition and acceptance of desire and its consequences that permits the film to follow the traditional reading of the avoidance of the real of desire.

One must surely notice the extraordinary amount of doubling going on here, not only in the texts I'm discussing, but also in the discussion itself. The scenario I have been describing, the fantasy of absolute paternal authority, is one that is already based on an unconscious repetition, as the detective repeats the original gesture of domination—nowhere more clearly than in Vertigo—with the "screen girl"; the scenario elaborated in "The Adventure of the Copper Beeches" is repeated in Vertigo, itself a repetition of Boileau and Narcejac's novel D'entre les morts. But there is an important distinction between "Copper Beeches" and Vertigo, a difference that involves repetition. Vertigo features yet *another* uncanny duplication in the back story of Carlotta Valdes. Carlotta functions as another "screen woman," in a self-conscious staging of the film's uncanny repetitions.

Gavin Elster originally hires Scottie Ferguson to investigate his wife. He claims to believe that she is possessed by the spirit of a woman who died tragically, Carlotta Valdes. Elster's wife "Madeleine" (it is already Judy dressed as Madeleine) compulsively revisits all of Carlotta's old haunts, all the while evincing a suicidal propensity that will later explain her "death," which will be the death of Elster's real wife. One should note here, however, that not only is Judy/Madeleine's apparent "possession" by Carlotta a prefiguration of the later compulsive reenactments in the film, but that Carlotta's story is itself another instance of the fantasy of absolute paternal authority. Pop Leibel, a bookstore owner well acquainted with the day to day events of old San Francisco, tells Scottie the story of Sad Carlotta and "a rich man, a powerful man," named Ives who "takes" Carlotta, builds her a house, and has a child with her:

> I cannot tell you how much time passed, or how much happiness there was. But then he threw her away. He had no other children; his wife had no children. So, he kept the child and threw her away. You know, men could do that in those days. They had the power . . . and the freedom. And she became the Sad Carlotta. Alone in the great house . . . walking the streets alone, her clothes becoming old and patched and dirty . . . the Mad Carlotta . . . stopping people in the streets to ask "Where is my child . . . have you seen my child?"

Again, the main action of *Vertigo*, revolving around Scottie, Judy/Madeleine, and Elster, describes a doubly doubled structure. First, Elster throws his wife from the tower (throws her away), a scene that Scottie repeats at the end of the film, only slightly less literally. We then noted that this overall scenario recalled Conan Doyle's "Copper Beeches," a story that already has the basic elements of obscene father, woman who must be put away, screen woman, and detective, but that *Vertigo* cleverly incorporates its own reliance on repetition within itself, both through the evidently real historical antecedent of Carlotta Valdes and through the dummy plot of ghostly possession in which the detective turns out to be the one possessed. The point to make here is that there is another famous scene of detection that intervenes historically between Conan Doyle and Hitchcock, one in which a different sort of detective, who was a serious reader of Conan Doyle, and who was, in turn, read by Hitchcock, makes a telling discovery about repetition and the "throwing away" of woman: I mean, of course, Freud in *Beyond the Pleasure Principle*, who noted his grandson playing with a reel and a piece of string. The child would "hold the reel by the string and very skillfully throw it over the edge of his . . . cot" (1920, p. 15). This is the famous *fort/da* (gone/there) game, in which Freud hypothesizes that the child is staging, again and again, the loss and return of the maternal object, devising an elementary game to be played with the object (a), in which it is repeatedly thrown away. Freud's initial theory that the game represents an attempt at mastery is already troubled by the fact that the child seems to prefer the first part, the loss, "which was repeated untiringly as a game in itself" (p. 15). He concludes somewhat hesitantly that "the child may, after all, only have been able to repeat his unpleasant experience in play because the repetition carried along with it a yield of pleasure of another sort" (p. 16), suggesting the possibility that there might be a pleasure in the repetition of an act that does not, in itself, deliver satisfaction—in other words, enjoyment.

To return to *Vertigo*, then, Madeleine/Judy plays not only the primary and secondary woman in the fantasy scene; she also functions as a kind of "screen woman" for this primal father, Ives, who "threw away" Sad Carlotta, modeling her appearance on a portrait of Carlotta that hangs in the Palace of the Legion of Honor. She does her hair the same way, wears an identical necklace, and holds a bouquet of flowers that is identical to the one in Carlotta's lap. Let me call attention particularly to the way the portrait functions as a screen (itself a "screen woman"), not only in the sense of something that blocks our view of a truth hidden behind it, but also in the cinematic sense: it is the screen of fantasy, where Gavin and Scottie's desires are projected.

The first two views we have of "Madeleine" also conspicuously double her image: the first is inside a restaurant where Gavin Elster has placed Scottie so that he may surreptitiously observe Elster's "wife." We should again note the theatricality here, the most superficial formal feature that the detective should notice but does not: he believes Elster has set a scene to deceive "Madeleine," but it is, of course, a scene to deceive him, Scottie. As the couple exits the restaurant, Scottie sees the embodiment of the entire scenario elaborated by the film: the doubling of the paternal power and the woman he wants to control, Elster and Madeleine exiting next to a floor-length mirror. The next day he follows "Madeleine" to a flower store. He observes her from behind a mirrored door that reflects her image; the resulting tableau repeats the mirror image of the previous night, with precisely the "illegitimate" substitution we would expect: Scottie standing in the place of Gavin (that is to say, Madeleine's reflection appears in the mirrored door, while Scottie's face appears next to hers through the open crack of the door left just ajar). Here it is the mirror that becomes the fantasy screen, akin to Carlotta's portrait.

How is one to understand repetition upon repetition, repetition as the excess of itself? Here repetition acquires an uncanny, compulsive quality, as if these early scenarios were possessing, reanimating, the later one, compelling us to repeat the fantasy of absolute paternal power. It is, again, not so much a question of desire as that of an automatic repetition. ("Pete and Repeat were in a boat. Pete fell out. Who was left?") In this continuous reenacting of the fantasy of paternal domination, there are at least two things to note. The first has to do with the term *fantasy*. Although we normally understand it as a form of wish fulfillment, we should recall that in Lacanian theory, "fantasy designates the subject's "impossible" relation to *a*, to the object-cause of desire . . . what the fantasy stages is not a scene in which our desire is fulfilled, fully satisfied, but on the contrary, a scene that realizes, stages, the desire as such" (Zizek 1992, p. 6). Fantasy, then, does not give satisfaction, or at least does not give satisfaction in the way in which we normally understand it; after all, the fantasy depicted in "The Adventure of the Copper Beeches" and in *Vertigo* is quite literally a description of an "impossible relation," a thing that is not allowed, a fantasy whose invocation also calls forth the detective in order to push the fantasy scenario into a hysterical breakdown. This leads to the second point, which has to do with *repetition*. In pushing the fantasy scenario into a hysterical breakdown, the detective also repeats it, exercising his own kind of absolute domination over the "screen woman." So, the scenario must be broken down, but it also must be repeated; it is this structure that allows the reader to remain in "a state that enable[s] him to postpone indefinitely his desire's full satisfaction . . . a state that reproduce[s] the lack constitutive of desire" (Zizek 1992, pp. 7–8). Or, to put it in slightly different terms, "*fantasy is the very screen that separates desire from drive*"; with the breakdown of the fantasy and its concomitant desire, all that is left is the repetition of drive (Zizek 1997, p. 32, original emphasis). Both of the texts I've been discussing demonstrate this, but it is *Vertigo* that makes particularly manifest the excessive nature of the repetition of the scenario that is constitutive of the genre, reveals it as fantasy rather than the fulfillment of desire. It does so perhaps most revealingly through the "superfluous" figure of Midge, Scottie's old friend. Midge is in love with Scottie (and must bear the irony of having once rejected his proposal), and wishes to write herself into the fantasy scene that he is repeating. She does so quite literally, using her artistic skills to duplicate the portrait of Carlotta Valdes that Madeleine

imitated to such uncanny effect, but with an unbearable, grotesque difference: her own face. The portrait of Carlotta, then, literally stands as the fantasy scene, a screen onto which the protagonists' desires are projected again
and again and again, indicating that this projection gives no satisfaction to
those desires. Indeed, in the case of poor Midge, her pastiche-like insertion
of herself into the fantasy scene produces only revulsion on the part of Scottie, and a kind of nervous laughter in the audience.[15]

More broadly, the constant repetition of the same scenarios in detective
fiction, the relentless insistence on identical situations, structures, gimmicks,
characters, even the insistence on serial adventures, the same detective
coming back again and again, points not to the satisfaction of a desire, albeit
a disavowed one, but rather to some other mechanism. Fortunately, we
have a psychoanalytic term that is well suited to the constant return to that
which does not give us satisfaction: *enjoyment*.

---

15. What is it that gives Midge's version of the portrait its unbearable, grotesque
quality? The portrait of Carlotta is fascinating not through any particular feature of Carlotta's,
although her necklace functions as the point of meaningless fascination, the object (a),
but precisely through its total anonymity, an impersonality that renders the image "open"
to the projection of fantasy. This is why pornography must also strip away markers of the
individual—it removes entirely, or attempts to remove, the question of the desire of the
other, the *che vuoi?*. In essence, the removal of the *che vuoi?* permits the unimpeded consideration of the *che voglio?*, the "what do I want?" But Midge's portrait features a blot that
insists on her absolute particularity, the marker of her inexplicable, unbearable desire, a
marker that frames that unbearable gaze: her glasses. Needless to say, this transforms the
portrait from a screen in the fantasy sense to a mere portrait, but one that carries traces of
the fantasy scenario; such a procedure renders acutely visible the embarrassing truth of
male pornographic fantasy. The same procedure was used, also with comic results and
with even greater clarity, in an episode of *Sex and the City* ("Hot Child in the City"). Charlotte, the preppy white socialite, has recently married her ideal man, Trey McDougal, only
to find that Trey is impotent. But then she discovers Trey masturbating to a pornographic
magazine; he is not precisely impotent, only incapable of an erection with Charlotte. The
indefatigable Charlotte goes to work on an art project that would make Martha Stewart
proud, recycling their excess wedding photos, and the episode ends happily with Trey
masturbating to his magazine again: he turns the page to discover that Charlotte's earnest,
smiling face has been pasted over the faces of all the women in the magazine. And so Trey's
masturbatory *jouissance* becomes a laborious chore, as he finds he cannot escape the *che
vuoi?*. What do you want from me, Charlotte? In the same way, Midge's spectacles under-
score her potential to usurp Scottie's role as spectator, a voyeur with desire.

ENJOYMENT

We could perhaps conceive of enjoyment as a kind of intermediate space between desire and drive. Whereas we normally conceive of desire as normal and non-pathological, fundamentally tied to the symbolic and the social, we think of drive as unnatural, inhuman, or, in terms of psychopathology, psychotic or autistic in its relentlessly mechanical nature, and fundamentally tied to the real, the reef on which desire and the symbolic break. To return to the cinematic examples in the previous chapter, the tragedy of Tom Ripley, as configured by Anthony Minghella, is his desubjectification, his gradual transposition from the realm of desire, the social order that he never fit very well into, to a regime of drive: a mechanical repetition of the same scenario, over and over again. To take three emblematic moments from that film—the opening credits, the climactic centerpiece, and the film's ending—they all describe precisely the same scene, a scene that Tom cannot escape from: he has always just killed someone on a boat. The contrast between (symbolic) desire and (real) drive is precisely the one that Tom articulates when he says that he would rather be "a fake somebody than a real nobody." And the creature of drive is precisely that, a "real nobody," a thing that has been evacuated of all subjectivity. What is noteworthy about this distinction between desire and drive, the normal and the psychotic, however, is the excluded middle, the space of "the psychopathology of everyday life." If we have a kind of ideal normalcy on the one side, and psychosis on the other, what has happened to the space of the neurotic, the space to which (let's be honest) most of us belong? Enjoyment is obviously socially acceptable, if frowned upon (one might think of all the little repetitions and dirty little habits that characterize everyday neuroses—chewing on one's fingernails, smoking cigarettes, and so on—all of which fail to give a satisfaction that would put an end to the desire that motivates them), and yet has the circular and automatic character of drive. One might even note that enjoyment becomes a kind of instantiation of Lacanian anxiety, which is produced when we approach too close to the satisfaction of our desire.

As helpful as this conception of enjoyment, the middle realm between desire and drive, may be, we might note that, in discussing the object (a) and the way that it both *provokes* desire and stands as its *impediment*, Zizek writes:

The final step to be taken is to grasp this inherent impediment in its *positive* dimension: true, the *objet a* prevents the circle of pleasure from closing, it introduces an irreducible displeasure, but the psychic apparatus finds a sort of perverse pleasure *in this displeasure itself*, in the never-ending, repeated circulation around the unattainable, always missed object. The Lacanian name for this pleasure-in-pain is of course enjoyment (*jouissance*), and the circular movement which finds satisfaction in failing again and again to attain the object . . . is the Freudian *drive*. [2001, p. 48, emphasis original]

Here we have to note that enjoyment appears not so much as an intermediate space that manifests features of both the symbolic/social and the real/autistic, but rather a "positive dimension" of drive. This is a rather more nuanced way of understanding desire, drive, and enjoyment: as simultaneous registers or dimensions of the subject's relation to the object (a). This is why Lacanian theory often gives the impression of having terms that constantly shift meaning. The object (a), for instance, appears at one moment as the *object* of desire, in another moment, the *cause* of desire, in another moment, the *impediment* of desire. It is, in fact, all three. Or, to return to the citation above, the object (a) causes desire, but as desire's impediment, it also produces a circular movement within the psychic apparatus that returns again and again, seeking satisfaction and failing to find it: hence it is drive. An excellent example of this is the split character Madeleine/Judy in *Vertigo*. When Scottie discovers Judy, she is clearly the *cause* of his desire, that is, she is the thing that provokes his desire to have Madeleine back again (the *object* of that desire). At the same time, however, Judy is herself, in her Judy-ness, the *impediment* to the realization of that desire; she is the stubborn material that has to be molded into the shape of Madeleine, and she resists throughout. Now the viewer knows, of course, that Judy and the Madeleine that Scottie knew are the same person, and so this object (a) plays all three roles. This "impossible nature" of the object (a) becomes clear in the moment when Scottie finally manages to fully transform Judy back into Madeleine. Not only is this the moment in which he *loses* the object/cause of his desire (i.e., discovers that "Madeleine" and Judy were in fact the same person, that he has been duped), but she appears to him as something untouchable, ungraspable, as something that will always exceed his reach: a ghost, literally translucent. (Hitchcock is using some kind of process shot here, giving the impression that Madeleine initially appears as a phantasm, who takes on weight and solidity as she moves forward toward the camera.) In other words, seeing Judy is the cause of

Scottie's desire, Madeleine is the object of that desire, and Judy/Madeleine is simultaneously also the impediment to the satisfaction of that desire, a kind of inherent impossibility within the object itself. Judy-into-Madeleine is the "missing piece" that the viewer and detective circulate around, quite literally in several shots in the film, typifying the "there and yet not there" nature of the object (a).

If we connect the beginning and end of this causal chain that runs from the object (a) as the cause of desire to the object (a) as the impediment to desire, to the object (a) as the "foreign body" that precipitates the circular movement of drive in search of an impossible satisfaction, we discover that *drive and its enjoyment are features inherent to desire itself.* This is not to say that desire is drive, that they are the same thing, but rather that we should always attend to the *dimension* of drive, and hence enjoyment, the "positive dimension" of drive, in the overall libidinal field. This is why the Zizekian imperative (to enjoy one's symptom) is *not*, in fact, a contradiction of the Lacanian imperative (to not give up on one's desire). It is precisely through persistence in my enjoyment that I might not give up on my desire.

This conception of desire, drive, and enjoyment permits a more nuanced understanding also of this project. In turning to enjoyment as a category for analyzing detective fiction, I am not casting aside the question of desire and its avoidance, which I take to be a constitutive feature of the genre. What I wish to do, however, is attend to this other register implicit in that desire, the desire of the detective, the desire of the reader. To return, then, to the earlier concrete examples of "The Adventure of the Copper Beeches" and Hitchcock's *Vertigo*, it is not that *Vertigo* nearly overcomes the avoidance of the real of desire that is so visible in "Copper Beeches." Rather, *Vertigo* pursues the logical chain of "desire, object (a), enjoyment, drive" very nearly to its full logical conclusion. The total pursuit of desire, not giving up on one's desire, leads to the negative dimension of the libidinal field, namely drive. Scottie's relentless pursuit of the object of his desire is the transformation of Judy into Madeleine. Note that, unlike what is normally supposed about the movie, what Scottie wants is not Madeleine, but the transformation of Judy into Madeleine, the complete repetition of the scene that Gavin Elster had already played out with the real Madeleine (whose very name already, via Proust, points to the involuntary character of this repetition), down to the final fall that prevents Scottie from actually having the object of his desire. Scottie is not in love with Madeleine and attempting to get her back. He is, on the contrary, endeavoring to do what

Gavin did, what Ives did before him: in the words of Pop Leibel (or the actions of Freud's grandson), he is frantically endeavoring to recreate her only in order to "throw her away," an injunction that Scottie manages to take quite literally. In other words, *Vertigo* makes manifest a feature of detective fiction that is present already in Conan Doyle, and which becomes fully explicit in *Monk*, namely, the central importance of repetition and its enjoyment, "the never-ending, repeated circulation around the unattainable, always missed object."

We should note that this claim casts an entirely different light on a claim that has been made about detective fiction by both Joan Copjec and Slavoj Zizek, namely that the break between classic detective fiction and hard-boiled/*noir*, conceived of as the most historically important break within the genre, is a break between a regime of desire and a regime of drive. Joan Copjec gives a very memorable account of this split in *Read My Desire*, part of a larger, "general historical transition" from desire to drive (1994, p. 182). She goes on to explain how the transition to a regime of drive and *jouissance* explains a number of *noir's* structures and devices (the empty public space, the voice-over from the dead body, and so on). Near the end of the essay, however, she also notes that there are "defenses against the drive, . . . means of curbing its satisfactions" (p. 196) within the genre. She particularly notes a way in which desire is reintroduced, through the use of deep focus photography, wide-angle lenses, and chiaroscuro-like lighting that generate a space that is mysterious and unknown—an "ersatz symbolic" (p. 197) space of desire that acts as a compensatory defense against drive. There are many things that are appealing about Copjec's analysis, and this is one of them: even while discussing a genre that she claims is quintessentially "on the side of drive," she still attends to the dimension of desire. What is missing from her analysis (and it is emblematic of the overall emphasis on the part of New Lacanian cultural studies critics on *noir* rather than classic detection), however, is how precisely the opposite occurs as well—how repetition, for instance, already demonstrates the presence of drive and enjoyment in *classic* detective fiction. It is true that the workings of drive emerge more clearly in, say, Hitchcock, whom one must certainly place *after* the historical break between classic and hard-boiled, than in Conan Doyle, not as a radical break with his progenitors but rather as the logical outcome of a dimension that was always present within the genre. Again, *Monk*, which operates exclusively within the constraints of classic detective fiction, follows all of its rules, and makes use of all of its devices, could not be more explicit about how the repetition compulsion is central to the genre.

Here, by the way, we can finally account for one of the features of detective fiction that has always bewildered its (here in a negative sense) critics: How can readers consume novel after novel that is exactly the same? Of course, it is precisely the identical repetitions of scene, structure, trope, plot, character, gimmick, and so on (the room with the dead body locked from the inside, the hapless sidekick-as-narrator, the "fatal appointment," the endless return of the detective to yet another crime—if Poirot was retired just before *The Mysterious Affair at Styles*, then he would have been about 115 years old at the time of his last adventure) that *are* the appeal of detective fiction, and of genre fiction more generally. Attending to the question of "enjoyment," the return again and again to what does *not* give us satisfaction, suggests, however, that these constantly repeated structures are deliberately constructed in order to *foil* our satisfaction (a suggestion that I will explore more fully in the next two chapters), not in order to provide it. Perversely, to return to the Lacanian conception of anxiety, this deliberate structure of dissatisfaction is precisely why genre fiction, specifically detective fiction, soothes us. It is not because it offers us the familiar, or reassures us that the social hierarchy is intact, or because it promises a kind of general order in the universe, although all of these things may be the case, but rather because all of its basic tropes are aimed at frustrating our desires, at casting us back into a circular movement in search of the "always missed object." We are soothed by the certain knowledge that our desire will not be fulfilled, that at the end of the story, we will be able to say, once again: "repeat."

6

VIOLENCE: *Christie | Poe | Gadda*

MY DEAR JAMES

The following letter appears at the beginning of Agatha Christie's *Hercule Poirot's Christmas* (originally published in 1938) as a kind of authorial introduction. It is not part of the story, but a chance for Christie to address one of her readers directly, and all of her readers by implication:

> My dear James,
>   You have always been one of the most faithful and kindly of my readers, and I was therefore seriously perturbed when I received from you a word of criticism.
>   You complained that my murders were getting too refined—anaemic, in fact! You yearned for a "good violent murder with lots of blood." A murder where there was no doubt about its being murder.
>   So this is your special story—written for you. I hope it may please.
>
> Your affectionate sister-in-law,
Agatha [2000a, p. i][16]

---

16. The novel has appeared under two other rather more pulpy titles: *Murder for Christmas* and *A Holiday for Murder*.

This slightly tongue-in-cheek beginning establishes many of the co-ordinates that will be key to understanding the workings of the detective novel and its readers. Most obvious is, of course, the appeal to the socially transgressive desire for violence and its resulting thrill. At first glance, the letter seems to contain nothing more than a kind of inevitable appeal from the reader of genre fiction, any kind of genre fiction: shock me into a new appreciation of what has become a stale formula! And Christie, who was certainly a master at delivering what her reading public wanted, eschews in this novel the "anaemic" crimes that her brother-in-law objected to in previous tales (poison is particularly criticized here as a bloodless method of murder). It is true that Christie's two previous Poirot novels (*Appointment with Death,* originally published in 1938 and *Dumb Witness,* originally published in 1937) featured poisoning exclusively. However, one doesn't have to look far to escape this recent "anaemia"—*Death on the Nile* (originally published in 1937, just one year before *Hercule Poirot's Christmas*), with its shootings and stabbing; *Cards on the Table* (originally published in 1936) with a stabbing and attempted drowning; or *The A.B.C. Murders* (originally published in 1936) with bludgeoning, strangling, and stabbing. This last novel contains a dialogue expressing a similar desire with a metaphor that is as delightful as it is distancing and aestheticizing. Poirot asks Hastings to order a crime as if he were ordering dinner. The amiable but dull Hastings replies with character-breaking wit: "Let's review the menu. Robbery? Forgery? No, I think not. Rather too vegetarian. It must be murder—red-blooded murder—with trimmings, of course" (1977, p. 10). One should also notice that there is a lightly veiled discourse of "virility" at work in these requests for violence, not to mention a concern about getting enough iron in one's diet.

The letter also establishes an important dichotomy between two seemingly antagonistic facets of detective fiction itself: the anemic and refined (typically associated with the detective and his investigation) and the violent and bloody (the criminal and his crime). Traditionally, classic detective fiction has been understood as the triumph of the former over the latter, and in turn, the triumph of law, order, and rationality over crime, chaos, and the irrational. Indeed, the letter also points at a related function of detective fiction: typically, detection also repairs a domestic breach, a violent opening into the safe space of the bourgeois home, just as the letter from Christie attempts to resolve a "perturbation" between her and her brother-in-law back into a happy domestic world of "faith," "kindness," and "affection."

But Christie's opening letter might already begin to indicate that this scenario is not completely satisfactory. To begin with, there is already a wound, a kind of bloodletting, even before Christie addresses her brother-in-law's complaint: a cutting word of *criticism*. In other words, violence can also lead to violence, rather than inexorably to its refined solution. And this cut is preceded by a cut of Christie's own: James's letter is omitted, and we are left only with a citation from it, the phrase "good violent murder with lots of blood." Second, there is a question of enjoyment. She hopes that this "good violent murder with lots of blood" will give pleasure. Do readers of detective fiction derive pleasure from a "good violent murder" or "lots of blood"? How can we square the reader's putative desire for blood with a simultaneous putative desire for triumph of law, order, and rationality? Finally, one has to wonder about the tone of Christie's last two lines. Might there not be another way to hear the phrase "I hope it may please"? A hope for a kind of *displeasure*? A suspicion that the reader is perhaps not ready for his own desire? Perhaps Christie is not so ready to satisfy James after all, and by extension, her other readers. Perhaps Christie has understood perfectly clearly that satisfaction is what is to be avoided at all costs in the detective genre.

Hercule Poirot's Christmas tells the story of the death of a family patriarch, Simeon Lee. The entire family (indeed, more of them than anyone suspects), fraught with long-standing resentments and grudges, is gathered together for Christmas when Simeon Lee gleefully decides to rewrite his will, presumably in favor of a prodigal son who has recently returned home and a beautiful half-Spanish granddaughter who has also just turned up and whom a number of men in the family, including Lee, appear to be unwholesomely, incestuously intrigued by. Lee is murdered before he can rewrite the will, and Poirot conducts an investigation alongside the official police investigation. When the murder is solved at the novel's end, most everyone is a bit older and wiser, and the family seems to have resolved at least some of their rancor. This is not an atypical structure in the detective novel: murder as therapy. As far as Christie's novels go, *Poirot's Christmas* is merely average; it has none of the structural complexity that makes *The Murder of Roger Ackroyd* or *Murder on the Orient Express* so memorable. As is typical of her work, the characters are flat and the prose is uninspired, but the narrative machinery is, as always, compelling. More to the point here, the novel begins with Christie's unusually explicit appeal to the presumed pleasure in taking in the spectacle of violence, in the certain knowledge that the law has been transgressed. The reader is being offered "the real thing," precisely akin to the transgressive thrill of reality television: the knowledge that these are not actors, but "real people" engaging in acts of pitiless scheming, backstabbing, and revenge, all of it voyeuristically visible to the "accidental observer" who is here the detective. The cut-throat behavior is fully public, on stage, and altogether literal in detective fiction.

When the murder victim is discovered in *Poirot's Christmas,* naturally, in a room locked from the inside, the scene allows no room for "doubt about its being murder," as the victim's throat has been cut. What follows is a scene of violence, but what jumps out is how curiously detached the narrative voice is; one is tempted to say that there is a great deal of blood, as James requested, but very little violence.

> There had clearly been a terrific struggle. Heavy furniture was over-turned. China vases lay splintered on the floor. In the middle of the hearthrug in front of the blazing fire, lay Simeon Lee in a great pool of blood . . . blood was splashed all round. The place was like a shambles. [2000a, p. 71]

What gives the scene this detached character is the elision of any agency. Everything is given to the reader in the passive voice ("furniture was overturned," "blood was splashed") or through passive verbs and agency-free constructions ("vases lay splintered," "there had been a struggle"). This, of course, will later turn out to be a clue to the nature of the scene, namely that it is a "scene," a staged, theatrical presentation, but for now, let us read it as it was meant to be read. In addition to the curiously unaffecting "great pool of blood," the "shambles" of the room also points to a violent struggle, as does the most singular feature of the murder that is inevitably both part of the murder scene just described and simultaneously "not there," part of an "other scene" located elsewhere: the long, horrendous scream of the victim, which each of the witnesses describes differently, but all with a shudder. Let us be clear about how this "partial presence" works in the description of the murder scene. There is a great deal of blood, but effectively no *person*; there is a name that lies on the carpet, but no identity, no personality or history or affective content attached, not even a body in any real sense. The very English narrative voice appears more concerned with the lack of tidiness than with the old man.

Christie next engages in what we will see is the classic procedure for dealing with violence in detective fiction, a kind of intellectual aestheticization. It is the conversion of violence into ratiocination, and hence, the triumph of refinement and order over brutality and chaos, and, simultaneously, the renunciation of the reader's *desire*. This conversion takes place immediately, as the murder scene is a locked room mystery, probably the most historically venerable feature of the genre, and the one most consistently repeated: Simeon Lee's body is discovered in a room locked from the inside, with no other means of entrance or egress readily apparent. Christie takes the reader to a further level of aestheticization a few pages later when she has her characters engage in a typical Christie moment of self-referential irony: the Chief Constable (a Colonel Johnson) and Poirot engage in a conversation that replicates the exchange between Agatha and James in the novel's opening letter. "Always an awkward business, a poisoning case . . . give me a straightforward case. Something where there's no ambiguity about the cause of death," declares the Constable. Poirot replies with his typically awkward Gallic syntax: "The bullet wound, the cut throat, the crushed-in skull? It is there your preference lies?" (2000a, pp. 74–75). But the most remarkable moment in the conversation is the conversion of blood into an intellectual problem rather than a sign of violence, as several characters discuss the condition of the body with the doctor:

> Johnson turned to the doctor.
> "What about bloodstains?" he asked. "Surely whoever killed him must have got blood on him."
> The doctor said doubtfully:
> "Not necessarily. Bleeding was almost entirely from the jugular vein. That wouldn't spout like an artery."
> "No, no. Still, there seems a lot of blood about."
> Poirot said:
> "Yes, there is a lot of blood—it strikes one, that. A lot of blood. . . . There is something here—some violence. . . . Yes, that is it—*violence*. . . . And blood—an insistence on *blood*. . . . There is—how shall I put it?— there is *too much blood*." [2000a, pp. 89–90, original emphasis]

Readers of detective fiction, even in Christie's time, are on familiar ground here. Between the now proverbial "dog that didn't bark in the night" in Conan Doyle's "Adventure of Silver Blaze" and the "*too* plain, *too* self-evident" letter in Poe's "Purloined Letter," they have been trained to be alert to lack and excess as markers of a hidden truth. What we see in this scene is the conversion of quantity into quality: *blood* is a sign of violence, a personal trauma or a sociological or historical manifestation, but *too much blood* is an intellectual problem that must be solved. There is indeed a moment of violence, albeit rhetorically attenuated and as temporary as possible. What is entailed in the intellectualization of violence is precisely the misrecognition of what came before, forgetting the "good deal of blood" in favor of "too much blood." This sleight-of-hand is apparent in theories of the detective novel, as when W. H. Auden writes that the body of the victim "must shock not only because it is a corpse but also because, even for a corpse, it is shockingly out of place, as when a dog makes a mess on a drawing room carpet" (1968, p. 151). In fact, the corpse as a corpse in classic detective fiction is not shocking at all; it is always treated, as it is here in Christie's novel, as quintessentially symbolic in Lacanian terms, something that is always "out of place," a mobile and slippery signifier that calls for interpretation. Still in Lacanian terms, Simeon Lee's real body is not there at all—the only piece of him the reader sees is his name. In short, the problem is not that there is a dead body, but that there is a terrible social *faux pas,* and here one understands why classic detective fiction is fundamentally English, even if it was invented in America. *A dead body in the drawing roo*m! Good heavens! The guests might see it! What is avoided here, as in Žižek's "avoidance of the real of desire," is the corpse as the kernel of the real: something incomprehensible, uncanny, traumatic—a cognitive stalemate. In David Grossvogel's phrase, detective fiction begins with "a corpse to which is attached no sense of death" (1979, p. 15), but I am not at all sure that *Hercule Poirot's Christmas* gives us even that much.

So far, I have only suggested that Christie is engaged in what I characterized as the traditional triumph of rationality over the brutality of violence. But the cut in Simeon Lee's neck cuts a different way, as well. On the one hand, it absolves Christie of her brother-in-law's criticism, and so undoes or heals a familial cut, while on the other hand, it denies him precisely the spectacle he seems to have requested, and accomplishes this denial precisely through a spectacle, that is, a staged, theatrical contrivance without the danger of "authentic" violence. To return to the metaphor I used before, this is *exactly* like reality television; it offers a voyeuristic pleasure of seeing "the real thing" (that is, people behaving badly, in a literally cut-throat manner), with the fetishistic recognition that this "real thing" is completely staged and artificial. The theatrical, if you like, is disavowed, but not denied. The effect is quite the opposite of what one might experience in watching, for instance, a videotape of Islamic extremists beheading a kidnapped hostage.

In Christie, as *blood* becomes *too much blood*, it evaporates any pleasure or horror to be found in a socially transgressive desire for violence.

Blood, the victim's perforated body, the denaturing hollow space left in the social network by what was once a subject—all this must be forgotten in favor of a pleasure that is intellectual and aesthetic. Yet all the same, this is a kind of violence, too: the denial of the reader's desire and the erasure of the victim's trauma. This becomes the explicit procedure of the novel, for the solution, as Poirot reveals at the end, is that the blood is fake (a vial of animal blood mixed with sodium citrate to prevent it from coagulating), and the "shambles" of the room indicating a violent struggle are equally manufactured. In other words, the prominent use of the passive voice serves precisely to point to the deliberate artificiality and staging: "blood was splattered about." Lastly, the drawn-out, eerie wail attributed to the victim is actually an air bladder (a novelty item called a "Dying Pig") deflating. The killing had occurred hours earlier, and this entire scene was manufactured so that the murderer would have a safe alibi. In short, the blood requested by "dear James" has been, on the one hand, provided, and on the other hand, taken away through a theatrical *mise-en-scène*. If James wished to see a good violent murder, to have such a scene conjured up for him, he would surely be disappointed by this theatrical and absolutely fictive spectacle, if he ever remembered, after the intellectual distractions that comprise the substance of the book, that there was in fact a murder, in a scene that *neither he nor any other reader was ever privy to*. This is the curious status of violence in detective fiction: it must be there, but it must also be taken away. Indeed, in this novel, it was never really "there" in the sense of being present to the reader, a formula we will see again when we turn to Poe's "Murders in the Rue Morgue." The staging of violence is perhaps the clearest example of how detective fiction regularly makes use of the repeated scenes I referred to in the chapter on "Repetition." Violence is staged for the reader's pleasure, but it is precisely that staging, precisely the *mise-en-scène* itself, that removes from the violence the pleasure it is supposed to bring us.

In the bravura and complexity of these esoteric explanations that are so typical of Christie, but also the entire classical detective novel (deflating pig bladders and sodium citrate mixed with blood in *Hercule Poirot's Christmas*, a Dictaphone hooked up to a timer in *The Murder of Roger Ackroyd*), something is crucially lost, *forgotten*: someone died. Simeon Lee was murdered. The throat was cut, and there was blood. But the operations of the classic detective novel are entirely bent toward making the reader forget, turning, as quickly as possible, *blood* into *too much blood*. The detective does precisely what we normally ascribe to the killer: his actions *conceal the body* in classic detective fiction, exchanging a corpse for a corpus of evidence and deduction. This is the first, and perhaps the fore-most, fact to keep in mind in our approach to a genre that is so often theo-rized as "cognitive," that is, one principally concerned with inference, deduction, justification, logic, and so on: its fundamental cognitive proce-dure is *forgetting*.

BLOOD AND THEORY

Detective fiction is, broadly speaking, still under-theorized, although this is less true with each passing year. Much of the supposedly critical litera-ture on the detective novel, for instance, still consists of reader's guides to individual authors, to a particular subgenre, to recent women writers of detective fiction, and so on, rather than theoretical or interpretive texts that address how detective fiction works, or what a given work might mean beyond the level of plot. Probably the best-known theoretical approaches to detective fiction have been formalist, such as Shklovsky (1990) or Todorov (1977), with an emphasis on generic structures and formal pat-terns (the locked room mystery, the detective's conventional sidekick, etc.).[17] There have also been, especially recently, a number of significant ideological, sociological, or historical interventions, such as representations of race, class, and gender; crime fiction as a response to modernity; or the relationship between the development of crime fiction and Empire.[18] Most reader-based approaches to detective fiction stress its cognitive and active nature; it involves the reader directly in hermeneutic activity, according to these accounts. That is, there is the perception that the reader sleuths along-side the detective, or that the detective offers a kind of model behavior for the reader to pursue in his reading. This is particularly the case with clas-sic detective fiction, which appeals to ratiocination considerably more di-

---

17. Of course, Umberto Eco and Thomas Sebeok's work in *The Sign of Three* (1983) is a little more wide-ranging in its implications. For a more recent example of formal or genre-based criticism, see Marty Roth (1995).

18. Within just the past few years, for instance, on race alone there have been Maureen T. Reddy, *Traces, Codes, and Clues: Reading Race in Crime Fiction* (2003); Gina Macdonald, *Shaman or Sherlock? The Native American Detective* (2002); Megan E. Abbott, *The Street Was Mine: White Masculinity in Hardboiled Fiction and Film Noir* (2002); and Andrew Pepper, *The Contemporary American Crime Novel: Race, Ethnicity, Gender, Class* (2000). This interest in representations of race became particularly prolific at the begin-ning of the 1990s.

rectly than, say, the hard-boiled novel. "The reader must make conjectures about motives and outcomes in the textual design," writes one critic (Hernández Martín 1995, p. xi), and "the armchair reader equals the armchair sleuth," writes another (Lehman 2000, p. 198).[19] A frequent comparison is made between reading detective novels and doing crossword puzzles, a comparison that does shed some light.[20] Both are "escapist" leisure activities, both proceed by inference (guesses that are confirmed or modified as further information emerges), and the enjoyment of both depends on a promise of full revelation and the unary solution. As always, promises are made to be broken: the convention of the unary solution has been broken in both forms, as in Christie's *Murder on the Orient Express,* where one murderer is revealed as twelve, and two solutions are offered by Poirot to boot, or *The New York Times* crossword the day of the 1996 Presidential election (November 5). The crossword's principal horizontal clue was "lead story in tomorrow's newspaper," and could be solved in such a manner as to give the name of *either* of the major parties' candidates (this necessitated all of the intersecting vertical clues having bivalent answers, as well) having won. Nothing impinges on the promise of a full solution, however, the fundamental tenet of *solubility.*

The comparison between crossword puzzles and reading detective fiction also produces an analogy between reader and puzzle solver that suggests an active hermeneutic enterprise on the part of the reader: an accumulation of facts and clues, inferences and deductions. I will suggest

---

19. David Grossvogel discusses the genre's putative "desire to engage the participation of the reader," and claims detective fiction "invites the reader instead to participate . . . to play the game actively rather than through the passivity of a demonstration" (1979, p. 16). Probably the principal theoretical articulation of reading detective fiction as active gaming (based on Gadamer's notion of "transformed play") is George N. Dove's *The Reader and the Detective Story* (1997).

20. For example, Willard Wright notes a strong similarity between "the structure and mechanism of the crossword puzzle and of the detective novel" (1976, p. 35). Even an opponent of detective fiction such as Edmund Wilson (tongue-in-cheek) associates detective novels with "vices" like smoking and "crossword puzzles" (1950, p. 263). There is an entire mini-tradition of crossword puzzles as the basis of detective fiction, as in Dorothy Sayers's "The Fascinating Problem of Uncle Meleager's Will" (1995), or Nero Blanc's seven (to date) crossword-based detective novels, such as the awkwardly titled *Corpus de Crossword* (2003), or the equally forced *A Crossword to Die For* (2002). I will go on to discuss the connection between psychoanalysis and detective fiction, especially within Lacanian and New Lacanian theory, and so perhaps I should also recall Lacan's advice to a young analyst: "do crossword puzzles."

particularly in the next chapter that such a model is profoundly flawed, but the example of Christie that I opened this chapter with (and violence in detective fiction generally) is already a case in point: the reader, far from engaging in cognitive activity, is engaged in *forgetting*, forgetting real violence in favor of a spectacle manufactured for his passive enjoyment. The genre promises full revelation, even in the etymological sense of *detection* (to raise the roof, to lift the lid, as it were), but is founded perhaps principally on concealment.

Leaving aside for a moment the question of theories of detective fiction, we should note that detective fiction itself plays a significant supporting role in a major branch of theory: psychoanalysis. Several detective narratives have foundational roles in psychoanalytic theory. Quite famously, Jacques Lacan's seminar on "The Purloined Letter" spawned a series of theoretical interventions that are still ongoing, including Derrida, Johnson, Irwin, and Žižek.[21] I will certainly not try to answer the much-vexed question of how often the letter arrives at its destination here, but rather would like to point out that there is something noteworthy in this choice of Poe stories. As the originary text in this longstanding debate, Poe's tale acquires a particular importance for theoretical purposes. "The Purloined Letter" is an important story in the history of detective fiction, but it is hardly the most important or influential. Indeed, by some standards—perhaps the most important ones, including the role of violence in the story—it is quite anomalous. Its central role in psychoanalytic discourse, then, bears some significant scrutiny. It is especially worth examination because psychoanalysis itself seems as if it should have much to offer in an understanding of violence, enjoyment, and the kinds of knowledge both produced and erased by detective fiction.

"The Purloined Letter" has a much more important predecessor within the context of detective fiction and its generic conventions: "The Murders in the Rue Morgue." "Murders" is almost universally considered to be the first "proper" detective story, producing an unproblematic effect of familiar recognition in the modern reader. It is one of the most widely imitated pieces in the genre, and offers an amazing array of the genre's standard devices in Poe's very first foray (the locked room, the eccentric genius detective and his decidedly more mundane sidekick who serves as a nar-

---

21. I would be remiss if I didn't mention another important detective story (*ante litteram*, to be sure) for psychoanalytic theory: *Oedipus Rex*.

rator, the "trivial" opening episode of deduction unrelated to the investigation that follows, and many more).[22] And, unlike "The Purloined Letter," "Murders in the Rue Morgue" is quite violent—one is tempted to say unusually so, violent in a way that shows how a narrative *might* resist the facile forgetting that Christie so ably and successfully employs. Ultimately, Poe's story does employ such mechanisms—that is to say, it ultimately stages for us "the real thing" precisely as a way of distracting us from the real: all the *frisson* of an approach to the real with none of the danger—a kind of Real Lite. The scene of the killing is once again a room in shambles, but this time the blood is minimal and the violence perpetuated against the two victims, a mother and daughter, Madame and Mademoiselle L'Espanaye, is maximized:

> The apartment was in the wildest disorder—the furniture broken and thrown about in all directions. There was only one bedstead; and from this the bed had been removed, and thrown into the middle of the floor. On a chair lay a razor, besmeared with blood. On the hearth were two or three long and thick tresses of grey human hair, also dabbled in blood, and seeming to have been pulled out by the roots. . . .
>
> Of Madame L'Espanaye no traces were here seen; but an unusual quantity of soot being observed in the fire-place, a search was made in the chimney, and (horrible to relate!) the corpse of the daughter, head downward, was dragged therefrom; it having been thus forced up the narrow aperture for a considerable distance. The body was quite warm. Upon examining it, many excoriations were perceived, no doubt occasioned by the violence with which it had been thrust up and disengaged. Upon the face were many severe scratches, and, upon the throat, dark bruises, and deep indentations of finger nails, as if the deceased had been throttled to death.
>
> After a thorough investigation of every portion of the house, without farther discovery, the party made its way into a small paved yard in the rear of the building, where lay the corpse of the old lady, with her

---

22. Just as Christie's readers would have recognized "*too much blood*" as a paraphrase of Dupin's "*too self-evident*," they might also recognize the strange scream that every character describes differently as a kind of "citation" from "Murders in the Rue Morgue," where every character hears the killer speak a different language, but always one that is foreign. In both cases, this clever device is a way of approaching, but also safely normalizing, something that is "other," brutal and bestial. In fact, in both cases the sound is produced by an animal or an animal part (an orangutan and a pig bladder).

throat so entirely cut that, upon an attempt to raise her, the head fell off. The body, as well as the head, was fearfully mutilated—the former so much so as scarcely to retain any semblance of humanity. [1966, p. 8]

The passage is remarkable: it owes much of its efficacy to the fact that, at first glance, the bodies of the victims are not there, only "thick tresses of grey human hair," and also to its grotesque and uncanny inversion of the daughter's body, uncanny because the head-down figure in the "narrow aperture" is certainly a repetition of the baby in the birth canal, now certain to be stillborn.[23] The reader is left to imagine the force and violence necessary to push a human body up a fireplace upside-down (note Poe's use of the passive voice, almost a kind of ablative absolute, "it having been thus forced up the narrow aperture for a considerable distance," which leaves the agency responsible unnamed), not to mention the unspoken but suggested possibility that the daughter was still alive when this occurred ("the body was quite warm"). The entire passage has the especially disturbing effect of dehumanizing the victims. We begin with uprooted "human hair" and end with a body that scarcely retains "any semblance of humanity," while the "trick" or "misdirection" of the story involves precisely the "humanizing" of the murderer. Every character, as well as the reader, assumes the killer is a human being, but quite famously, it is eventually revealed to be an "Ourang-Outang," whose bestial nature and climbing ability explain the lack of motive for the crime and the apparently impossible egress from the room.

The presence of the orangutan points at a prior violence, however, one that is common to much (one is tempted to say nearly *all*) nineteenth century detective fiction: the primate is abducted from an excursion into Borneo and brought back to Europe for sale. It is colonial violence, then, that permits the rest of the narrative (as in Collins's *The Moonstone*, Conan Doyle's *The Sign of Four*, or, for that matter, Brontë's *Jane Eyre*), a clear instance of the return of the repressed, in the figure of the oppressed. In Poe's text, the orangutan also points to the working out of anxieties about a specifically American form of colonial violence: this almost human-seeming animal, who speaks what sounds like a human language, who must be controlled with a whip, brought from a distant foreign land to be sold

---

23. This is a typical instance of the corpse in detective fiction as an uncanny repetition of some earlier "primal scene," noted from the very first by Marie Bonaparte in *The Life and Works of Edgar Allan Poe: A Psycho-analytic Interpretation* (1949).

here for profit, who places the local women at risk. This figure is obviously the African slave (Poe himself was an apologist for slavery). Jon Thompson, in *Fiction, Crime and Empire,* recognizes that Poe's detective stories are American "wish-fulfillment fantasies" (1993, p. 45), but oddly misses this possible reading, even when discussing slavery.

As remarkable as this passage is, what is more remarkable still is that Poe nevertheless manages to aestheticize and intellectualize, to compel the forgetting of violence. "You will see," Dupin says, once his ratiocination is under full steam, turning the reader's attention from the trauma done to the two victims to the entirely narcissistic question of how and why this scene was staged for our benefit, "that I have shifted the question . . ." (1966, p. 19). Poe layers narrative upon narrative—three newspaper accounts, including one that prints twelve individual witnesses' accounts; Dupin and the narrator's investigation, and the sailor's final tale, each of which progressively distances us from the uncanny violence, and each of which is bent entirely on either perplexing the reader (How did the murderer escape? How could each witness hear the killer speak in a different language?) or assuaging his or her resulting intellectual anxieties through explanation. The final line of the story is Dupin's contemptuous description of the Prefect of Police, a quotation from Rousseau's *Nouvelle Heloise*: the Prefect has "*de nier ce qui est, et d'expliquer ce qui n'est pas*" [to deny what is, and explain what is not] (1966, p. 26). Such a sentence literally posits explication and explanation in detective fiction as a compensation for a corresponding denial, the denial of violence. In this respect, as well then, "The Murders in the Rue Morgue" is a genuine prototype for the genre. Why, then, does it not play a similarly central role in psychoanalytic theory?

Lacan and others appreciate "The Purloined Letter" for its insistence that truth is hidden on the surface of things, and that the detective or the analyst might access that truth by a careful attention to superficial forms.[24]

---

24. Freud himself was a "regular and careful reader" of Sherlock Holmes stories, according to his patient, the "Wolf-Man," "precisely on account of the parallel between the respective procedures of the detective and the analyst" (Žižek 1990, p. 29). Žižek illuminates a whole series of parallels in this article between the detective's analysis of the crime and the analyst's hermeneutic effort in a patient's interpreting dreamwork and narratives: the necessity of the false solution, the intersubjective nature of seemingly loony (i.e., pathological) behaviors by either the criminals or the innocent, the detective/analyst as *le sujet supposé savoir*, the "subject supposed to know," and so on.

The psychoanalytic lessons, however, in "Murders in the Rue Morgue," are no less suitable to the demands of Lacanian theoretical discourse. The scene of the ape attempting to shave with a straight razor in front of a mirror, a sight that produces an excessive shock and horror on the part of the on-looker, seems tailor-made for a Lacanian excursus, not to mention the series of misrecognitions that afflict all of the witnesses. "The Purloined Letter," however, permits the psychoanalytic theorist to recognize himself or herself in the scene of analysis presented by the text, whereas "Murders" does not. Note that I am not saying that "Letter" offers a better analogue to the analytic scene—just that its textual mechanisms better facilitate an iden-tification with the figure of the detective. It is only a short step from here to suggest that this is an imaginary identification, or, to use Lacanian ter-minology, a *méconnaissance*. In fact, what makes "The Purloined Letter" so appealing for the psychoanalytic theorist and "Murders" so unsuitable is the apparent eccentricity of the detective, the way he seems to stand out-side of the circuit and circle of desire and enjoyment.

Žižek, for example, is quick to point out (a little *too* quick, Dupin might say) that the detective's payment is what enables him to opt out of the symbolic debts and libidinal economy that governs the other characters, just as the analyst's fee enables him or her to stand outside of the libidinal circuit that traverses the patient. As a result, the classic detective "accepts with accentuated pleasure payment for the services he has rendered" (Žižek 1992, p. 60). The detective's enjoyment must remain confined to a purely monetary realm. Žižek would like to contrast the situation in classic de-tective fiction to the detective in later hard-boiled or *noir* narratives who is, he claims, involved in the libidinal circuit but uninterested in money. Even if such a procedure worked (which indeed seems doubtful—Lacan [1966, p. 48] calls money the *"signifiant le plus annihilant qui soit de toute signification"* [the most destructive signifier that there might be of all signi-fication], whereas as any reader of nineteenth century novels knows, there are few signifiers more *productive* of signification), there is every reason to believe that Dupin is constantly caught up in his own circuit of symbolic debts and pleasures, long before he receives payment or possesses the let-ter, most notably in his constant and intense pleasure at humiliating the Prefect of Police and Minister D———. Dupin's love of humiliating others is already clear in "Murders in the Rue Morgue."

Unfortunately, the scene of "accentuated pleasure" over the detective's payment is exceedingly rare in classical detective fiction. It is almost never the case in the Sherlock Holmes stories. In *A Study in Scarlet*, Holmes mentions once near the beginning that he normally receives a "fee," but at the end of the novel, he receives only a "testimonial" that grossly under-represents his role in the case. No fee is ever mentioned in *The Sign of Four*, and indeed, Watson wonders aloud at the end: "You have done all the work in this business. I get a wife out of it, Jones gets the credit, pray what remains for you?" (Conan Doyle 2001, p. 118)—the answer being cocaine. Out of the twelve *Adventures of Sherlock Holmes*, Holmes only explicitly accepts payment in one ("The Adventure of the Beryl Coronet," where fully three-quarters of the payment is what Holmes had to pay to recover the jewels), and explicitly refuses monetary recompense in "A Scandal in Bohemia" and "The Adventure of the Speckled Band," where he states that the solution is its own reward. In fact, he strongly suggests that his policy is to accept only a voluntary defraying of his expenses; it is implicitly clear that in a majority of the stories, he does not take payment. Certainly there is no "accentuated pleasure" in payment. It is equally rare if not more so in Christie's novels. Does Miss Marple *ever* accept payment for her services? Payment is only rarely mentioned in the Poirot novels, and a description of the actual scene of payment, let alone Poirot's pleasure, is even more rare. In fact, even in Poe's three detective stories, only one features Dupin actually accepting payment: "The Purloined Letter."

It is no accident that "Letter" is also the only Dupin story to be free of the kind of explicit violence that so heavily marks "Murders in the Rue Morgue." And herein lies the other reason that "Murders" does not assume a central role in psychoanalytic theory: its fundamental cognitive/libidinal procedure—the forgetting of violence—is the seeming opposite of the scene of analysis. In other words, detective fiction relies on a *méconnaissance* by the reader, a misrecognition of the content of the story: I thought this was a story about a traumatic and violent breach, but now I see that it is an intellectual puzzle to be solved.[25] What is remarkable about the privileging of "The Purloined Letter" in psychoanalytic discourse is that it repeats precisely this misrecognition. It forgets the "Purloined Letter"'s violent past, just as it turns a blind eye to its own enjoyment, preferring to believe that it can buy its way out of symbolic debt and a tainted pleasure in the suffering of the characters investigated by the detective. As Dupin says, notably using language that combines pleasure and economics, "an inquiry will afford us amusement" (Poe 1966, p. 13). The detection of violence is what

---

25. This is in fact a double *méconnaissance*, as detective fiction encourages a misidentification of itself as an intellectual and hermeneutic puzzle, whereas in reality "all the tension of the work is directed, through a detailed organization of invisibility, toward *the prevention of thought*" (Bayard 2000, p. 25, original emphasis).

buys the detective pleasure, buys him into the tissue of the narrative and a sequence of symbolic debts that may, but usually do not, include a fee. And here we come to the key that unites violence, payment, and enjoyment: *the detective's "real" or proper fee has always already been paid in detective fiction, but paid by someone else.* Madame L'Espanaye, for instance.

I would suggest that the rare "other" scene of payment is indeed always a destabilizing and dangerous surplus that functions not to *cancel out* a symbolic debt but precisely to *initiate* one, to mark the detective as embroiled within the same libidinal economy that regulates the other subjects in the text, and, by extension, the reader as well.[26] The example of payment at the end of the film version of Christie's *Murder on the Links* (1995) is very clear on this point: Poirot has made a bet with the blustering detective Giraud about who will solve the case first. If Poirot does, Giraud will give him his trademark pipe; if Giraud does, Poirot will shave off his trademark moustache. At the end of the novel, Giraud arrives to surrender his pipe. Poirot refuses his proper payment, but precisely in order to make it clear that there is an entirely different payoff at stake for the detective: his rival's humiliation, and his own sneering, contemptuous superiority. This is not to suggest that the detective's "eccentric" position has been misunderstood. As I will argue in the chapter on "Enjoyment," the classic detective is almost invariably marked as socially defective or debilitated, a bar to any normal satisfaction of desire. Rather, his sole contact with the social field takes place precisely in this series of sadistic gestures (humiliation, superiority, gloating, and the like). The novel *Murder on the Links* (originally published in 1923) confines its payment to a bet of 500 francs, plus a whole series of humiliations that end up with Giraud having a nervous breakdown and returning to Paris. On rare occasions, the detective may himself be the butt of such humiliations, as in Doyle's "A Scandal in Bohemia," but most often, the reader is invited to share in the detective's rare pleasure in humiliating his colleagues and sidekick, and, by extension, as I argue in "Enjoyment," the reader. How are we

---

26. A full-fledged critique of psychoanalysis is certainly beyond the scope and outside the focus of this project, but this certainly raises the question: If detective fiction and psychoanalysis are, in fact, analogous, then the patient, too, has always already "paid the price" in the form of a traumatic and pathology-inducing brush with the Real, a brush that "affords some amusement" to the analyst. What does this make of the analyst's fee? It is perhaps no accident that it is precisely at the moment when he arrives at the corpse that Žižek claims that "the homology between the procedure of the analyst and that of the detective reveals its limits" (1990, p. 39). Perhaps instead this is precisely the point where the homology also reveals itself most fully.

to refer to this monomaniacal, egocentric, antisocial character who is capable of interacting with others only through humiliation and cruelty if not a sociopath? Psychoanalysis might do well to think twice before taking the classic detective as a model.

To sum up what I have tried to articulate so far: although many theoretical approaches to detective fiction emphasize the active role of the reader, working alongside the detective accumulating evidence and facts, the actual set of cognitive tropes employed by classical detective fiction consists primarily of misdirection, omission, and forgetting. A consideration of violence affords several striking examples of the detective genre as a genre of forgetting, from its earliest examples (Poe's first stories), to its classic instantiations in detective fiction's "golden age" (Christie's novels), to its theoretical appropriations by psychoanalysis. This structure of forgetting, however, must also leave open the possibility of remembering. To return to psychoanalytic theory, it must leave open the possibility of the return of the repressed. I have already suggested in Christie's novel that the repression of real violence in the narrative returns in a series of critical cuts toward her brother-in-law, undermining the domestic and familial tranquility seemingly produced by the mystery's solution at the end. I would like to turn now to an example of detective fiction that is highly self-aware, highly attuned precisely to questions of forgetting and its epistemological and ideological consequences.

LITTLE NOODLES

Italy has a curious relationship to detective fiction: the political, ideological, and historical coordinates that configure classic British detective fiction, for example (i.e., late nineteenth, early twentieth century upper-middle class nostalgia in a state with a strong national identity on the verge of losing its Empire), largely do not apply to Italy at the same time.[27] At the end

---

27. For a long time, virtually the only history of Italian detective fiction was Loris Rambelli's *Storia del "giallo" italiano* [History of the Italian "Whodunit"] (1979), which just barely missed the publication of Italy's only truly famous mystery novel: Umberto Eco's *Il nome della rosa* [*The Name of the Rose*] (1980). Recently Luca Crovi has added two volumes to the bibliography: *Delitti di carta nostra: Una storia del giallo italiano* [*Crimes of Our Pages: A History of the Italian Whodunit*] (2000) and *Tutti i colori del giallo: il giallo italiano da De Marchi a Scebanenco a Camilleri* [All Kinds of Whodunit: The Italian Crime Novel from DeMarchi to Scebanenco to Camilleri] (2002).

of the nineteenth century, Italy had only recently politically unified in 1861, remained linguistically fragmented with a very strong sense of regional identity, had a small middle class, was largely illiterate, and was only beginning what would be a very belated and troubled relationship to empire. As the Marxist theorist Antonio Gramsci famously noted years later, even in the middle of the twentieth century, Italy had no national popular literature into which a genre like detective fiction could be inserted. It would be safe to say that Italy acquired a national popular culture quite late, largely through television, and it is an open question whether there is even today what could be called a national popular literature. Certainly almost all genre fiction in Italy is imported. Moreover, Italian literature after the Middle Ages and Renaissance has a marginal relationship to the other Western European literatures. All of this works to make Italian detective fiction stand at the margins of the margins, as it were. And indeed, the early examples of formulaic detective fiction (there are examples of crime fiction like Emilio De Marchi's *Il cappello del prete*, originally published in 1887, that have a more Dostoyevskian character) are all marked by a strong parodic or ironic feel, occasionally, as in Luciano Folgore's *La trappola colorata,* originally published in 1934, so strong as to render the narrative almost surreal or oneiric. Whatever the sources of pleasure and fascination in classic detective fiction, it is clear that a writer like Folgore, like so many other writers of early detective fiction in Italy, didn't "get it." However, these early ironic texts are often effective, if somewhat adolescent, at exposing the genre's most problematic presumptions: they ridicule and lay bare the detective's belief in totalizing knowledge, his trivial deductions, the episodic and mixed-genre nature of classical detective fiction.[28]

Italian detective fiction also arrives belatedly, in the first years of the 1930s. Alessandro Varaldo's *Il Sette bello,* originally published in 1931, is generally credited as the first Italian detective novel. Given fascist censorship, the Italian relationship to this predominantly Anglo-French genre was

---

28. Loris Rambelli notes that Alessandro Varaldo's *Il Sette bello,* for example, depends on "il capriccio del caso" [the whim of fate], "incredibili coincidenze" [incredible coincidences] that result in the most "inverosimili" [inverosimilar] behaviors by the characters, not to mention a preference for the irrational rather than the scientific (sleepwalking, dreams that foretell the future, and so on) (1979, p. 38). He also mentions its pastiche-like, although not intentionally parodic, qualities of the novel, as well (p. 33). Arturo Lanocita's *Quaranta milioni,* originally published in 1931, is, however, along with Folgore's *La trappola colorata,* probably the best example of the early Italian detective novel as parody of the genre. Lanocita's version is rather more sophisticated, and his production of parodic novels continued into the 1940s.

potentially quite complex. Virtually all detective fiction in Italy appeared in translation, but what was written by Italians (Varaldo, Augusto de Angelis, Arturo Lanocita) was initially tolerated by the fascists under the rubric of national self-sufficiency, or autarchy. Italy was supposed to produce everything her citizens needed, from food and raw materials to cultural goods, although the problem of representing crime in the fascist state would remain difficult. Writers like de Angelis feature the occasional obligatory exclamation "quello non poteva essere il delitto di un italiano!" [that could not have been the crime of an Italian!] (1963, p. 86). The citation is from *L'Albergo delle Tre Rose,* originally published in 1936, and is worthy of comment in the often racialized and nationalistic context of classic detective fiction. In Conan Doyle, foreigners are suspect and indeed, many of the threats do emerge from abroad, but as often as not, an Englishman plays a central role in the commission of the crime. In *The Sign of Four,* for instance, the pygmy Tonga is a source of violence and horror, but Jonathan Small receives the lion's share of the text's blame. Agatha Christie regularly has her proper British subjects suspect the foreigners in the group, but typically as a way of mocking their insular small-mindedness. De Angelis's text is instead typical of a kind of ideological schizophrenia produced by fascist censorship: the detective frequently exclaims, apropos of nothing and with no justification, that the killer could not be Italian, a kind of transcendental and a priori truth. At the end of the day, both the crime's mastermind and the actual killer are Italian, tainted by foreignness, to be sure (an Italian-American and an Italian woman with an English name), but nonetheless Italian. Not coincidentally, de Angelis was jailed and harassed for his anti-fascism. Still, the Italian government eventually decided that detective fiction was irremediably marked by foreignness, and banned any new publication of detective fiction and recalled much that was already published in August of 1941. This was followed by the Ministry of Popular Culture's sequestration of all detective fiction in Italy, regardless of when it was printed, in June of 1943.

So what does it mean for an Italian writer to choose classical detective fiction as a model? A history of irony and exclusion from both the outside (the marginal status of post-Renaissance Italian culture) and the inside (official censure of the genre as insufficiently Italian), suggests it might mean a certain freedom from the genre's generic, ideological, epistemological, and psychic structures and procedures.[29] This is certainly the case

---

29. For an Italian writing in the immediate aftermath of World War II, like Carlo Emilio Gadda, it also can probably be fairly seen as a repudiation of fascism and its isolationist

for what is one of the most remarkable literary achievements in postwar Italian literature: Carlo Emilio Gadda's *Quer pasticciaccio brutto de via Merulana* [*That Awful Mess on Via Merulana*]. Readers who have even a modicum of Italian will realize from the title alone that there is something linguistically strange here. Gadda's writing is self-consciously positioned within Italy's linguistically fragmented milieu. The novel's prose densely and rapidly combines Venetian, Neapolitan, Roman, and Molisan dialects (occasionally simultaneously), "standard" Italian from the deeply vulgar to the most courtly and literary, technical jargon from crystallography to philosophy, and a smattering of French, English, German, and of course, Latin and ancient Greek. It is very hard to read, not to mention untranslatable, despite William Weaver's best efforts,[30] and yet deliberately positioned outside of Italy's official literary language and modeled on a popular and foreign generic model.

It is also worth mentioning, as it will have obvious consequences for writing a detective novel, that Gadda never finished even a single one of his major works. It is certainly the case that his manipulation of the conventions of classic detective fiction is wholesale—that is, it is not confined solely to the omission of the generic requirement of full revelation at the novel's end. There is no final revelation of the truth and concomitant final arrest of the criminal, but the detective is also explicitly situated within the circle of desire and symbolic debt—and there is no forgetting of the violence. Similarly, Gadda makes every attempt to mark his detective, don Ciccio Ingravallo, with the stain of desire, from the very first description: his eyes may be "metafisici" [metaphysical], (1993, p. 3) but his lapel also bears "una o due macchioline d'olio" [one or two little oil stains] (p. 3). Likewise, his philosophical inclination to "riformare in noi il senso della categoria della causa . . . quale avevamo dai filosofi, da Aristotele o da

---

policies of national superiority. Gadda also had other reasons for choosing detective fiction as a template for his novel: its cognitive pretensions and discourses on method left him ample opportunity for "filosofare a stomaco vuoto" [philosophizing on an empty stomach], as Gadda says of his detective protagonist (1993, p. 5).

30. Weaver has translated both of Gadda's major novels, *Quer pasticciaccio brutto de via Merulana* [*That Awful Mess on Via Merulana*] (1965), and *La cognizione del dolore* [*Acquainted with Grief*] (1969) as well as anyone could, but often Gadda's simplest wordplay remains inert, especially in American English. Perhaps an entire novel whose narration rapidly oscillated between and cross-contaminated Cockney, Scottish dialect, and upper crust English, with frequent excursions into Kant and Aristotle that featured alarming vulgarities, would come close.

Emmanuele Kant" [reform our notion of the category of cause . . . which we have from philosophers, from Aristotle or from Immanuel Kant] (p. 4) is stained by his relationship to women, of whom he has "una certa conoscenza" [a certain knowledge] (p. 3). Ingravallo frequently repeats, as a truism, "ch'i femmene se retroveno addó n'i vuò truvà," [that ya find wimmin right where ya don't wanna] (p. 5), which Gadda mocks as a "tarda riedizione italica" [late Italian re-issue] of the French *cherchez la femme.*[31] But after uttering this phrase, Ingravallo "pareva pentirsi, come d'aver calunniato 'e femmene, e voler mutare idea" [would seem to repent, as if he'd slandered wimmin, and wished to change his mind] (p. 5). In other words, Ingravallo is situated from the beginning of the text in an unstable relationship to women, a potentially paralyzing double bind of suspicion and adoration.

The example that follows is the description of the body of the murder victim, Liliana Balducci. A "proper" citation from Gadda would necessarily require dozens if not hundreds of pages, as every scene is always enmeshed, situated within a subdigression of a digression from what appeared to be a principal plot. Ingravallo is found at last by one of his subordinates, who informs him confusedly that there has been a murder in Via Merulana. The victim is something more than an acquaintance of Ingravallo's. His subordinate uses language that explicitly situates the detective and the victim in a set of oedipal coordinates, as do numerous other references in the novel: "Hanno tajato la gola, ma scusi . . . so che lei è un po' parente . . . Volevo dire, amico" [Dey cut her throat, but sorry . . . I know that yer kinda a relative . . . I mean, friend] (p. 45). After a long digression on the state of Liliana's underwear (a typical Gaddian obsession), Ingravallo finally raises his eyes to the wound, and here we cannot help notice how radically different Gadda's description of a cut throat is from Christie's:

Un profondo, un terribile taglio rosso le apriva la gola, ferocemente.
Aveva preso metà del collo, dal davanti vero destra, cioè verso sinistra,

---

31. I mentioned before that Gadda was untranslatable. The best translations of his work, like Weaver's, adopt a neutral, standard English, but unfortunately lose the macaronic tissue of his language; this seems better, however, than a series of non-standard Englishes that do not properly "map" onto the deformations of the original. I have adopted the latter approach, however, in these examples, because it is precisely these deformations that work to keep the body of the victim from ever being forgotten, from ever becoming "too much blood."

per lei, destra per loro che guardavano: sfrangiato ai due margini come da un reiterarsi dei colpi, lama o punta: un orrore! da nun potesse vede. Palesava come delle filacce rosse, all'interno, tra quella spumiccia nera der sangue, già raggrumato, a momenti; un pasticcio! con delle bollicine rimaste a mezzo. Curiose forme, agli agenti: parevano buchi, al novizio, come dei maccheroncini color rosso, o rosa. 'La trachea,' mormorò Ingravallo chinandosi, 'la carotide! la iugulare . . . Dio!' [1993, p. 47]

A deep, a terrible red cut opened her throat, ferociously. It had taken up half of the neck, from the front toward the right, that is toward the left, for her, right for those who were looking: fringed at the two edges as if by a reiteration of blows, blade or point: a horror! Ya just couddn't lookaddit. It was as manifest as certain red threadlets, on the inside, amid that black frothling o' blood, already gummed up, moments ago: a mess! with some small bubbles left in the middle. Strange shapes, to the agents: they looked like holes, to the novice, like little macaroni noodles, colored red, or pink. 'The trachea,' Ingravallo murmured, bending over, 'the carotid! The jugular . . . God!'

Here, unlike Christie or Poe, the actual wound is depicted as a breach in the body, a fringed slit in the throat. The sexual nature of the image is not atypical for Gadda; the wound is described as if it were a repulsive horizontal vaginal aperture, a symbolic compensation for the immaculate and impenetrable "candore affascinante" [fascinating candor] (1993, p. 46) of Liliana's undergarments. The erotically charged description of Liliana's underwear that precedes it marks the wound as a violation, one that Gadda crucially compels us to see *from the perspective of the beholder, but also from that of the victim*: "It had taken up half of the neck, from the front toward the right, that is toward the left, for her, right for those who were looking."[32] The passage is especially marked by the disturbing presence of diminutives (*filacce, spumiccia, bollicine*; threadlets, frothling, small bubbles), which culminate in the classically grotesque *maccheroncini*, or little noodles. The severed blood vessels in Liliana's neck appear to the agents in cross-section, and so seem like hollow tubes of red or pink pasta. Food in the throat, in yet another uncanny repetition.

Liliana and her violated body haunt the rest of the novel, just as her suffering and bloodied body literally haunt the theater and film adapta-

---

32. Images of castration abound in Gadda, particularly in this novel. See Pedullà, 1997, especially pp. 24–44, on castration as a positive force in Gadda.

tion, where, as other characters discuss her fate, she wanders the stage after her death, perhaps nowhere so clearly as the *Pasticciaccio*'s final scene.[33] Ingravallo has gone to confront Assunta, one of Liliana's former maids, hoping she will tell him the name of the killer. Her reply, and Ingravallo's reaction, form the novel's final sentences:

> 'No, nun so' stata io!' Il grido incredibile bloccò il furore dell'ossesso. Egli non intese, là pe llà, ciò che la sua anima era in procinto d'intendere. Quella piega nera verticale tra i due sopraccigli dell'ira, nel volto bianchissimo della ragazza, lo paralizzò, lo indusse a riflettere: a ripentirsi, quasi. [1993, p. 264]

> 'No, it waddn't me!' The unbelievable cry blocked the fury of the man obsessed. He didn't comprehend, den and dere, what his soul was on the verge of comprehending. That black vertical fold between the two eyebrows of rage, in the girl's white, white face, paralyzed him, propelled him to reflect: to repent, almost.

Liliana's wound appears again here, now located on Assunta's forehead, a *piega nera verticale*, a black vertical fold. This reminder, this remembering, is also a dis-membering, as it leads to a castrating language of arrest and blockage, incomprehension, a return to the original shock and cognitive stasis produced by the violence done to Liliana's body. Ingravallo "non intese" (didn't understand) and is "paralyzed"; the promise of being "in procinto d'intendere" (on the verge of comprehending) and of a repentance are all belied by the novel's final word "almost." Dombroski calls the *piega* in Assunta's forehead "a fold in the tissue of narration" (1999, p. 103) and I would like to adopt this phrase in a slightly different sense. This *piega nera verticale* produces a Möebius-like fold in the novel, a return to the "profondo . . . terribile taglio rosso" [deep . . . terrible red cut] in Liliana's neck. This Möebius fold also quite literally returns the reader almost to the novel's first page, to Ingravallo's libidinal-epistemological deadlock with regard to women, his desire to "pentirsi" [repent] (Gadda 1993, p. 5) for his slander of women, a deadlock we find unchanged here at the end. In

---

33. The various adaptations postulate different killers: Virginia Troddu in Gadda's own screenplay, *Il palazzo degli ori*, to have been directed by Antonioni but tragically never made; Assunta in Luca Ronconi's theater and film version of the novel; one critic argues that the logic of Freudian negation, among other proofs, demonstrates that the *Pasticciaccio* does indeed reveal the killer (Assunta) in Amigoni (1996).

other words, Gadda's *Pasticciaccio* is a remembering—even an obsessive remembering—of violence and of the tissue of its own narrative. The wounds in the body become traumatic incisions that mark its extraction from the Symbolic network: it becomes the hole of the Real that both supports and frames Symbolic reality, no longer re-normalized by the detective's intellectualizing of violence and ultimate solution, but left as a "foreign body" to disrupt the subject's enjoyment. This extraction, or hole, that frames and supports reality, and that remains as a foreign body is also identified as the object (a) (see Žižek 1992, pp. 94–95 and Žižek 2001, pp. 48–49).

We are now, I think, in a position to give a psychoanalytic explanation of the curious status of the body in detective fiction, why there must be "a good violent murder with lots of blood" that is, at the same time, taken away from the reader. The body is immediately identifiable with the stain of the real, "this remainder of the real that 'sticks out'" (Žižek 1992, p. 93), a term Žižek employs principally within a cinematic context. It is the distant dot of the approaching biplane in *North By Northwest*, or the glow of Thorwald's cigarette in *Rear Window*. In short, it is the mark that not all is well with the world, a minute stain that deforms and denatures the entire frame. This is assuredly the role of the body on the carpet in the drawing room, again, "shockingly out of place," as W. H. Auden says (1968, p. 151), which immediately renders the entirety of the social/symbolic network unstable, a stain that spreads to transform every character into a suspect, and denatures (in classic detective fiction) the stolid middle-class domestic world into a place that is uncanny, surreal. At the same time, it is the extraction of this bit that "sticks out" that *frames* reality, indeed gives it its "realistic" (i.e., normal) nature; again, it is the task of the detective to *conceal* the body, to extract it from the frame in order to restore the social and symbolic network, an extraction that is as much of a cut as the one on Simeon Lee's or Liliana Balducci's neck.[34] The body, then, becomes merely a memory of something seen in the corner of one's eye, a stain that was

---

34. This certainly suggests that the detective is always left holding the object (a), becomes a kind of custodian of the traumatic kernel of the real. He carries and conceals the entirety of the Žižekian stain, then, by the end of the classic detective novel. And this is what is so remarkable about Ingravallo, who remains visibly marked by his "macchioline" (little stains) from the novel's first pages, and who refuses to carry this burden, letting the stain continue to spread, perhaps even beyond the edges of the text, perhaps even as far as the reader.

revealed as something like an optical illusion, only perceived when "looking awry." Agatha Christie's brother-in-law James posits the violated body as a potential source of enjoyment ("may it give you pleasure," writes Christie), but the object (a) is precisely "the reef, the obstacle which interrupts the closed circuit of the 'pleasure principle'" (Žižek 2001, p. 48). In this view, it is the aim of detective fiction *to deny the reader's pleasure*, precisely through the inevitable and immediate loss of the object (a), the body. Žižek goes on to outline a psychic movement that has always been evident in readers of detective fiction, an obsessive pathology that has always proved the principal fodder for critics of the genre like Edmund Wilson (1950): the novels are all the same, and readers consume them as if they were chain smoking—more precisely, that as a vice, it "ranks somewhere between smoking and crossword puzzles" (1950, p. 263). How is this possible?

> The final step to be taken is to grasp this inherent impediment in its *positive* dimension: true, the *objet a* prevents the circle of pleasure from closing, it introduces an irreducible displeasure, but the psychic apparatus finds a sort of perverse pleasure *in this displeasure itself*, in the never-ending, repeated circulation around the unattainable, always missed object. The Lacanian name for this pleasure-in-pain is of course enjoyment (*jouissance*), and the circular movement which finds satisfaction in failing again and again to attain the object . . . is the Freudian *drive*. [Žižek 2001, p. 48, italics original]

Is there not, in this discussion of Gadda, Poe, and Christie, an implicit sense that Gadda's novel is "superior" in some way? After all, his novel is an acknowledged literary masterpiece in Italy (although it is virtually unknown in the rest of the world), rich in stylistic and philosophical subtleties, featuring textual mechanisms that emphasize remembrance over forgetting, providing altogether a sense of honesty and forthrightness when contrasted to Christie's "bad faith." Wouldn't James have been happier with Gadda's "good, violent murder with lots of blood" in a way that he could not possibly have been with Christie's? After all, the murder of Liliana Balducci is truly violent, not a simulacrum of violence; there is truly "no doubt about it being murder" and the blood there is real, not chemically manufactured. Perhaps above all, she is human, and her death is human. No animal intervention (orangutans, pig's blood, and pig bladders) is required or used.

Although this is all true, Žižek's observation about enjoyment and drive turns this scenario on its head: it is *Christie's* text that follows the

Žižekian imperative to "enjoy your symptom!" Gadda's novel, on the other hand, along with so much other so-called anti-detective fiction, short-circuits readers' perverse enjoyment by actually giving them what they want—the body—thus following the Lacanian imperative to "not give up on one's desire" (*ne pas céder sur son désire*). The problem lies in the fact that this short-circuit of drive and enjoyment has precisely the opposite effect that it is supposed to achieve: it offers a "normal," "healthy" model of desire that aims to destroy the pathological or "loony" behavior of the compulsive mystery novel reader. Finally, we can stop all of that compulsive serial reading that so troubles commentators on the detective novel, reading one novel after another, when they are in fact all the same. For all of the insistence that detective fiction is politically and ideologically conservative, it might make us suspicious that reading literary fiction, including those works that are inspired by detective fiction, from Gadda to Pynchon, receives a tacit or explicit social approval. If these texts truly promote a radical confrontation with the real of desire, then they do so in a way that is remarkably socially acceptable, even socially esteemed. Reading Christie and even Poe, at least in the United States where he is still seen as a children's writer, is, on the other hand, a frivolous waste of time, a "guilty pleasure" to use a term I will make much of in the next chapter. Why should we enjoy our symptom? Precisely because something in this enjoyment disturbs the powers that be, not in the sense of a radical call to arms, but in an unpreventable and everyday fashion, an obstinate persistence that *annoys* rather than challenges. Readers of detective fiction may now join the ranks of cigarette smokers, gum chewers, and teenagers who play their music too loudly: addicts (to anticipate another term from the next chapter) who bother us with their obstinate, public enjoyment, addicts who refuse to be cured of their addiction.

7

ENJOYMENT: *Conan Doyle* | Monk | *Eco*

REPETITION AND ADDICTION

My students are often surprised to discover that Sherlock Holmes was addicted to cocaine. It is an aspect of the detective's image that, unlike his deerstalker cap, which never actually appears in the novels and stories, and magnifying glass, has largely failed to seize the popular imagination, particularly as we have decided to receive Conan Doyle principally as children's literature. Nonetheless, one could make a persuasive case that Holmes's addiction is no less iconic than his cap and glass, and I will make the case in this chapter that it is considerably more important, not only for Conan Doyle, but for the entire genre. Addiction appears early as a trope within detective fiction, and although it rarely appears in the explicit form that it takes in Conan Doyle, I will argue that it continues to appear as a constitutive feature of the detective within the "classic" form of the genre. (In this chapter I will confine my analysis to detection of this classic variety.) The beginning of Conan Doyle's *The Sign of Four*, originally published in 1890, suggests that Sherlock Holmes actually alternates between morphine and cocaine, and is rather alarming to the modern reader for the depth of Holmes's addiction. Contemporary readers would not have been as well acquainted with the drug's dangers, but it still would have represented a significant character flaw, a weakness or defect in this otherwise super-human rationality:

> Sherlock Holmes took his bottle from the corner of the mantelpiece, and his hypodermic syringe from its neat morocco case. With his long, white, nervous fingers he adjusted the delicate needle and rolled back his left shirtcuff. For some little time his eyes rested thoughtfully upon the sinewy forearm and wrist, all dotted and scarred with innumerable puncture-marks. Finally, he thrust the sharp point home, pressed down the tiny piston, and sank back into the velvet-lined armchair with a long sigh of satisfaction.
>
> Three times a day for many months I had witnessed this performance, but custom had not reconciled my mind to it. . . .
>
> Yet upon that afternoon, whether it was the Beaune which I had taken with my lunch or the additional exasperation produced by the extreme deliberation of his manner, I suddenly felt that I could hold out no longer.
>
> "Which is it to-day," I asked, "morphine or cocaine?"
>
> He raised his eyes languidly from the old black-letter volume which he had opened.
>
> "It is cocaine," he said, "a seven-per-cent solution. Would you care to try it?" [2001, pp. 5–6]

The passage owes its efficacy in large part to the adjectives (the *neat morocco* case, the *delicate* needle, the *sharp* point, the *tiny* piston, the *velvet-lined* armchair), which frame a language of obsessive precision and exactitude with a language of luxury (that is, "neat morocco" and "velvet-lined" frame, serve as bookends for, "delicate . . . sharp . . . tiny").[35] The effect produced is a kind of precise superhuman control over this decadent enjoyment, betrayed only by those "long, white, nervous fingers" that roll back the left sleeve with such precision. (Note that the narrator's control

---

35. Luxury of any kind in this novel is tainted by an Eastern (i.e., Orientalist) deca-dence, already visible here in the "neat *morocco* case." Nowhere is this more clear than in our introduction to Thaddeus Sholto's home, whose "Eastern luxury" consists of an "Ori-ental vase," "two great tiger-skins," and "a huge hookah" (2001, p. 24). The hookah, not coincidentally, is the marker of yet another kind of addiction, for Mr. Sholto says: "Well, then, I trust that you have no objection to tobacco-smoke, to the balsamic odour of the Eastern tobacco. I am a little nervous, and I find my hookah an invaluable sedative" (2001, p. 26). Holmes, of course, has no objection, as tobacco is another one of his addictions.

fails here as well, with a sudden excess of description.) Such control serves only to make the enjoyment itself more threatening, and this is the passage's other emphasis, namely the *excess* of this enjoyment: *Three times a day!* For *many* months! *Innumerable* puncture-marks!

Not surprisingly, Holmes's addiction and the twin coordinates of overwhelming control and overwhelming drive are reflected in Watson, but in a poorer, attenuated, more socially acceptable form. Watson is not addicted, but merely intoxicated ("the Beaune which I had taken with my lunch"), and his perfectly ordinary and unthreatening source of enjoyment is matched by a perfectly ordinary and unthreatening lack of control ("I suddenly felt that I could hold out no longer"). Once again, Watson is banal and ordinary, whereas Holmes is extraordinary. For Holmes, detection is the only activity that is capable of breaking his obsessive-compulsive rhythm: "Give me problems, give me work, give me the most abstruse cryptogram, or the most intricate analysis, and I am in my own proper atmosphere. I can dispense then with artificial stimulants" (2001, p. 6). Holmes here opposes the natural stimulation of detection to the artificial stimulation of cocaine. And in fact, the mystery of *The Sign of Four* is successful at distracting Holmes from his addiction—for a time. It is remarkable how often classic detective fiction presents us with this "pathological" detective, given over to a whole series of manias, phobias, addictions: Holmes with his cocaine, Poirot with his obsessive care of moustache and shoes, poor shell-shocked Peter Wimsey, John Rebus and his alcoholism. . . . What this opposition between the detective's addiction and his investigation serves to mask, however, is a fundamental indifference: the investigation is, of course, nothing but the detective's most elementary addiction.

In a revealing touch, the film version of Agatha Christie's *Murder on the Orient Express* (1974) has Poirot appear wearing a bizarre prosthetic device to protect his moustache at night while sleeping. Such a device is never mentioned in Christie, but it is perfectly consonant with the standard procedure of classic detective fiction, which, as much as the detective is the "subject supposed to know" who guarantees a coherent narrative, also aims at presenting a *debilitated* detective. What is key for my purposes here is that this debilitation seems invariably to block the detective's pleasure, his satisfaction in ordinary life. The convention of the debilitated detective has recently found a kind of contemporary culmination in the television series *Monk*, whose eponymous protagonist suffers from obsessive-compulsive disorder brought on by the trauma of his wife's death. (The show is entirely Sherlockian in its nature, frequently borrowing from Conan Doyle for its devices and plot twists.) Monk's disorder impairs normal social contact, his love life, and, in a kind of "limit case" for the genre, *the detection itself*, normally the detective's only consolatory pleasure. A nearly invariable feature of each episode is a scene where Adrian Monk (Tony Shalhoub), in order to obtain a clue, must shake hands with a sewage worker, crawl into a garbage dumpster, climb a tall tower, or otherwise subject himself to the dirt, disorder, and phobias he compulsively avoids. At times he cannot overcome his disgust and fear and must pursue another course; at other times, he can, and the audience witnesses his psychic degradation, invariably shot as comic relief. The show's success demonstrates that the fundamental aspect of this convention is not detection as *compensatory* pleasure for the detective, but rather the necessity of blocking the detective's normal social satisfaction, short-circuiting the "normal" path of desire into the mechanical, repetitive, even autistic behaviors that characterize enjoyment and drive.

In "Mr. Monk Goes to the Theater," Monk pursues a female suspect to a singles meeting. In order to speak to her, he must participate in a social exchange, an exchange fundamentally of *desire*. He must first speak with a number of women also there looking for a romantic match. The meeting is a kind of round robin, where every man meets with every woman for a minute or two, a "speed dating" service, hoping that sparks will fly, and Monk self-consciously refers to his upcoming experience as being like "Dante's seventh circle of hell." Monk transforms each encounter into a social short-circuit, again, to comic effect. He transforms one woman's sexual advances into incomprehension. On learning that he was a policeman, she purrs, "Do you still have your handcuffs? Maybe you'd like to show them to me sometime . . ." "Wh– Why?," he stammers in helpless bewilderment. He reduces another woman to tears when he spends their two minutes together telling her about his dead wife, and how much he loved her. Finally, he performs a brilliant piece of deduction when a woman claims to be 38 years old. "It's hard to meet men when you're my age," she says, fishing for a compliment. He proves instead that she is at least 42. "All right," she snarls, "I'm 43—are you happy now?" But Monk, of course, is never really happy. These forced and agonizing social exchanges culminate in a scene repeated too often for comfort in the series: after extracting information from his suspect, he dashes away, leaving the young African-American woman who was next in line to conclude that Monk's flight is racist revulsion.

Although this takes us briefly away from the topics at hand—addiction and enjoyment—it is so frequent in *Monk* that it is worth commenting on. This racist "mistake" appears repeatedly as a kind of throwaway joke, often enough that it begins to appear as a lightly masked version of white paranoia: a white person's most innocent symptoms are constantly and incorrectly perceived as prejudice by racial others. The *mise-en-scène* of this paranoia thus conceals a kind of resentment against the racial other for having always disrupted an "innocent" enjoyment, a resentment that masquerades as a comic misunderstanding.[36] One is reminded here of Freud's joke about the two Jews on the train: "Where are you going?" asks the first Jew. "To Cracow," says the second. "Liar!" says the first. "You say you are going to Cracow only in order to make me think you are going to Lemberg, when you are really going to Cracow. Why are you lying to me?" In other words, the net effect of *Monk's mise-en-scène* of racial paranoia is to say: "How dare you mistake my repulsion for repulsion?!" This racial repressed returned musically in a series of advertisements for the second season of the show that place Monk into an explicitly parodic relationship with blackness. The advertisements remade the often parodied theme song from the "blaxploitation" film *Shaft* as a song about Monk, as well as the classic Parliament song "Give Up the Funk (Tear the Roof Off the Sucker)," with the lyrics now saying "Monk" instead of "funk": "we want the Monk . . . we need the Monk . . . we gotta have that Monk. . . ." Monk's own racial identity is never explored or mentioned, although the actor Tony Shalhoub is, of course, not normatively white, either.

One might, in light of *Monk* and its debilitated detective, also consider Mark Haddon's recent *The Curious Incident of the Dog in the Night-Time* (2003), whose protagonist/detective is an autistic teenager much taken with Sherlock Holmes and his methodology. It is not, properly speaking, classic detective fiction (indeed, it is not even really detective fiction at all). One could easily imagine, however, a classic detective of this type, his serial adventures, and his "normal" (i.e., socially normal, but stupid) sidekick. Indeed, such imagination is no longer necessary, since the USA network,

---

36. This paranoia in *Monk* appears in other forms of fear about non-normative subjects, as well. In an earlier scene in the same episode, Monk accompanies Sharona and her mother to a beauty salon so they can get a manicure. He discovers an important clue by idly scanning the appointment book, but the "price" he must pay in this instance is the fawning and lisping attentions of the gay African-American stylist: "the curl in your hair— it's *fabulous!*" he croons, touching Monk's hair. What bothers Monk more: the overly intrusive approach of another person (he does not, of course, like to be touched by anyone), or the proximity of Blackness? Both the gay and the Black are coded (not least by the show *Monk*) as yet another form of cultural "dirt" (see Douglas 1995).

having correctly understood the appeal of the debilitated and compulsive detective, decided to introduce (and shortly thereafter cancel) a show with a similar, if possibly more extreme, premise. The hero of *Touching Evil* is David Creegan, who was an ordinary police officer until he was shot in the head and suffered, in the words of the amused *New York Times* review, "character-building frontal-lobe damage" that transforms him into an amazing detective.[37] Such a transformation is exceedingly unlikely, although Creegan's disregard for the rules is one possible response to this kind of injury, but one should note that the most likely outcome of frontal-lobe damage is a profound kind of *social impairment*, an inability to feel empathy or sympathy, to understand humor and irony, and a lack of what neurologists call "behavioral spontaneity"—in other words, a kind of extraction of the subject from normal social enjoyment through autism, obsessive-compulsive disorder, brain damage, whatever it takes.[38] If *Touching Evil* made the necessity of this exchange evident—no classic detection without social impairment—*Monk* was not willing to be any less explicit: the third season of the show ended with an episode entitled "Mr. Monk Takes His Medicine" in which Monk discovers a drug that frees him of his obsessive-compulsive disorder, finally allowing him to socialize normally, to relax, to enjoy himself, in the everyday sense of the phrase. It also, of course, makes him strictly ordinary, no more clever, no more extraordinary than

---

37. Heffernan (2004). The show was based on a British show of the same title. Since the success of *Monk*, *The Curious Incident,* and others, there has been a sudden explosion of new shows and texts based on the idea of the "defective detective," ranging from ABC's *Blind Justice* (blinded in the line of duty, Detective Jim Dunbar returns to the force to investigate, his other senses sharpened by his loss of vision), CBS's *NUMB3RS* (dreamy mathematician Charlie Eppes is recruited by his more practical and realistic brother to work for the FBI), and Howard Engel's *Memory Book*, (2005) (the detective Benny Cooperman, like the author in real life, suffers from *alexia sine agraphia*, a rare syndrome that permits one to write but not to read, as well as causing a variety of memory and cognitive disturbances), among others.

38. Intriguingly, Anne Perry has written a series of novels set in Victorian London that also postulate a debilitated but brilliant detective named Monk with brain damage, one who also suffers from a kind of social impairment, an obsessiveness that has made him distrusted and disliked by his coworkers. In the first of these novels, the detective awakens with amnesia after a serious head injury; his amnesia both constitutes who he is as a character and interferes with his detection (Perry 1990). Although the novels appear to have no connection to the show *Monk*, it is nonetheless curious that the protagonist of Perry's books is named Mr. Monk, and his sidekick, exactly as in the television show, is his nurse.

Watson at the beginning of *The Sign of Four*. The episode is slightly more complex than the mere exchange of detection for normal socialization. Monk is even more unbearable on the drug than he usually is, adopting a new lounge lizard-like persona, "the Monk." The episode is unusually moralistic and sentimental for the show as well: Monk stops taking the drug because he can no longer "commune" with his dead wife, Trudy, when he is on it (these scenes of "communing" are a creepy and unfortunate novelty introduced in this episode). In its more clear-thinking moments, such as "Mr. Monk and Mrs. Monk," however, *Monk* makes clear exactly the opposite, namely that Trudy is the "absent center," the hole that Monk's subjectivity is organized around. It is not that "without her, he is nothing," but precisely the opposite: it is the loss of Trudy that brings him into being in the first place.

The increasing tendency to make use of "defective detectives" appears at times to have sent mystery writers in search of innovative protagonists to the books of Oliver Sacks (*The Man Who Mistook His Wife for a Hat* and others), in which the neurologist chronicles the most fascinating cognitive "deficits" he has encountered over the years. (I place "deficits" in scare quotes since Sacks is, of course, absolutely dedicated to showing the rich and active mental life of his patients.) In addition to American detectives who suffer from frontal-lobe damage, autism, obsessive-compulsive disorder, or the painkiller-addicted Dr. House, we find that this tendency has crossed national borders: Sandrone Dazieri has penned a series of extremely successful Italian detective novels with an equally esoteric detective, with titles like the 1998 *Attenti al Gorilla* [*Beware of the Gorilla*] and the 2001 *La cura del Gorilla* [*The Gorilla's Cure*]. The detective is also named "Sandrone Dazieri" (although his friends mostly know him as "Gorilla") and shares a significant amount of biography with the author, as well. But Dazieri (the author) has cleverly reduplicated the idea of the novelistic protagonist as the author's alter ego by giving the Gorilla an alter ego, as well. The Gorilla suffers from a kind of multiple-personality disorder, acquired in childhood. When he falls asleep, his other personality (whom he calls his "Partner"), wakes up. The two personalities inhabiting this same body, the Gorilla and the Partner, work together in a series of comical hard-boiled adventures, adventures that are—as is typical of the contemporary Italian detective novel—reflective of larger social concerns, from homeless teenagers to immigrants from outside of the European Union. The novels are narrated by the Gorilla, who virtually never has access to his other half (only under the influence of certain drugs can the two directly converse), and here is the real innovation of Dazieri: the Gorilla's Partner is smarter than he is, but socially incapacitated. He is paranoid, and—surprise—obsessive/compulsive. Once again, the detective capacity is figured as a kind of compensation for a psychic wounding. Indeed, it is perhaps not so much a *compensation* for this hole in the symbolic/social network as a *marker* of the wound itself. Although the overall tenor of the series is both comic (the Partner takes over just as the Gorilla is about to make love with a beautiful woman, or hands control back to the Gorilla in a particularly difficult moment) and hard-boiled (the Gorilla is constantly beaten up, and solves the mysteries primarily through his obstinate insistence, two markers of the hard-boiled), there are occasional flashes of genius, logical reasoning, and the other hallmarks of the classic detective. Not surprisingly, these invariably emerge from the Partner, the socially excluded, paranoid, compulsive, and debilitated half of the protagonist.

One can't help but notice that the compulsive quality that I've been outlining characterizes the entire genre, with its endlessly repeated formalist tics. Of the principal types of modern genre fiction (including the romance novel, horror, science fiction, fantasy, and the western), detective fiction, especially in its classic formulation, is by far the most formulaic, the most conservative. It has many subgenres (the cozy, the police procedural, the hard-boiled, the forensic), but what is remarkable is that most of these subgenres manifest a set of generic tics that, although different from those in classic detective fiction (indeed, in some cases, such as the hard-boiled novel, deliberately opposed), are no less compulsive. Conan Doyle's Sherlock Holmes stories offer a model case of this compulsive repetition; as Todorov showed, each scene can effectively be known in advance. We begin in Holmes's studio: a conversation between Holmes and Watson results in one of Holmes's astonishing deductions that is unrelated to the case; a knock at the door, and a supplicant arrives begging for Holmes's assistance; the exposition of the case and Holmes's questions; the investigation of the scene of the crime typically featuring Holmes examining the grass or making use of his magnifying glass; and so on. On the one hand, this is surely an attractive feature of Conan Doyle's fiction: the stories are familiar, and make use of a narrative structure that obviously works. On the other hand, familiarity breeds contempt, and more than one critic of detective fiction has wondered how a reader can consume so many novels that are effectively all the same. Often, even the minimal variations permitted in the genre are extremely limited, so although one would think the method of murder would show a great deal of inventiveness, its conventional possibilities are relatively few in number.

The Parker Brothers board game *Clue* is perhaps the ideal example of the genre's claustrophobic limitations: a generically Christie-esque cast of characters mechanically named after colors (Miss Scarlet or Professor Plum), a generic, depersonalized victim (Mr. Boddy), a set of potential generic locations (the parlor or the dining room), and a set of possible killing implements (a noose, a knife, or—my personal favorite when I was a child—the candlestick). One immediately notes the game's perfect assimilation of the genre's essential traits. It structurally excludes the questions that are, after all, irrelevant to the reader of classic detective fiction, such as motives, personal histories, or psychological depth to the characters. Its attention is instead devoted entirely to a reconstruction of the *scene* of the crime: who, where, and how. This aspect is not incidental, as it reveals detective fiction's preference for theatricality, for proceeding through a series of scenes that are conditioned by an invisible "other scene" that remains hidden until the end. (In the game *Clue*, this "other scene" is described by a series of cards that remain hidden in an envelope until a player is ready to guess the truth.) This game, an ideal example of Derridean *jeu sûr* if there ever was one, is entirely combinatorial: no question is admitted into play other than a selection from column A (which character?), one from column B (which room?), and one from column C (which killing implement?). As a result, one could simply generate an algorithm that would exhaustively list every possible combination of the characters, rooms, and weapons in order to produce the entirety of the narrative possibilities inherent in the game.[39] If this sounds like a dismally boring prospect, we should note that Italo Calvino, as part of his work for OuLiPo, Raymond Queneau's group dedicated to exploring the mathematical and combinatorial possibilities of literature, attempted to put it into literary practice. His short story "L'incendio della casa

---

39. There are thus 324 possible outcomes to the game, given 6 possible suspects, 9 possible rooms, and 6 possible weapons. Relatively speaking (compared, for instance, to chess or cards) this is a claustrophobically small number of possible end-states for a game. I must confess to a certain professional curiosity about Professor Plum. Although the other characters in *Clue* represent easily recognizable types from Christie's fictions (the stolid British military man, the exotic foreign seductress, the charming if potentially deadly old lady, and so on), I cannot recall any professors in her corpus, particularly not prominent suspects. From where does this image—professor as murderer—emerge?

abominevole" ["The Fire in the Abominable House"] (1993) attempts just such a mechanical investigation into a case of arson, and the results are in fact, nearly unreadable, anti-ludic in their mechanical rigidity.[40]

Imagine for a moment someone who plays *Clue* every day, each time with the same breathless anticipation of a surprise, the revelation of a mystery, the pleasure of a solution. To someone on the outside of the game's action, what is most striking is the radical *pointlessness* of such an activity. Every possibility is already foreseen, mechanically. To play the game repeatedly would seem, in the Žižekian sense, *idiotic*, that is, mechanical, irrational, completely counterproductive. Sue Grafton's "alphabet series" is a perfect example of *idiotic* detective fiction in this sense. After reading *A is for Alibi, B is for Burglar, C is for Corpse*, how can one feel anything other than boredom at the prospect of *T is for Terror*, or *X is for X–acto Knife*?[41] A few repetitions would be sufficient to show that the results of the "investigation" are entirely arbitrary, a point made perfectly by the comic film based on the board game I have been discussing. After the main action of *Clue* (1985) comes to an end, it is followed by a whole series of alternate endings that reinterpret the same previous visual material to come to completely different solutions. Now consider someone who plays the game the way a chain smoker smokes cigarettes. With the revelation that this time it was Miss Scarlet in the library with a wrench, the player immediately starts a new game that will eventually reveal that this time it is Mr. Green in the dining room with a rope, after which a new game immediately begins proving that. . . . This behavior passes from the idiotic to the *pathological*. Yet many readers of detective fiction read in precisely this way, a kind of chain-reading that demonstrates a certain addictive quality. "Which is it to-day," one feels tempted to exclaim in irritation, "Conan Doyle or Christie?" "Conan Doyle," they reply languidly from their enjoyment. "Would you care to try it?"

---

40. Calvino's story is not based on *Clue,* a game that, as far as I know, he was not acquainted with, but is virtually identical in its procedures: who, where, how. The story shares the "mechanical" character of Calvino's worst writing, such as *Il castello dei destini incrociati* (1973).

41. The first series of Grafton titles are real, but the latter are my parodic, although not entirely improbable, inventions. Grafton's latest, at the time of this writing, *S is for Silence* (2006).

ADDICTION AND IDENTIFICATION

The Sign of Four tells the story of a Miss Morstan who solicits Holmes's assistance in searching for traces of her long-lost father and the curious benefactor who has been sending her expensive pearls. As Holmes investigates, it becomes clear that Captain Morstan is dead, caught up in a mystery surrounding a hugely valuable treasure taken from colonial India, the "Great Agra Treasure." This treasure always stays one step ahead of Holmes and its "rightful" owner, Miss Morstan (it certainly cannot belong to the Indians from whom it was originally stolen!). Many clever deductions and a romantic subplot involving Watson and Miss Morstan later, the novel culminates in a dramatic riverboat chase on the Thames in which the Treasure is recovered, and the culprit apprehended. Watson carries the heavy iron chest back to Miss Morstan, only to open it and find that "it [is] absolutely and completely empty" (2001, p. 93). This permits a satisfactory resolution to the romance (Watson can now ask Miss Morstan to marry him, as she will not be above his financial and social station), and serves as a satisfactory resolution to the detective plot as well. The Treasure is, after all, only a McGuffin which, once it has thrown the narrative into forward motion, can disappear. If there is satisfaction to be had in reading detective fiction, it is not in the recovery of so many jewels or bits of gold. It is worth noting, however, that the Treasure appears in *The Sign of Four* as an object that is "always missed," initially always one step out of reach, and then later not there, never having been there at all. This is already a kind of dream-logic, best exemplified in the sufferings of Tantalus, who is condemned to repeat again and again the same "tantalizing" gesture of attempted and failed satisfaction.

Many critics and many readers of detective fiction assume that the reader identifies in some way with the detective in the story, thus deriving an imaginary pleasure, the vicarious satisfaction of temporarily being a genius. There can be no doubt, for instance, that the narrative voice in classic detective fiction is constantly inviting the reader to laugh at the detective's sidekick and his obtuseness and, in a very clever touch, this stupidity is associated with the position of the *writer* rather than the reader, insofar as the sidekick is invariably the narrator of the story. "I may be very obtuse, Holmes," says Watson in *The Sign of Four*, "but I fail to see what this suggests" (2001, p. 19). "This is all an insoluble mystery to me," he says again later, "It grows darker instead of clearer." "On the contrary," Holmes replies, "it clears every instant. I only require a few missing links to have an entirely connected case" (p. 40). *Yes, yes*, thinks the reader, *only a few more links, Watson, you idiot*. And yet the reader has no more notion of what those links might be than Watson does. Film versions of the Sherlock Holmes stories have typically exaggerated Watson's bumbling for comic effect, as one critic notes: "If a mop bucket appeared in a scene, his foot would be inside it, and if . . . he managed to stumble upon an important clue, he could be depended upon to blow his nose in it and throw it away" (Conan Doyle 1986, p. vii). Christie takes the pleasures in the sadistic mistreatment of the sidekick to the next level: Poirot refers to Hastings as his "mascot" and occasionally compares him to a dog.

Indeed, it would be safe to say that the historical arc leading from Poe to Conan Doyle to Christie is one of ever increasing sadism and humiliation of the sidekick. Dupin never engages the narrator in the solution, or expects him to make a contribution. The function of the narrator/sidekick seems to be to express horror at the crime and wonder at the genius detective's solution. In Conan Doyle, however, exchanges such as the following are common:

> "What is your theory, then, as to those footmarks?" I asked eagerly when we had regained the lower room once more.
> "My dear Watson, try a little analysis yourself," said he with a touch of impatience. "You know my methods. Apply them, and it will be instructive to compare results."
> "I cannot conceive anything which will cover the facts," I answered.
> "It will be clear enough to you soon," he said, in an offhand way.
> [2001, pp. 43–44]

In Conan Doyle, these exchanges typically function in the key of impatience or classically Victorian irritation. We should note immediately that this is a beautiful instance of misdirection and misrecognition: the reader should indeed be impatient and irritated here, but not at Watson. These exchanges are invariably a technique of the author for delaying a revelation of truth, or more commonly, withholding it entirely until the end of the story. It is precisely Watson's inability to *"cover the facts"* that successfully covers the facts, that is, that hides them from view, conceals them. By the time of *The Valley of Fear* (1986, originally published 1914), Conan Doyle could open the novel with the following exchange between his good detective and "one of the most long-suffering of mortals," namely Dr. Watson, that makes clear the ever-increasing irritation with the sidekick's obtuseness:

"I am inclined to think—," said I.

"I should do so," Sherlock Holmes remarked impatiently. [1986 vol. 2, p. 149]

In Christie, Poirot never tires of humiliating Hastings. In its most extreme and "open" form, these humiliations sound like this: "How many times am I to go over this? . . . Come Hastings, you are not so stupid as you like to pretend . . . The trouble with you is that you are mentally lazy . . . You do not like to work with your head . . . You are obstinate and extremely stupid . . . You cannot use your grey cells as you do not possess them" (1993, pp. 71–73).

More often, however, Poirot's little barbs are more subtle and go unnoticed by the poor Hastings. In addition to blocking any hermeneutic desires the reader might entertain, these humiliations also provide an exemplary occasion to drive an "identificatory wedge," as it were, between the reader and sidekick. They function precisely to create a space of irony in which the reader recognizes the sidekick's humiliation, *but the sidekick does not realize it himself*. It should be clear by now where I am heading: every textual mechanism at work in the depiction of the sidekick aims at preventing the reader from seeing that *this is exactly his own position in the text*. It is the *reader* who, at all costs, must be kept from conceiving "anything that will cover the facts," who does not recognize his own humiliation. Each abasement of the sidekick, each eruption of impatience on the part of the detective, is an expression of contempt for us, for our structural position of total non-mastery. Now we can understand why there is an arc of increasing humiliation of the sidekick in classic detective fiction: it creates a *méconnaissance* that is necessary to the basic function of the mystery novel. The reader *must* misrecognize: interpret clues incorrectly, fail to recognize a character in disguise, fail to recognize the importance of a chair that has been moved, fail to see a letter that is hanging in plain view, step in a bucket, blow his nose on the important clue. This is a first reason readers of detective fiction read serially, rather than rereading (many critics have noted that mystery novels are "self-destructing," meant to be read only once): to prevent the possibility of, in its etymological sense, any *re-cognition*, any rethinking of their own imaginary relationships. One might say that detective fiction depends on encouraging the most superficial modality of thinking—quite literally, "don't think twice." The question of the sidekick, then, becomes not a question of the pleasures of his sadistic mistreatment, but the reader's masochistic (disavowed, misrecognized) enjoyment.

If the reader is encouraged to project his own shortcomings onto the sidekick, and, in classic Freudian fashion, to manifest an increasing hostility and contempt for this doppelganger, there is a concomitant pressure to ally himself with the detective who expresses so clearly the contempt the reader feels for his alter ego ("have I not here my faithful dog to protect me also? My excellent and loyal Hastings!" [1993, p. 46]). Rather than recognize our position of absolute passivity, we misrecognize ourselves in the detective's frantic activity. Rather than recognize the impossibility of our solving the crime, we misrecognize ourselves in the figure of the "subject supposed to know," the absolute guarantor of coherent meaning in the investigation. And rather than recognize that the text, to use a juridical phrase, "holds us in contempt," we misrecognize that contempt as our own.

Now we are in a position to understand the absolute brilliance of the structural *double méconnaissance* entailed in classic detective fiction: we are encouraged to identify with the detective *in every way except the one respect in which we actually resemble him.* How is it that the reader of detective fiction resembles the detective? In what respect? Obsessive-compulsive addictive behavior. This behavior occurs in the only space in which the detective manifests a notable lack of introspection and observation, which is to say, his "idiotic" repetition, the failure to ask that most obvious of questions: "Why do I keep doing this?" or "Why does this keep happening to me?" The key here is that, in both cases, the reader's actual identifications only take place in the realm of blindness, the sidekick's stupidity and the detective's blind spot.

Monk once again provides a "limit case" of this theory. Monk's sidekick is Sharona Fleming the stereotypical single mother raising a child, an entirely sympathetic character, whereas it is the *detective* who is regularly submitted to humiliation as he is forced, as if on a reality TV show, to do the things he most dreads. Fleming's role in the show is quite different from the usual function of the sidekick. She is a nurse, and she is persistently found gazing at Monk in sorrow and sympathy for his debilitation. The psychic structure is unchanged, however; only its targets are different. We still fail to recognize our own obsessive-compulsive behavior in Adrian Monk, where it is instead seen as abnormal and extraordinary as compared to the eminently normal Ms. Fleming; in fact, in a classic instance of having one's desire and eating it too, Monk permits the viewer to gaze at his own debilitated figure in *sympathy and pity* without recognizing that he is seeing himself. The pleasure of entertaining a hostile relationship to one's own stupidity is not foregone, however: it is preserved in the figure of Lieutenant Randall Disher, who invariably rejects Monk's deductions (ultimately shown to be correct), while mocking Fleming's efforts in an inept form of flirtation. "Do I detect a hint of jealousy?" he sarcastically asks Sharona in "Mr. Monk and the Sleeping Suspect"; "If so, it's the only detecting you've ever done," she replies tartly, neatly transforming a manifestation of desire into the genre's mechanically repetitive conventions of enjoyment.

Let me return briefly to Sandrone Dazieri's "Gorilla," who suffers from multiple-personality disorder. Since the novels are narrated by the Gorilla, we almost never hear the Partner directly—we know him through the notes and occasional videotapes he leaves for the Gorilla, as well as the comically difficult situations he leaves our protagonist in. As I noted before, the Gorilla is socially gregarious and hard-drinking, but his Partner is not. On the contrary, the Partner is obsessive-compulsive, paranoid, rigorously logical, and socially incapable (he displays almost no affect). In short, Dazieri's innovation was to combine the hard-boiled detective and the classic detective in the same body, almost as if he wished to demonstrate that the two subgenres can—like the Gorilla and his Partner—never properly meet. It also quite cleverly allows him to make use of classic detection (including leaps of deductive logic) when the plot seems to require it.

While the Gorilla and his Partner represent one kind of primary duality in detective fiction—classic vs. hard-boiled—they also represent a different kind of split, one already visible in classic detection: the split between the detective and the narrator. Once again, the narrator always represents the actual state of the reader. The reader of Dazieri's novels has full access to the Gorilla's consciousness. He conceals nothing from us, but just as the Partner is an enigma to him, disclosed only through the bits of textual evidence he leaves for the Gorilla (notes and reports), he is an enigma to us. We never get to watch him directly, to hear his voice. Our protagonist, the Gorilla, will "wake up" in bed with a sleeping woman, or on a park bench in an unknown city, and the reader must reconstruct along with him how he got there, what city he's in, who the woman is. Far from vicariously enjoying the classic detective's powerful mind, that potent brain remains an unimaginable enigma for us, one that is uncannily embedded in our brain now. Perversely, the closer to us the genius of the classic detective comes, the more it becomes clear that it is a deadlock. Once it inhabits us directly, shares our brain with us, it becomes clear we can never know this other person, can never even meet him.

And again, just like Holmes and Watson, Poirot and Hastings, the Partner doesn't spare the Gorilla's feelings. The Gorilla may consider himself

"Sandrone Dazieri" and call this other person by the impersonal sobriquet "Partner," but as far as the Partner is concerned, *he* is Sandrone Dazieri, and he refers to the Gorilla with a nickname that is kinder that Poirot's canine metaphors for Hastings, but one that is clear about who is the senior partner in their collorative business: "Fratellino," or "little brother." In *La cura del Gorilla* (2001), he also clearly manifests his contempt for his Fratellino's methods, lifestyle, and intelligence. Moreover, he expresses his contempt for his Fratellino's *narration,* in language and terms that are a deliberate recollection of Holmes chastising Watson at the beginning of *The Sign of Four,* where Holmes complains about Watson's overly sentimental narratives:

> Il tuo problema è che non hai mai imparato a guardare la realtà senza ricamarci sopra. La fantasia può essere utile in molti mestieri, ma non in quello che ci siamo scelti. Meglio la concretezza . . . Sai, i tuoi resoconti sono sempre inutilmente prolissi sulle tue sensazioni ed estremamente stringati sulle tue esperienze dirette (p. 161).

> Your problem is that you've never learned to look at reality without embroidering on it. Imagination can be useful in many jobs, but not in the one we chose for ourselves. Concreteness is better . . . You know, your reports are always pointlessly verbose about your sensations and extremely stingy about your direct experiences.

If we return now to the opening scene of *The Sign of Four*, we might now perceive something else, and hear Sherlock Holmes's question to Watson somewhat differently:

> "Which is it to-day," I asked, "morphine or cocaine?"
> He raised his eyes languidly from the old black-letter volume which he had opened.
> "It is cocaine," he said, "a seven-per-cent solution. Would you care to try it?" [2001, p. 6]

What is this "old black-letter volume," and why is it that Holmes's response to cocaine, to his addiction, is to turn immediately to *reading*? Might Holmes and Watson be speaking of the book and its contents? That is, the detective's addiction is marked from the beginning by the scene of reading, quite literally, if one considers the Dupin stories, casually presented as an irrelevant "realistic" detail (the classic detective suffers from bibliophilia: Dupin, Holmes, Wimsey, and many others). In this light, Holmes is offering an invitation to the reader, a seven-percent solution that will be addictive, mechanically repeating itself in "innumerable puncture-marks." As it turns out, we *would* care to try it, despite, or precisely because, of the fact that it does not entail satisfaction. This is of course, the key feature of addiction, the feature that marks it as addiction as such: a dose of the drug creates not so much satisfaction as an increase in appetite for the drug. We might then say, along with Avital Ronell, that Sherlock Holmes is not simply on cocaine in this scene, but "on crack," the drug that "is only about producing a need for itself" (1993, p. 25).[42] This endless circular movement of longing that ends in a blockage of satisfaction, only to then repeat again and again, is called drive. What is remarkable is that it is the source for a kind of pleasure as well. As Žižek writes: "the psychic apparatus finds a sort of perverse pleasure *in this displeasure itself*, in the never-ending, repeated circulation around the unattainable, always missed object. The Lacanian name for this pleasure-in-pain is of course enjoyment (*jouissance*) . . ." (2001, p. 48, italics original). Or, as Dr. House says of his use of prescription painkillers on the FOX medical detective program *House*, "OK, I'm addicted. It's just not a problem."

Once again, *Monk* makes this connection between addiction, enjoyment, and the debilitated detective explicit, not only through an advertising campaign that proclaims Adrian Monk "America's Favorite Defective Detective!" but also through a key scene in "Mr. Monk Goes To Jail." Monk is trying to obtain a key piece of evidence in the prison kitchen, but is unbearably distracted by one of the cooks, a Rastafarian with a single dreadlock dangling out of his hair net. This is precisely the sort of disorder that Monk cannot bear. He makes repeated attempts to get the man to tuck in his stray lock of hair, but his social awkwardness produces only hostility from the cook. But it is Sharona who succeeds in resolving the situation when she realizes that Monk and the cook have something in common:

SHARONA: You been in rehab, right?

COOK: How did you know?

SHARONA: I'm a nurse, I can see the track marks [*gesturing to the cook's arm*]. So you know about addiction, right? Well, my boss has a jones for neatness, okay?

---

42. Ronell's claim is that Madame Bovary is "on crack," addicted to addiction itself in a kind of "epidemic of misfired *jouissance*" (1993, p. 54).

MONK: [*awkwardly attempting to use street slang*] It's my . . . jones.
SHARONA: And he needs a fix, real bad.

At least in detective fiction, it is imperative that the subject not recognize his enjoyment as such, as enjoyment entails an inevitable gap in the subject, a missing piece—namely the object (a)—that stands in the way of satisfaction, that the reader perceive it as hostility toward the sidekick or the criminal, for instance. The functioning of enjoyment as it works in the detective novel (and elsewhere) is represented perfectly in a joke—a dirty joke, of course:

> A man goes hunting in the woods and spies a bear. He shoots at the bear, but misses, and the bear rushes over, tears the gun out of his hands, throws him down on the ground, and has sex with him. The following week, the outraged hunter waits in the woods again with a new gun, sees the bear again, and shoots. Again he misses, and again the bear throws him on the ground and has sex with him. The following week, angrier than ever, the man returns to the woods with a bigger gun with a better scope, etc. He spies the bear, shoots—and misses. The bear tears the gun away, throws him on the ground, pauses and says to the hunter: "You don't come here for the hunting, do you?"[43]

One might just as easily ask the reader of detective fiction: "You don't come here for the detection, do you?" In point of fact, they do not, but it is crucial that they keep up appearances and appear to do so. (Here an extremely important feature of enjoyment emerges: it is an antisocial, unacceptable impulse that performs a kind of masquerade of social acceptability.) The reader of classic detective fiction is blocked from an active hermeneutic role, from "coming here for the detection." The author may misdirect his attention in a variety of ways (concealing an important clue, for instance,

---

43. I have left the sex act relatively unspecified here, but all versions of the joke suggest or specify that the bear is male (the hunter is always male, of course): some specify fellatio and others sodomy. Several versions have the bear present the hunter with a choice: "either I maul you to death or we have sex, you give me head, etc." In any event, the joke's humor lies in the revelation of *desire*. The repeated returns to the "always missed object" would seem to indicate that the hunter is trapped in a kind of autistic repetition, an inhuman drive—but thank goodness that it was actually my desire, albeit homosexual, bestial, and masochistic!

in a mass of seemingly irrelevant, realistic details), may omit key facts, or may rely on knowledge that no reader would be likely to have (see Bayard 2000, especially pp. 19–40). The idea that readers might solve the mystery on their own is exemplified in the "Van Dine Principle," part of a set of "rules" drawn up for classic detective fiction by the American author S. S. Van Dine: it states that a reader should, in theory, be able to solve the mystery at the same time the detective announces his solution. Naturally, the Van Dine Principle is itself another mechanism of detective fiction that encourages the same *méconnaissance* with the detective, allowing the reader to continue to believe that he comes to it "for the hunting." This misunderstanding characterizes a great deal of detective fiction theory, as well, which separates the fiction into its hermeneutic (the detection) and non-hermeneutic (the romantic subplot of *The Sign of Four*, for instance) parts. *There is no hermeneutic component to the detective novel.* The reader simply waits for the effortless dissipation of the problem, albeit misrecognizing his own waiting as some other activity, finding enjoyment like the hunter precisely in his "repeated circulation around the unattainable, always missed object." One is tempted to suggest that this structure in the detective story also explains the very *interminability* of the critical chain discussing Poe's "Purloined Letter," from Lacan to Derrida to Johnson to Irwin to Žižek to. . . .

Equally crucially, this indicates that the detective, too, doesn't come here for the detection. He, too, misrecognizes his enjoyment, believing, in spite of the obvious evidence, that he finds satisfaction in his work. Yet, time and time again, he is called back, finds himself once again nearby when a murder is committed, discovers a body quite by chance, receives a letter by accident meant for another that triggers yet another investigation. Perhaps nothing seems so improbable as the retiring, demure Miss Marple so invariably on hand, so close by, when murder is committed. One begins to wonder about these detectives, perhaps even suspect them, as murder seems to follow them to the most unlikely of places. In *Curtain*, originally published in 1975, Poirot is presented with his most devious opponent ever, one who leaves no evidence, no traces of any kind, precisely because he never actually commits the murder. Instead, he is a master manipulator based on Shakespeare's Iago, capable of inciting rage, jealousy, and so forth in others, eventually leading them to kill for him. There is simply no way to show that he is responsible, other than a kind of contiguity. Poirot explains how this opponent was connected to five seemingly unrelated murders:

"Let me put it this way. There is a certain person—X. In none of these cases did X (apparently) have any motive in doing away with the victim. In one case, as far as I have been able to find out, X was actually two hundred miles away when the crime was committed. Nevertheless, I will tell you this. X was on intimate terms with Etherington, X lived for a time in the same village as Riggs, X was acquainted with Mrs. Bradley. I have a snap of X and Freda Clay walking together in the street, and X was near the house when old Matthew Litchfield died. What do you say to that?"

I stared at him. I said slowly:

"Yes, it's a bit too much. Coincidence might account for two cases, even three, but five is a bit too thick." [1993, p. 20]

X is always suspiciously nearby, on hand, or otherwise connected to the case—but for the negative and uncanny effect of repetition he would appear to be a seemingly innocent bystander. My point here is that this figure of the repeatedly "innocent" bystander, accidentally nearby, by coincidence, by mere chance on hand for a murder again and again and again is none other than the figure of the detective. What does the detective want, other than the idiotic repetition of this scenario time and time again? He is, to use a phrase that must surely be the title of some pulp novel somewhere, "addicted to murder."[44] It is no accident that *Curtain*, the only text where X makes a direct appearance, is the very text where Poirot reveals himself as a murderer. It is only the play of condensation and displacement that allows the text to posit the detective and X as separate characters in the first place; the underlying libidinal logic indicates that they are the same. Hence the uncanny effect when Poirot says "*X is in this house.*" Again, it is the only real point of commonality between the reader and the detective: they both earnestly wish for someone's death as the object (a), the absolutely forbidden object that they can endlessly circle in their enjoyment.

Nowhere is the detective's dependence on the repetition of this scenario made more clear than at the ending of *The Sign of Four*, as Holmes and Watson discuss the aftermath of the case, particularly the successful conclusion to the romantic subplot (Watson and Miss Morstan are engaged

---

44. I was surprised to find that the title *Addicted to Murder* is only a true crime book about Dr. Harold Shipman, the British doctor who killed over a hundred and possibly many more of his patients (Sitford and Panter 2000), but happily, it is also the title of a low-budget vampire film from 1995 by Kevin Lindenmuth. Indeed it is a trilogy of films.

to be married) and the lack of success on the part of the police. (Inspector Jones has enthusiastically arrested a great number of people who, it turns out, are not guilty, but Holmes is a consulting detective who always lets the police take the credit for his correct solution.)

> "Well, and there is the end of our little drama . . . But you look weary."
>
> "Yes, the reaction is already upon me. I shall be as limp as a rag for a week."
>
> "Strange," said I, "how terms of what in another man I should call laziness alternate with your fits of splendid energy and vigour."
>
> "Yes," he answered, "there are in me the makings of a very fine loafer, and also of a pretty spry sort of a fellow. . . . By the way, apropos of this Norwood business, you see that they had, as I surmised, a confederate in the house, who could be none other than Lal Rao, the butler: so Jones actually has the undivided honour of having caught one fish in his great haul."
>
> "The division seems rather unfair," I remarked. "You have done all the work in this business. I get a wife out of it, Jones gets the credit, pray what remains for you?"
>
> "For me," said Sherlock Holmes, "there still remains the cocaine-bottle." And he stretched his long white hand up for it. [2001, pp. 117–118]

What remains for Holmes at the end of the adventure is repetition itself, addiction in its purest form. The psychic structures of detection fiction permit the reader to get something for nothing: pleasure in a contemptuous dismissal of the sidekick's stupidity, without recognizing that it is his own, or pleasure in the guilt of another, without recognizing his own guilt (see the chapter on desire). Likewise, they seem to permit, if that is the right term, the detective to get nothing for something. Others receive romantic and sexual satisfaction, honor, and credit. The detective's sole compensatory pleasure, and one of the many pleasures for the reader, is his capacity to recognize his enjoyment as such, to *enjoy his symptom*.

FROM *MONK* TO MONKS

In his excellent and unique book about addiction to cigarettes, Richard Klein asks, "Is there some logical necessity such that reflecting on cigarettes leads one inevitably to prophetic anticipations of apocalypse?" (1993,

p. 79).[45] This question about addiction and the End will also describe this chapter in some ways, as a reflection of the circular movement of enjoyment; always returning to the scene of its attempted satisfaction and always missing it again must inevitably lead one to wonder: When and how will it all end? We would, of course, prefer to think of enjoyment in the Žižekian sense, along with addiction, as pathological states, but it is perhaps telling that the end of addiction can only be visualized in terms of the apocalypse. What comes after enjoyment, when the pathology is over? Is there nothing after illness? Are illness and addiction all we have, all we can ever have? Such questions also lead us to what is probably the most carefully developed meditation on the addiction of bibliophilia and the Apocalypse in detective fiction, namely Umberto Eco's *Il nome della rosa* [*The Name of the Rose*] (1980). In what follows, I will argue that Eco's novel, in addition to the many other topics it undertakes, also attempts to dramatize the libidinal scenario that awaits the reader of detective fiction, as well as attempting to imagine an end to that scenario, an end to all enjoyment.[46]

We should begin by noting the importance of *prohibition* for enjoyment. What transforms the desire at the heart of detective fiction into an object (a), a foreign body that causes a skip or a stutter that changes satisfaction into the endlessly repeated circularity of drive, is precisely its socially transgressive character.[47] The social field marks the desire as off limits, as

---

45. Klein's claims for cigarettes will sound familiar, even though he avoids the term *jouissance*, preferring the category of the sublime: a "painful pleasure" (1993, p. 2) that arises out of a drive that simultaneously reflects a longing for death and for eternity. Are whodunits sublime? The "prophetic anticipations" he refers to are Freud's *Civilization and Its Discontents,* originally published in 1930, and Italo Svevo's brilliant *La coscienza di Zeno,* originally published in 1923, but one might equally note how Freud's reflections on compulsive repetition in *Beyond the Pleasure Principle,* originally published in 1920, also led him to a theory of the death drive.

46. In discussing a novel that has received a great deal of commentary, I will try to avoid repeating at length some of the most often noted points about the book—that is, I will take it for granted that readers know that Eco's description of William of Baskerville is a near citation from Conan Doyle, or that the scene involving the Abbot's horse is taken from Voltaire's *Zadig.* Readers who wish to pursue some of the allusions should see Cohen (1988).

47. Social prohibition, although the most obvious example, is not the only thing that can cause this skip or stutter, the blockage that obstructs the circuit of desire. Trauma can also generate the same effect, as the "thing you just can't get past," as Freud was at pains to show in *Beyond the Pleasure Principle.* And whereas detective fiction may, in fact, be replaying a number of traumas (the murder as a "primal scene," for instance), it is assuredly the social disapproval of light or frivolous reading that makes it, in a strict sense, *enjoyable.*

a foreign body (and in so many instances of detective fiction that desire is marked as literally foreign, typically belonging to the colonial sphere) that interrupts satisfaction. Hence we must immediately note the value of *authority*, which claims our desire for its own, and so the state becomes the only agent properly authorized to satisfy the appetite for violence. Classic detective fiction manifests a certain uneasiness about this operation, as the detective is always a kind of para-authority, a *supplement*, in the Derridean sense, to authority. Dupin, Holmes, Poirot, or for that matter, Adrian Monk, all work as adjuncts to the police, acting in no official capacity, taking no credit, and permitting the state to maintain the polite fiction of its exclusive provenance in the field of desire. As we have shown, however, the sole point of identification between the reader and the detective is precisely the libidinal field, and so the reader is allowed to play with the possibility of being "let in," to *almost* experience an authorization of his desire. The later convention of the "amateur sleuth" who is not even a para-authority is even more seductive, as the sleuth's position with respect to authority is even closer to the reader's, and hence his "transgression" in appropriating the functions of the official regulators of the libido is all the more daring.

Umberto Eco was hardly the first to set his detective novel in a monastery, but he certainly was successful at transforming the locale into yet another micro-genre of detective fiction.[48] The detective in the novel, William of Baskerville, is an obvious analogue of and homage to Sherlock Holmes, but it is remarkable how many classic detectives are monks of one kind or another. They are aesthetic souls, rigorous in their self-discipline and self-denial, and they are bachelors and spinsters all. Lord Peter Wimsey's novelistic adventures come to an end along with his honeymoon, for example. One need do no more than note Adrian Monk's last name to see that the detective's professed lack of desire is part of that super-human (one might just as easily say pathological) control of desire that serves to mask the desires that bring the story into being in the first place. The monk is an eccentric figure par excellence, constituted as being set outside the circle of desire and guilt that characterize the "normal" world. Eco's brilliance in setting the

---

48. If the hard-boiled and police procedural are examples of subgenres, we need a term to characterize the almost fetishistic repetition of motifs, locales, and personas that appear to form an even smaller generic unit, such as detective stories that prominently involve cats, or detective stories that are set in or around horse racing tracks, or detectives who are Medieval monks. Hence, a *micro-genre*.

story in a monastery was, of course, not to emphasize the detective's self-control and eccentricity, although it does, of course, have that function, but rather in order to create a whole series of guilty pleasures that characterize everyone within the abbey. One is tempted to say, in fact, that Eco's abbey runs on enjoyment. There are, of course, the predictable sodomitical desires that emerge during the course of the investigation, but the principal guilty pleasure in The *Name of the Rose*, the principal fuel for the abbey's motor of enjoyment is, without question, the unauthorized access to forbidden books.

Reading detective fiction has long been characterized as a guilty pleasure, something most serious scholars avoided admitting to until the 1970s. In the Anglo-American academy, marked by a Protestant work ethic, it is seen as marginal and frivolous because it is easy, light reading, and hence unworthy, not to mention its unseemly subject matter. In a European context, the problem is quite different: there detective fiction is unredeemably popular, if not downright vulgar. These same factors are at play, of course, for the "average" reader: mystery fiction and romance, in particular, although not pornography, seem to require a certain degree of furtiveness in their purchase and consumption, a desire to conceal the cover or the title from the sales clerk. In any event, the reader feels an imperative that emerges from the social field, with the force of authority behind it: Thou shalt not read detective fiction! In writing about a library filled with forbidden books, then, Eco was bound to choose a genre that also consisted of "forbidden books." He was bound to choose detective fiction for many reasons, not least because of his own admiring work on Conan Doyle in *The Sign of Three* (Eco and Sebeok, 1983).

The *Name of the Rose* tells the story of a Franciscan monk, William of Baskerville, who, in 1327, is engaged in a delicate diplomatic mission that brings him to an unnamed monastery possessed of the finest library in the Christian world where, it so happens, there has recently been a suspicious death, the illustrator Adelmo of Otranto. William, famous for his acumen and investigatory abilities, is charged with the inquiry, but alas, a whole series of deaths plague the abbey. Two facts are noted as the investigation proceeds: the deaths appear to fit, at least loosely, the descriptions of the seven days of the Apocalypse in the Bible, and the mystery appears to revolve around a precious book, a forbidden book, in the library. When William is charged with the investigation, he is, of course, authorized to do so by the chief authority of the monastery, the abbot, in a series of formal performative utterances that reach a kind of impasse when they arrive at the question of the book, and hence, at the question of enjoyment:

> "Bene," disse allora Guglielmo, "potrò porre domande ai monaci?"
> "Potrete."
> "Potrò aggirarmi liberamente per l'abbazia?"
> "Ve ne conferisco facoltà."
> "Mi investireste di questa missione coram monachis?"
> "Questa sera stessa."
> "Comincerò però oggi, prima che i monaci sappiano di cosa mi avete incaricato. E inoltre desideravo molto . . . visitare la vostra biblioteca . . ."
> L'Abate si alzò quasi di scatto, col viso molto teso. "Potrete aggirarvi per tutta l'abazia, ho detto. Non certo per l'ultimo piano dell'Edificio, nella biblioteca." [1980, p. 43]

> "Very well," William said then, "may I question the monks?"
> "You may."
> "May I move freely about the abbey?"
> "I grant you that power."
> "Will you assign me this mission *coram monachis* [in front of the monks]?"
> "This very evening."
> "I shall begin, however, today, before the monks know what you have charged me to do. Besides, I already had a great desire . . .to visit your library . . ."
> The abbot rose, almost starting, with a very tense face. "You can move freely through the whole abbey, I said. But not, to be sure, on the top floor of the Aedificium, the library." [1983, pp. 34–35][49]

Once again, the detective is provided with a kind of para-authority, half on the side of the paternal prohibition from the abbot, and half on the side of the prohibited desire, the reading of books that are frivolous or vulgar. You *ought to be* like the father (free to question, to move about, in a publicly recognized display of power), and you *may not be* like the father (you may not enjoy a specific kind of penetrating freedom, in this case, access to the library) (Freud 1923). If this prohibition is paternal in its first appearance, it is uncannily doubled and made more venerable and filled

---

49. I will use Weaver's translation throughout, with occasional modifications.

with authority when it comes from the old, blind Jorge de Burgos. The dead monk Adelmo was an illustrator who worked on marginalia, specializing in *babouins*, fantastic figures that represent the inverse of the normal world, often in a humorous way, and Jorge inveighs against the laughter that the illustrations provoke among the monks. "Cosa vogliono tutte queste nugae? Un mondo inverso e opposto a quello stabilito da Dio . . . ormai è più piacevole per il monaco leggere i marmi che non i manoscritti, e ammirare le opere dell'uomo anziché meditare sulla legge di Dio. Vergogna, per il desiderio dei vostri occhi e per i vostri sorrisi" (1980, p. 88) "What is the aim of all this nonsense? A world that is the reverse and the opposite of that established by God . . . by now it is more pleasurable for a monk to read marble [Jorge refers to the fantastic images sculpted in the capitals of the cloister] than manuscript, and to admire the works of man than to meditate on the law of God. Shame! For the desire of your eyes and for your smiles!" (1983, p. 80). No one is more adept at a disciplinary denial of these visual pleasures than Jorge, whose blind pupils are "bianc[he] come la neve" (1980, p. 86). "white as snow" (1983, p. 79) in their purity. Jorge is indeed presented as the perfect monk and the perfect paternal authority, rigorous and utterly removed from desire. Eco returns again and again to Jorge's concern with this frivolous and pleasurable marginal reading, and what emerges is that this kind of indulgence, this guilty pleasure might undermine the foundation of authority. The library is itself a prohibited text, a guilty pleasure for the detectives and the reader. It is a labyrinth in which each room is assigned a letter that permits one to chart a course through the rooms by spelling out the names of geographical locations, and hence it is also a textual map of the world. Within the textual possibilities afforded by the library's rooms is the word "leones" or lions, standing in synecdoche for Africa. But the section marked "leones" contains a hidden room, one with no apparent ingress. Prohibition upon prohibition, combined with the guilty pleasure of penetration and illicit books.[50]

Jorge's concern that humorous marginalia might shake the foundations of authority is the opposite of the normal concern about classic detective fiction, another frivolous and pleasurable marginal reading. Like the romance novel, the ideology of detective fiction is typically seen as conservative. It subjects the social field to disorder (criminal disruption,

---

50. And so desire for the forbidden book also becomes a kind of sodomy: if "normal" penetration of the library is forbidden to the monks, then this is a kind of secondary penetration into a space with no "easy way in" that is doubly off limits.

uncontrollable suspicion that temporarily brings different classes to the same level) only in order to reestablish and reaffirm the security and certainty of that same social order of a middle-class nostalgia for an aristocratic past. It introduces normally repressed desires for violence and criminality only in order to all the more effectively ban them, just as the romance introduces a series of threats to heteronormativity, principally in the form of hostility between the sexes, only in order to reaffirm its necessity. However, the mechanisms that I have examined so far in this chapter and the previous one might indicate that this is not the whole story. The detective novel introduces the forbidden desire and removes it in one breath (provides the violated body and makes it disappear at the same time), thus establishing enjoyment, and thus equally establishing a rhythm of a permanent return to precisely those antisocial desires that the text aimed to discipline and dissipate in the first place. In other words, the desire, the prohibition, the foreign body of the object (a) that interrupts the circuit of pleasure and satisfaction—all of these psychic formations are constituted simultaneously and reciprocally by each other. And because enjoyment can only occur in the context of an authoritarian and "impossible" prohibition (you must be like the father; you cannot be like the father), it is perversely always anti-authoritarian to enjoy. Therein lies the optimism with which Žižek can embrace even the most seemingly idiotic and banal of postmodern commercial slogans: "Enjoy Coke!" It is precisely by taking the dictates of authority in their most literal sense and in their most extreme form that we most effectively "resist" them.

Eco had a very specific context for his concerns about authority and resistance, namely the co-opting of the group of *sessantottisti*, those who participated in the social, political, and cultural upheavals of 1968 that extended broadly throughout Western Europe—the transformation of hippies into yuppies, as it were. The anonymous narrator of the Borgesian frame story ends his introduction to the supposedly found manuscript of *The Name of the Rose* by observing that the political changes of the last ten years have permitted a kind of enjoyment that was not possible before: "Negli anni in cui scoprivo il testo . . . circolava la persuasione che si dovesse scrivere solo impegnandosi . . . per cambiare il mondo. A dieci e più anni di distanza è ora consolazione dell'uomo di lettere (restituito alla sua altissima dignità) che si possa scrivere per puro amor di scrittura" (1980, p. 15) "In the years when I discovered the . . . volume, there was a widespread conviction that one should write only out of a commitment . . . to change the world. Now, after ten years or more, the man of letters (restored to his loftiest dignity) can happily write out of pure love of writing" (1983, p. 5). He goes on to note sarcastically that the story he will tell is "incommensurabilmente lontana nel tempo" ("incommensurably remote in time") and "gloriosamente priva di rapporto coi tempi nostri" (1980, p. 15) ("gloriously devoid of relevance for our day" (1983, p. 5)). He discovered the volume in, *naturalmente*, 1968, and pens the introduction in 1980.[51] But it is Remigio the cellarer who makes the context clear; having taken part in a series of carnivalesque egalitarian social experiments (i.e., the 1960s counterculture) as part of the Dolcinian heresies, he has attempted to conform to social conventions: "Vedi, un tempo ho tentato di ribellarmi ai signori, ora li servo . . ." (1980, p. 275) "You see, I once tried to rebel against the overlords; now I serve them . . ." (1983, p. 272). Another monk, Benno, initially champions the principle of free and unfettered access to the forbidden texts of the library, until he comes to possess the mysterious forbidden book, and elects not to read it, but rather to become an exclusionary authority, the new assistant librarian for the abbey. William notes that "da qualche ora Bencio è passato dall'altra parte" (1980, p. 398) "a few hours ago Benno joined the other side" (1983, p. 395); he now stands on the side of prohibition. In other words, Eco consistently associates broader questions of social and political freedom with access to forbidden and marginal literature, and vice versa.

Naturally, the abbot's prohibition, as well as Jorge's, creates nothing but a series of returns and repetitions to these guilty pleasures: William and his Watson-like sidekick Adso enter the library clandestinely again and again, seeking first clues and information, and eventually the forbidden book that is the cause of the murders. This book is, of course, the "always missed object" that is responsible for the reader's enjoyment, the object (a) whose extraction makes the reality of the narrative possible in the first place. The book is, just like the Great Treasure of Agra, a classic instance of the Hitchcockian McGuffin, the object that the entire narrative revolves around; it appears to be of paramount importance, but is, in fact, absolutely meaningless, serving only to motivate the plot. One thinks of the

---

51. Hans Kellner (1988) notes quite aptly that the disappearance of the narrator's beloved, which leaves "a great emptiness" in his heart, stands for the Soviet takeover of Prague, and the loss of the possibility of "socialism with a human face." It is one of the rare essays in English on Eco's first novel that attends to the political dimension, most losing themselves in the author's allusions to Borges, mirrors, chess, Peirce, semiotics, classic detective fiction, contemporary critical theory, and so on.

briefcase in *Pulp Fiction* or *Kiss Me Deadly*, the "secrets vital to air defense" in *The 39 Steps*, or the radioactive wine bottles in *Notorious*. This is precisely how the forbidden book of Aristotle functions in *The Name of the Rose*, in a room marked, as in the joke that gave the McGuffin its name, with the sign of nonexistent *leones*.

This forbidden book passes from monk to monk, producing again and again the same effect: death. Two monks, Venantius and Berengar, die with their fingers and tongues stained black; another (Severinus, the herbalist, smart enough to wear gloves), his head crushed by an armillary sphere; then Malachi, the librarian (stained fingers again), and finally, the abbot himself. Each time, William and Adso arrive on the scene too late: the object is again extracted, and again the detectives are plunged back into this "never ending . . . circulation." So far, this is no different than the pursuit of the Treasure of Agra in *The Sign of Four*, a pursuit that must turn up empty-handed in order to render the text's bibliophilic addiction enjoyable. At the end of the novel, William and Adso return to the library to confront the architect of all these deaths, and, they hope, recover this most rare and precious of texts, the only copy of the second book of Aristotle's *Poetics*, the book on comedy. Naturally, this final confrontation involves not only an illicit penetration of the library, but a secondary (sodomitical), even more prohibited zone, the *finis Africae*, the chamber with no apparent entrance.

The architect of the crimes in the abbey is of course Jorge, the ideal paternal authority who enjoins all enjoyment (happily, *enjoin* has a double sense of both "to impose with authority" and "to prohibit with authority," as it is the authoritarian prohibition itself that imposes the enjoyment), who declares: "la licenza della plebe venga tenuta a freno e umiliata, e intimorita con la severità" (1980, p. 479) "the license of the plebeians must be restrained and humiliated, and intimidated by sternness" (1983, p. 475). Here, in the novel's final confrontation, William and Jorge behave according to the rules of classic detective fiction: William explains his brilliant deduction, which Jorge confirms or corrects, each praises his adversary's acumen and intellect, and they have a final opportunity to debate the merits of frivolous enjoyment. The reason Jorge hates Aristotle's book so much, is willing to kill to prevent others from reading it, is that it is an *endorsement of enjoyment*, an endorsement from the ultimate medieval authority, a figure so massively important in all learned reasoning that he was referred to simply as The Philosopher. And what happens when Authority legitimates enjoyment? It transforms, according to Jorge, the insignificant, vulgar, and plebeian resistance of heretics like Dolcino into art and philosophy, into "la scintilla luciferina che appiccherebbe al mondo intero un nuovo incendio" (1980, p. 478) "the Luciferine spark that would set a new fire to the whole world" (1983, p. 475). Perversely, in this view, laughter would allow us to take the revolution seriously. Jorge believes that a world in which the frivolous and the marginal become legitimated is a world in which no order can stand, in which "del centro si perderebbe ogni traccia" (1980, p. 479) "every trace of the center would be lost" (1983, p. 475). (It is not surprising, by the way, that Jorge seems to have read Derrida, as William quotes Wittgenstein at the novel's end.) William disagrees; the legitimation of laughter would instead eliminate "l'arroganza dello spirito, la fede senza sorriso, la verità che non viene mai presa dal dubbio" (1980, p. 481) "arrogance of the spirit, faith without smile, truth that is never seized by doubt" (1983, p. 477). In other words, it would generate a kind of utopian authority that William imagines throughout the novel, where the wise make only such prohibitions as are necessary to protect the simple, maximizing social freedom and uplifting the people through relatively unfettered access to information— a modern, Western European democracy run by moderate socialist intellectuals, in other words. William is, of course, completely wrong.

Such a claim runs the risk of creating a kind of ethical imperative that merely reverses the direction of the authoritarian prohibition without changing the essentially authoritarian nature of it—you *must* read detective fiction! You *owe it to society* to read detective fiction!—that would rob us of our enjoyment in reading (the dead body, the useless frivolity, the marginal status of the literature, are all no longer a "foreign object" blocking satisfaction and creating enjoyment), and turn our subversive *jouissance* into a laborious chore, what Todd McGowan calls "commanded enjoyment." McGowan goes on to note that this commanded enjoyment, however, "*in no way allows subjects within the social order to enjoy themselves*, any more than they were ever able to" (2004, p. 37, original emphasis).[52] That is, the faintly democratic and liberal desire at work here to free up detective fiction and other kinds of marginal knowledge, to loosen the strictures

---

52. Throughout McGowan's book, and quite possibly this one, as well, there is the constant problem of enjoyment being used in both its technical sense (the constant return to what does not give satisfaction, and the pleasure in that lack of satisfaction) and in its everyday sense (taking pleasure in something). Commanded enjoyment, in other words, gives no satisfaction. Indeed, it provides less satisfaction because it does not even permit the negative pleasure of *jouissance*. Commanded to read frivolous literature, the subject can then only turn to another guilty pleasure: sneaking a quick peek at Shakespeare or Kant in a plain brown wrapper, perhaps.

of canon formation, once again constitutes a mystification of desire and enjoyment, suggesting that our enjoyment has been wrongly pathologized. Such a course, although typical of "self-esteem" based therapies, which invariably begin with a litany of reassurances that "it is normal" to engage in whatever kind of neurotic behavior the patient is engaging in, is merely a way of avoiding the traumatic kernel of the real, the object (a) that causes our desire to stutter and skip into *jouissance*, in this instance, our addiction to detective fiction. We can, of course, "enjoy our symptom," but only insofar as it is a symptom.

Perversely, this places Jorge on the side of enjoyment, even if he doesn't know it. He is willing to kill to preserve the extracted disruptive status of the object (a), whereas it is *William* with his good intentions who risks turning popular fiction into a kind of socialist realist text, filled with socially salubrious "subversive" potential that will keep "the wise" philosopher- or semiotician-kings in authority from arrogance and oppression. William has his own addiction, his own enjoyment, of course, mentioned in one of the early passages in the novel that is most clearly drawn from Conan Doyle, "some herb" that he regularly eats, especially "nei momenti di maggior tensione" (1980, p. 24), "at the moments of greatest tension" (1983, p. 16). I mention socialist realism here as one instance of what happens when subjects are commanded to enjoy nominally subversive literature (i.e., communist propaganda). It becomes a mind-numbing, formulaic chore free of any trace of *jouissance*, but far worse is what happens when subjects begin to enjoy their own obedience to such commands. This is what fascism and Stalinism had in common, the essence, as it were, of totalitarianism: their ability to elicit the subject's enjoyment of obedience.

What follows next is a truly remarkable scene, as it and the scenes that follow it undo all of the "good intentions" that characterize the rest of the novel. What can happen at the end of this story? Eco is deeply indebted to classic detective fiction, so despite the faintly paternalistic promise of greater access to forbidden texts, there is no question that we will get our object (a)—the Treasure of Agra *must* turn up empty. What happens in *The Sign of Four* is instructive here. In that novel, the object (a) remains a gap that stops the circuit of pleasure, but we are still left with the cocaine in the library, the sign of our own addiction to reading detective novels, our return to the beginning of this libidinal short circuit. What Eco offers, on the contrary, is the answer to the question I asked earlier about enjoyment: Where and how will it end? The text suffers a psychotic breakdown and imagines an apocalyptic end to all enjoyment, to all text, sweeping away in one gesture both the question of authority and prohibition and the consolatory bottle of cocaine.

"Tutto questo non è servito comunque a nulla," gli disse Guglielmo. "Ora è finita, ti ho trovato, ho trovato il libro, e gli altri sono morti invano."

"Non invano," disse Jorge. ". . . E affinché non siano morti invano, un'altra morte non sarà di troppo."

Disse, e incominciò con le sue mani scarnite e diafane a lacerare lentamente, a brani e a strisce, le pagine molli del manoscritto, ponendosele a brandelli in bocca, e masticando lentamente . . .

Guglielmo lo guardava affascinato e pareva non si rendesse conto di quanto avveniva. Poi si riscosse e si protese in avanti gridando: "Cosa fai?" Jorge sorrise scoprendo le gengive esangui, mentre una bava giallastra gli colava dalle labbra pallide sulla peluria bianca e rada del mento.

. . . Rise, proprio lui, Jorge. Per la prima volta lo udii ridere . . . Rise con la gola . . . Jorge . . . si ritrasse stringendo il volume al petto con la sinistra, mentre con la destra continuava stracciarne le pagine e porsele in bocca. . . . Il vecchio rise ancora, questa volta più forte . . .

. . . Il suo volto, al chiarore rosso del lume, ci apparve ora orrendo: i lineamenti alterati, un sudore maligno gli striava la fronte e la gote, gli occhi di solito bianchi di morte si erano iniettati di sangue, dalla bocca gli uscivano lembi di pergamena come una belva famelica che si fosse troppo ingozzata e non riuscisse più a trangugiare il suo cibo. Sfigurata dall'ansia, dall'incombere del veleno che ormai già serpeggiava abbondante nelle vene . . . la figura venerabile del vegliardo appariva ora disgustosa e grottesca . . . [1980, pp. 483–486]

"All of this, in any case, has been to no avail," William said to him. "Now it is over. I have found you, I have found the book, and the others died in vain."

"Not in vain," Jorge said. ". . . And to ensure they have not died in vain, one more death will not be too many."

He spoke, and with his fleshless, diaphanous hands he began slowly tearing to strips and shreds the limp pages of the manuscript, stuffing them into his mouth, slowly chewing . . .

William looked at him, fascinated, and seemed not to grasp what was happening. Then he recovered himself and leaned forward, shouting, "What are you doing?" Jorge smiled, baring his bloodless gums, as yellowish slime trickled from his pale lips over the sparse white hairs on his chin.

. . . He laughed, he, Jorge. For the first time I heard him laugh . . .

He laughed with his throat . . . Jorge . . .drew back, clasping the volume to his chest with his left hand while his right went on tearing the pages and cramming them into his mouth. . . .The old man laughed again, louder this time . . .

    . . . His face, in the reddish glow of the lamp, now seemed horrible to us: the features were distorted, a malignant sweat streaked his brow and cheeks, his eyes, usually dead white, were bloodshot, from his mouth came scraps of parchment, and he looked like a ravening beast who had stuffed himself and could no longer swallow his food. Disfigured by anxiety, by the menace of the poison now flowing abundantly through his veins . . . the venerable figure of the elder now seemed disgusting and grotesque. [1983, pp. 480–483]

This scene, curiously enough, allows us to address the question of Eco's "postmodernism." Notwithstanding its panoply of postmodern devices (anachronistic citation, parody, homage, pastiche), *The Name of the Rose* is the work of a committed structuralist and semiotician, one, moreover, with a clear sociopolitical program. It is no more postmodern than Borges. Certainly William's stance in the novel functions as a completely non-ironic center that endeavors to subvert the arrogant authority of the abbot or Jorge without actually putting into doubt the notion or necessity of authority itself, as William/Eco, the ideal philosopher-king, could attest. But something quite different occurs in this breakdown of the patriarch here at the end of the novel. Žižek writes that the "postmodern shift affects radically the status of paternal authority: modernism endeavors to assert the subversive potential of the margins which undermine the Father's authority, of the enjoyments which elude the Father's grasp, whereas postmodernism *focuses on the father himself and conceives him as 'alive,' in his obscene dimension*" (2001, p. 124, original emphasis). We can now see that, whereas Eco almost certainly believed he was writing a modernist novel in this sense (that is, asserting "the subversive potential of the margins which undermine the Father's authority"), *his text is postmodern in spite of itself,* postmodern in a way that dissolves William's (and Eco's) "good intentions."

    Žižek is here discussing the figure of the "anal father," the father who appears insane, as a "nauseous debauchee, threatening yet ridiculously impotent . . ." (2001, p. 127), and here indeed Jorge is transformed from a lean tower of paternal authority, the venerable elder, or *vegliardo*, with that word's suggestion of surveillance in Italian, into a bloated "debauchee" with bloodshot eyes. This psychotic breakdown is also an absolute breakdown of the "Big Other," the symbolic order that represents the disembodied social field, complete with its authority and prohibitions. Jorge attempts to maintain the prohibition against frivolous, marginal literature by literally consuming that "poisoned text." He inevitably also feels the enjoyment that comes with this guilty pleasure, the consumption of what is forbidden, and it transforms him from the stern and humiliating figure of the Father of Law into the obscene and revolting figure of the Father of Enjoyment, the "anal father," or perhaps one should call him here the "anal grandfather." Not coincidentally, this may permit us to also finally successfully analyze Eco's curious decision to install this ever-so-thinly veiled version of Jorge Luis Borges (another blind, Spanish-speaking librarian) as the revolting villain of his novel. In this scene, Eco can grotesquely dissolve a quintessential master of modernism, reveal him not as an authority to be subverted or one-upped, but as an obscene figure of enjoyment.

Žižek specifically links this figure that is now obscenely "alive," burning with enjoyment, to Freud's dream figure of the burning child. The "clean," patriarchal Jorge that we begin with is "dead," with his literally dead white eyes (*bianchi di morte*) and his "fleshless, diaphanous hands." Žižek writes:

> The father qua Name of the Father, reduced to a figure of symbolic authority, is "dead" (also) in the sense that *he does not know anything about enjoyment* . . . Which is why the famous Freudian dream of a son who appears to his father and reproaches him with "Father, can't you see I'm burning?" could be simply translated into *"Father, can't you see I'm enjoying?*—can't you see I'm alive, burning with enjoyment?" [2001, pp. 124–125, italics original]

What happens here is that the Big Other and the symbolic order learn about enjoyment, a knowledge that their prohibitions would normally prohibit to themselves as well. They consume detective fiction and are transformed first into something repulsive, and then into nothing: ". . . the social bond dissolves itself. A catastrophe ensues . . ." (Žižek 1992, p. 73). Once again, reflection on enjoyment leads inevitably to a consideration of catastrophe, Apocalypse. Jorge's transformation makes him first appear as a "nauseous debauchee," but within pages he is literally burning: sensing Adso's lamp near his face, he knocks it out of Adso's hand and sets the library and himself on fire. The abbey burns "per tre giorni e per tre notti" (1980, p. 499) "for three days and three nights" (1983, p. 497), fulfilling the apocalyptic pattern of the deaths in the abbey, a pattern that also dissolves into chaos, as it turns out it initially was an accident, and later an idea that Jorge encouraged as a false lead for William to follow. The conflagration, along with Jorge's consumption of the forbidden book, leaves nothing but "brandelli di pergamena . . . qualche foglio . . . il fantasma di una o più parole . . . mezzo foglio . . . un incipit, un titolo" (1980, pp. 501–502) "scraps of parchment . . . a few pages . . . the ghost of one or more words . . . a half page . . . an incipit . . . a title" (1983, p. 500) that Adso compulsively attempts to piece together to form something, to decipher a message. But the obscene dissolution of the Name of the Father into the "anal grandfather" in *The Name of the Rose* does not permit a reconstruction of *jouissance*, the solace of an addiction (to cocaine, to detective fiction, to text), and Adso becomes convinced that his textual collage "non contiene alcun messaggio . . . non dice e non ripete . . ." (1980, pp. 502–503) "contains no message . . . says and repeats nothing . . ." (1983, p. 501) but his own fantasies, imaginings—and so gives up. Without our paternal prohibitions, there is nothing left to enjoy, no serial reading, no endless circling, no carnival of 1968. Only scattered words, the "nomina nuda" (1980, p. 502) that the novel ends with. This is how postmodernism transforms what should be, in Dominick LaCapra's (1999) terms, a historical *loss* (after a certain point in history, we have to recognize a different relationship to the idea of paternal authority) into a structural *absence*. In other words, Eco transforms the enjoyment of *drive* (idiotic and yet antiauthoritarian) into the nostalgic *desire* of the liberal European intellectual, with an Apocalypse of enjoyment forever standing between him and his never-to-be-fulfilled dreams of '68.

References

Abbott, M. E. (2002). *The Street Was Mine: White Masculinity in Hardboiled Fiction and Film Noir*. New York: Palgrave Macmillan.

Abramovich, I. (2004, December). American scene: this month on the design beat. *House & Garden*, p. 77.

Amberg, G. (1969). L'avventura: *A Film by Michelangelo Antonioni*. New York: Grove.

Amigoni, F. (1996). *La più semplice macchina: lettura freudiana del «Pasticciaccio»* [*The Simplest Machine. A Freudian Reading of the "Pasticciaccio"*]. Bologna: Il Mulino.

Auden, W. H. (1968). The guilty vicarage. Notes on the detective story, by an addict. In *The Dyer's Hand, and Other Essays*, pp. 150–153. New York: Vintage.

Barron, S. (2002). *Jane and the Prisoner of Wool House*. New York: Bantam.

Bayard, P. (2000). *Who Killed Roger Ackroyd? The Mystery Behind the Agatha Christie Mystery*, trans. C. Cosman. New York: The New Press.

Blanc, N. (2002). *A Crossword to Die For*. New York. Berkeley Books.

———— (2003). *Corpus de Crossword*. New York. Berkeley Books.

Bonaparte, M. (1949). *The Life and Works of Edgar Allan Poe: A Psycho-analytic Interpretation*, trans. J. Rodker. London. Imago.

Božovič, M. (1992). The man behind his own retina. In *Everything You Wanted to Know about Lacan (But Were Afraid to Ask Hitchcock)*, ed. S. Žižek , pp. 161–177. New York: Verso.

Calvino, I. (1973). *Il castello dei destini incrociati.* [*The Castle of Crossed Destinies*]. Torino: Einaudi.

——— (1993). *Prima che tu dica «Pronto».* [*Numbers in the Dark*]. Milano: Mondadori.

Camilleri, A. (1996a). *Il cane di terracotta* [*The Terra-Cotta Dog*]. Palermo: Selleria.

——— (1996b). *Il ladro di merendine* [*The Snack Thief*]. Palermo: Selleria.

——— (2002). *The Terra-Cotta Dog*, trans. S. Sartarelli. New York: Viking.

——— (2003). *The Snack Thief*, trans. S. Sartarelli. New York: Viking.

——— (2006). *La vampa d'agosto* [*The Blaze of Summer*]. Palermo: Selleria.

Christie, A. (1977). *The A.B.C. Murders.* New York: Pocket Books, 1936.

——— (1984). *Murder on the Links.* New York: Berkeley Books, 1923.

——— (1993). *Curtain.* New York: Harper Paperbacks, 1975.

——— (2000a). *Hercule Poirot's Christmas.* New York: Berkeley Books, 1938.

——— (2000b). *The Murder of Roger Ackroyd.* New York: Berkeley Books, 1934.

——— (2000c). *Murder on the Orient Express.* New York: Berkeley Books, 1934.

——— (2004). *And Then There Were None.* New York: St. Martin's Griffin.

Cohen, M. (1988). The hounding of Baskerville: allusion and apocalypse in Eco's *The Name of the Rose.* In *Naming the Rose: Essays on Eco's* The Name of the Rose, ed. M. T. Inge, pp. 65–76. Jackson: University Press of Mississippi.

Conan Doyle, A. (1986). *Sherlock Holmes: The Complete Novels and Stories.* Two volumes. New York: Bantam Books.

——— (2001). *The Sign of Four.* New York: Penguin Putnam, 1890.

Copjec, J. (1994). *Read My Desire: Lacan against the Historicists.* Cambridge, MA: The MIT Press.

Crovi, L. (2000). *Delitti di carta nostra: Una storia del giallo italiano* [Crimes of Our Pages: A History of the Italian Whodunit]. Bologna: Editrice PuntoZero.

——— (2002). *Tutti i colori del giallo: il giallo italiano da De Marchi a Scebanenco a Camilleri* [*All Kinds of Whodunit: The Italian Crime Novel from De Marchi to Scebanenco to Camilleri*]. Venice: Marsilio Editori.

Dazieri, S. (1998). *Attenti al Gorilla* [*Beware of the Gorilla*]. Torino: Einaudi.

——— (2001). *La cura del Gorilla* [*The Gorilla's Cure*]. Torino: Einaudi.

de Angelis, A. (1963). *Il Commissario De Vincenzi: tre romanzi polizieschi italiani* [*Commissioner De Vincenzi: Three Italian Detective Novels*]. Milano: Feltrinelli.

Dombroski, R. (1999). *Creative Entanglements: Gadda and the Baroque.* Toronto: University of Toronto Press.

Douglas, M. (1995). *Purity and Danger: An Analysis of the Concept of Pollution and Taboo.* New York: Routledge.

Dove, G. N. (1997). *The Reader and the Detective Story.* Bowling Green, OH: Bowling Green State University Popular Press.

Eco, U. (1980). *Il nome della rosa* [*The Name of the Rose*]. Milano: Bompiani.

——— (1983). *The Name of the Rose*, trans. W. Weaver. New York: Harcourt Brace Jovanovich.

Eco, U., and Sebeok, T. (1983). *The Sign of Three: Dupin, Holmes, Peirce*. Bloomington, IN: Indiana University Press.

Engel, H. (2005). *Memory Book*. New York: Penguin.

Freud, S. (1913). Totem and taboo. *Standard Edition* 13:1–131.

——— (1920). Beyond the pleasure principle. *Standard Edition* 18:7–64.

——— (1923). The ego and the id. *Standard Edition* 19:1–59.

——— (1925a). Negation. *Standard Edition* 19:235–239.

——— (1925b). Some psychological consequences of the anatomical distinction between the sexes. *Standard Edition* 19:248–258.

——— (1930). Civilization and its discontents. *Standard Edition* 21:57–145.

Gadda, C. E. (1965). *That Awful Mess on Via Merulana*, trans. W. Weaver. New York: Braziller.

——— (1969). *Acquainted with Grief*, trans. W. Weaver. New York: Braziller.

——— (1993). *Quer pasticciaccio brutto de via Merulana*. [*That Awful Mess on Via Merulana*]. Milano: Garzanti.

——— (1996). *La cognizione del dolore* [*Acquainted with Grief*]. Milano: Garzanti.

Grafton, S. (1987). *A is for Alibi*. New York: Bantam.

——— (1987). *B is for Burglar*. New York: Bantam.

——— (1987). *C is for Corpse*. New York: Bantam.

——— (2006). *S is for Silence*. New York: Bantam.

Grossvogel, D. (1979). *Mystery and Its Fictions: From Oedipus to Agatha Christie*. Baltimore: Johns Hopkins University Press.

Haddon, M. (2003). *The Curious Incident of the Dog in the Night-Time*. New York: Vintage.

Hammett, D. (1992a). *The Maltese Falcon*. New York: Vintage Crime.

——— (1992b). *Red Harvest*. New York: Vintage Crime.

Haycraft, H. (1974). *The Art of the Mystery Story*. New York: Simon and Schuster.

Heffernan, V. (2004). Orders come from a talking lion (made of wax). *The New York Times*, March 12, p. B22.

Hernández Martín, J. (1995). *Readers and Labyrinths: Detective Fiction in Borges, Bustos Domecq, and Eco*. New York: Garland.

Horsley, L. (2005). *Twentieth-Century Crime Fiction*. Oxford, NY: Oxford University Press.

Irwin, J. (1994). *The Mystery to a Solution: Poe, Borges, and the Analytic Detective Story*. Baltimore: Johns Hopkins University Press.

Kellner, H. (1988). "To make truth laugh": Eco's *The Name of the Rose*. In *Naming the Rose: Essays on Eco's* The Name of the Rose, ed. M. T. Inge, pp. 3–30. Jackson: University Press of Mississippi.

King, H. (1999). "All the shapes we make": *The Passenger*'s flight from formal stagnation. *Qui parle* 11.(2): 115–125.

Klein, R. (1993). *Cigarettes Are Sublime*. Durham, NC: Duke University Press.

Knight, S. (2004). *Crime Fiction, 1800–2000: Detection, Death, Diversity*. New York: Palgrave Macmillan.

Lacan, J. (1966). *Écrits*. Paris: Éditions du Seuil.

────── (1975). *Le Séminaire de Jacques Lacan, Livre XX (Encore) 1972–1973*. Paris: Éditions du Seuil.

LaCapra, D. (1999). "Trauma, Absence, Loss." *Critical Inquiry* 25: 696–727.

Lehman, D. (2000). *The Perfect Murder: A Study in Detection*. Ann Arbor: University of Michigan Press.

Levine, L. (2003). *This Pen for Hire*. New York: Kensington Books.

Macdonald, G. (2002). *Shaman or Sherlock? The Native American Detective*. Westport, CT: Greenwood.

Maclean, A. (2004). *Louisa and the Missing Heiress*. New York: Signet.

Malmgren, C. (2001). *Anatomy of Murder: Mystery, Detective and Crime Fiction*. Bowling Green, OH: Bowling Green State University Popular Press.

Mankell, H. (1995). *Villospår* [*Sidetracked*]. Stockholm: Ordfront Förlag.

────── (1996). *Den femte kvinnan* [*The Fifth Woman*]. Stockholm: Ordfront Förlag.

────── (1997). *Steget efter* [*One Step Behind*]. Stockholm: Ordfront Förlag.

McGowan, T. (2004). *The End of Dissatisfaction? Jacques Lacan and the Emerging Society of Enjoyment*. Albany: State University of New York Press.

Miller, D. A. (1989). *The Novel and the Police*. Berkeley: University of California Press.

Nowell-Smith, G. (1997). *L'avventura*. London: British Film Institute.

Pedullà, W. (1997). *Carlo Emilio Gadda: Il narratore come delinquente* [Carlo Emilio Gadda: Narrator as Delinquent]. Milan: Rizzoli.

Pepper, A. (2000). *The Contemporary American Crime Novel: Race, Ethnicity, Gender, Class*. Edinburgh: Edinburgh University Press.

Perry, A. (1990). *The Face of a Stranger*. New York: Random House.

Poe, E. A. (1966). *Complete Stories and Poems of Edgar Allan Poe*. Garden City, NY: Doubleday.

Porter, D. (1981). *The Pursuit of Crime: Art and Ideology in Detective Fiction*. New Haven, CT: Yale University Press.

Rambelli, L. (1979). *Storia del «giallo» italiano* [*History of the Italian Whodunit*]. Milano: Garzanti.

Reddy, M. T. (2003). *Traces, Codes, and Clues: Reading Race in Crime Fiction*. New Brunswick, NJ: Rutgers University Press.

Rohdie, S. (1990). *Antonioni*. London: British Film Institute.

Ronell, A. (1993). *Crack Wars: Literature, Addiction, Mania*. Lincoln: University of Nebraska Press.

Roth, M. (1995). *Foul and Fair Play: Reading Genre in Classic Detective Fiction*. Athens: University of Georgia Press.

Sayers, D. (1995). The fascinating problem of uncle Meleager's will. In *Lord Peter*, pp. 35–55. New York: Harper Collins.

Scaggs, J. (2005). *Crime Fiction*. New York: Routledge.

Shklovsky, V. (1990). Sherlock Holmes and the mystery story. In *Theory of Prose*, trans. B. Sher, pp. 101–116. Elmwood Park, IL: Dalkery Archive Press.

Sitford, M., and Panter S. (2000). *Addicted to Murder*. London: Virgin Books.

Svevo, I. (2001). *La coscienza di Zeno [Zeno's Conscience]*. Milano: Mondadori, 1923.

Thompson, J. (1993). *Fiction, Crime and Empire: Clues to Modernity and Postmodernity*. Urbana: University of Illinois Press.

Todorov, T. (1977). The typology of detective fiction. In *The Poetics of Prose*, trans. R. Howard, pp. 42–52. Ithaca, NY: Cornell University Press.

Van Dine, S. S. (1929). "Twenty Rules for Writing Detective Stories." In Haycraft (1974): 189–193.

Wilson, E. (1950). Who cares who killed Roger Ackroyd? In *Classics and Commercials*, pp. 257–265. New York: Farrar & Straus.

Wood, R. (1965). Rear Window. In *Hitchcock's Films*, pp. 61–70. New York: A. S. Barnes.

Wright, W. (1976). The great detective stories. In *The Art of the Mystery Story*, ed. H. Haycraft, pp. 33–70. New York: Biblo and Tannen.

Žižek, S. (1990). The detective and the analyst. *Literature and Psychology* 4: 27–46.

———— (1992). *Looking Awry: An Introduction to Jacques Lacan Through Popular Culture*. Cambridge, MA: October Books.

———— (1997). *The Plague of Fantasies*. New York: Verso. (2004).

———— (2001). *Enjoy Your Symptom! Jacques Lacan in Hollywood and Out*. New York: Routledge.

———— (2004). *Iraq: The Borrowed Kettle*. New York: Verso.

Index